KEVIN KEEGAN
—BLACK & WHITE—

KEVIN KEEGAN

— BLACK & WHITE —

JOHN MOYNIHAN

CollinsWillow
An Imprint of HarperCollins*Publishers*

First published in 1993
by CollinsWillow
an imprint of HarperCollins*Publishers*, London

© John Moynihan, 1993

**A CIP catalogue record for this book
is available from the British Library**

ISBN 0 00 218536 9

Printed in Great Britain
by Butler & Tanner Ltd

*Colour plate section credits: Allsport,
Bob Thomas Sports Photography,
Coloursport and Mail News*

CONTENTS

For Philip and Linda Evans

ACKNOWLEDGEMENTS

The author would like to thank his son, Leo Moynihan, for his caring support in helping research this biography; Amanda G. Smythe for typing the manuscript against a tight deadline; and the following for their kind assistance: Bryon Butler, Erich Biegert, Beverly Ceci (Pegler, Ltd), Alex Granditsch, Ian Hargreaves, Frank Keating, John Gaustad (Sportspages), Joe Latham, Bob Cass, Brian Moore, Brian McNally, Louise Taylor, Arthur Rotmil, Jack Rollin, Jeff Powell, John Watt, Peter Wise, Brough Scott and David Lacey. Special thanks to the Willow team at HarperCollins: Tom Whiting, Rachel Smyth and Deborah Kayser.

INTRODUCTION

The summer of 1993 was one of particular satisfaction for Joseph Kevin Keegan, OBE. Newcastle United, the team Keegan had taken over in his first managerial role only a year before, had reached the Premier League. His chairman, Sir John Hall, was already discussing the North East club's involvement in a European super league within the next decade. For Keegan, the challenges of meeting his old clubs Liverpool and Southampton; the Premier League champions Manchester United; and the FA Cup holders, Arsenal, lay around the corner.

There was time now for Keegan to relax on a Barbados beach with his wife of nearly 19 years, Jean, and daughters Laura Jane and Sarah, and savour the knowledge that, in an almost ludicrously short period, he had made it as a football manager, one of the least enviable and unsettling professions going. Relaxation was not a common pastime of Keegan's, but he had been determined to take his family far away for a rest. Moreover, as the England team he had once captained with pride sank that summer into new levels of mediocrity, the media were turning towards him as a possible successor to the incumbent manager, Graham Taylor. Keegan might have found it difficult coping with such distractions following the mass adoration heaped on his shoulders by Geordie fans after Newcastle had won their way, with a flourish, into the Premier League. This was followed by Keegan being named Barclays League First Division Manager of the Season.

It was perhaps too early to think of Keegan turning his attention to running an ailing national team so soon after curing an equally ailing Second Division club. Nevertheless, the idea of him taking over the England job did not seem too far-fetched, despite his inexperience. As a player at Liverpool under the admiring father-figure influence of Bill Shankly, Kevin Keegan had been determined to build up his career to become a world-class player; this sort of dedication to the game began in his boyhood as a miner's son living in Doncaster and was first noticed by mother Doris ('Kevin was always into football'). When Don Revie made him captain of England, Keegan admitted it was his proudest moment of all. By then, he had the strength of character to do well on the international scene. He was well paid, full of confidence, and had a plan to follow.

When the *Sun's* John Sadler and the *Daily Express's* Steve Curry named Keegan as a manager with the necessary charisma to sort out the England mess, they did so as experienced journalists who had not only followed England's fickle progress since the Alf Ramsey era, but had also observed Keegan's role in the front line, both as international captain and a club player with Liverpool, Hamburg, Southampton and, lastly, with Newcastle United before his retirement in 1984. Both knew Keegan well enough to know he could make a good job of running the international team, even though it might take a year or two of Premier League experience before he did so. Jasper Rees, writing in the *Independent on Sunday* under the headline 'Awaiting a Grand Entrance', put Keegan's name forward among nine other alternatives to take over Taylor's job.

'Keegan is the hot tip. No coaching qualifications, but that didn't stop Franz Beckenbauer. Drastic action is needed and Keegan's record at Newcastle shows he can do a short-term job. No doubts about his powers to motivate; an England under him would not have given up in Oslo. He has bags of international experience, and is hugely popular.'

How much was Keegan's decision to become a football manager – after denying he would ever do so during eight years of voluntary exile on a Spanish golfing green – caused by a hidden desire to take over a once-hallowed responsibility now besmirched by failure? Derek Pavis, the Notts County chairman, who played golf with Keegan in Spain, believes there was always a burning ambition inside the former England player to go into football management.

'My belief is that Keegan wanted the England job all along, and came back to give himself four or five years of experience. Kevin didn't have much reason to come back otherwise. He had plenty of money and a healthy life. But when he did come back, I have to say he did a very good job at Newcastle. The England job won't be far off in his mind.'

Keegan used to say during his early days at Liverpool that he wanted to become another Bobby Charlton or Bobby Moore. Through hard work, he did become a very popular member of the England team, even if it did not encompass the winning of a World Cup medal. His record at Newcastle had been almost too much of a fairy story, but given time and experience in the Premier League, and what Jack Charlton calls 'his self-belief in his own method', Keegan had every reason to expect success in the higher echelons.

After all, had he not always shown such success could be earned by ruthless self-discipline and hard work, displeasing those critics who believed he was a self-manufactured product without the natural gift of such magicians as Stanley Matthews and George Best? There was nothing wrong, however, with such effort, as Rome saw all too vividly one early summer's night in 1977. Doris Keegan's boy had proved on a European stage that he was a world-class player, as Liverpool beat Borussia Moenchengladbach to take home the European Cup.

'I was not at all surprised Keegan did so well in getting Newcastle into the Premier League,' Tommy Smith, his old Liverpool cohort in that final, reflected. 'I know he is the sort of person who sets out to do what he wants to do and also, by being superbly fit for a man of his age, he could impress his own determination on others. As a player himself, Kevin had 75 per cent ability, 150 per cent fitness. He wasn't like Kenny Dalglish, who was a player who didn't have to train so hard to play at such a high level. He had to do it by hard work, and it influenced others when he became manager. He couldn't have chosen a better time to do it at Newcastle than when he did.'

The 'Mighty Mouse', as he was known at Anfield and at the Volkspark Stadium, Hamburg, became the first English footballer to live the life of a superstar. The Football League president and former chairman of Newcastle, Gordon McKeag, compares Keegan to Nick Faldo for the way they drove themselves on from modest backgrounds to the top. 'Both have the same dedication and will to win.' Brian Moore, the veteran ITV Big Match commentator, recalls that, 'Kevin was the first private jet-setting, Arnold Palmer-style footballer of his time. His programme made us all dizzy. That's his life-style. You can't really change it.'

Such energies will surely promote Keegan to the England manager's post one day soon. That is certainly the opinion of former England coach, Don Howe.

'Keegan is the man in the street's choice. Now that Brian Clough has retired, Keegan will be the manager they want. I think it's a stone cold certainty Kevin will get the job.'

Keegan's initial priorities, however, lay with building a Newcastle team for the fans to be proud of.

1
'HE'S M' GOD'

A minor domestic drama was unfolding on that clear, summer-like evening of Thursday, 6 May 1993, somewhere out there in the grey urban landscape that sprawls away from the city centre of Newcastle-upon-Tyne.

This was not the night for a housewife to lose her door keys. Normally, she would have been forgiven by her other half, but that evening was different. Quite simply, her husband, like so many of the male population of Tyneside, had managed to get tickets for the football match at St James's Park where Kevin Keegan's Newcastle United were celebrating their ascension to the Premier League.

From the top of the new sprawling Jack Milburn stand, which from the highest tiers offers a panoramic view of the surrounding cityscape, the housewife's predicament only came into focus via a message on the stadium tannoy. It was just before kick-off, and Keegan's heroes were about to make their entrance for the match against Oxford United in front of the rapturous 'Toon Army' of fans. The message was announced clearly enough, but was still hard to hear as the fans at the Gallowgate End, Newcastle's equivalent of Liverpool's Kop, erupted into some wild chanting.

'Would Mr Blaydon [or a name sounding like that] go home immediately because his wife has locked herself out of their home?'

As all routine life outside the bounds of the stadium had been packed away for the evening, the plight of the husband became an object of uncontrollable mirth.

The crowd roared in sympathy. One loyalist among the all-ticket crowd of 29,438 was being torn away from his beloved football team just as they were about to celebrate reaching the pinnacle of success. It must have taken a brave woman to wrench her hubby away from his shrine, or to even contemplate such a dubious action. Whether the husband baled out and left was never disclosed, but a Geordie who abandoned such an important match would be a rare specimen.

Kevin Keegan also left earlier than expected. His excuse for leaving the dug-out zone in the charge of his assistant manager, Terry McDermott according to official sources, had to do with an upset tummy, which perhaps was understandable. Newcastle had claimed the Barclays League First Division pennant only two evenings before at Grimsby Town. Goals by Andy Cole and David Kelly had diffused all the suffocating tension and pressure the manager and his assistant had endured over all those matches since August. Messrs Keegan and McDermott had sniffed the clear air, even of fishy Grimsby, and McDermott, in a state of obvious ecstasy, proclaimed, 'Keegan's vision got us here'.

However, according to colleagues near to Keegan, the decision to leave the ground before Newcastle scored their two winning goals was caused by Keegan's in-built disciplinary code which never allows high standards to decline. Unfortunately, the mastermind of Newcastle's incredible success since arriving in February 1992, had missed strikes by the North East Footballer of the Year, Lee Clark, and his most risky but eventually crucial £1.75 million buy from Bristol City, Andy Cole.

That night of joyous celebration at St James's Park would be followed the next Sunday afternoon with an ITV-relayed Big Match Geordie party as the Newcastle team were presented with the First Division Barclays League championship trophy. The Gallowgate 'Toon' lads had gone berserk as their team thoroughly trounced Leicester City 7–1. Kevin Keegan had urged his team to keep up the standards he had. demanded throughout the long season. Against Leicester City he got his wish; against Oxford United, before his team scored, he hadn't.

'There will be a lot of people coming to St James's Park wanting to celebrate. They want to see us finishing in style,' said Keegan.

Oxford were mean enough to offer stern resistance, even taking into account the home side's shooting lapses. Keegan had decided, according to a St James's Park steward, 'to scarper off – the lads weren't playing in the style the boss wanted'.

Whatever the reasons for the sudden departure of the Newcastle boss, it must have been the first time in the history of the Football League that a manager had his team's progress relayed to him in the car over the mobile telephone. McDermott was frequently on the line as Keegan drove to the house on chairman Sir John Hall's estate at Wynard in Durham – into which he and his wife Jean had moved after he joined the club – on that warm spring evening.

'He must have been in Washington, Tyne and Wear, when our first went in and near Peterlee when we scored our second,' recalls McDermott.

To have witnessed as a 'neutral' those highly emotional matches over four almost Rio carnival-like days and nights, would have seemed like looking in on another world; a world where Geordie fans genuinely loved the local football team with a passion, leading one small boy to describe the resident manager with the words, 'He's M' God'.

When he took over from the dismissed Ossie Ardiles, Kevin Keegan had become the saviour of a club which had been grimly treading black Tyne water in the depths of the old Second Division. At the start of the 1992/93 season, he inspired the team to an eight-match winning run, which laid the foundations for taking the championship. 'But why all the fuss?' an outsider might ask.

Keegan would have been the first to tell a stranger to Newcastle why the winning of the championship prompted such a festive atmosphere in a community otherwise depressed by recession and the threat of job losses at Swan Hunter, the last shipyard on the Tyne.

'It is because Newcastle United are an unbelievable club. You only have to look over at St James's Park and you see a new stand going up and millions of people coming in and out and so much happening. Newcastle are a club on the move. So it was important when our fans turned up for the celebration games, that we were worthy champions. The reception they gave us was fantastic.'

The value of Newcastle United to a local community craving success was viewed so highly by the local council that they decided to honour the club, lock, stock and barrel with the freedom of Newcastle.

'Geordies all over the world have taken an enormous pride in the achievements of the club. Now is a fitting moment to commemorate their contribution to the life of the city and the region,' said Jeremy Beecham, leader of the council.

His comments couldn't have explained more accurately why so many Geordie boys and girls were running about with faces painted black and white, supremely happy, and singing the 'Blaydon Races' in Trader Jacks opposite the station and up towards the Strawberry Pub near the ground. Also, he hardly could have missed the Keegan fervour abounding in the 'toon'. If it wasn't Chairman Sir John Hall pulling a pint for the fans as skilfully as the Queen Mother!

The ubiquitous Keegan had a constant workload. It usually started with training at the team's new rented ground at Durham University, through a midweek match, and then on to Saturday afternoon. There was never time to waste with Kevin Keegan. He gave his all in every aspect of managerial life following on from his life style as a player. There were golfing jaunts, including a visit to the Belfry, the Ryder Cup headquarters, and a workout under the benevolent gaze of the Aston Villa manager, Ron Atkinson, at his team's training ground nearby – minor deviations from the club's routine schedule perhaps, but in Keegan's view, vital ingredients to prevent staleness setting in. Such comparatively inconsequential detours made news among the local fans because everything Newcastle did and everything Keegan was setting out to do on the promotion path, was news. It was something to talk about when the prospect of the dole was only just around the corner. Waiting until seven o'clock on a Sunday evening until the pub opened, could be as bleak as it was for your Dad, in the days when heroes like 'Wor' Jackie Milburn and Frank Brennan took their minds off rainy days and a few mouths to feed back in Blaydon.

Keegan was rarely out of the North East radio sports bulletins, and the build-up to winning the championship was nursed along by his own articulate, breezy Doncaster self. So much so, that he could have been coming and going simultaneously from the bench to the microphone or television studio as a Big Match analyst, almost as if the two jobs were linked together. They weren't of course; Keegan took on a comparatively minor role in the broadcasting stakes, although he carried out these duties, many experts said, with almost professional zeal.

What he did have to say was quickly devoured by Newcastle ratepayers. Beecham and his council members were thankful that his side was creating something morale-boosting to keep Geordie chins up high, as another 6,000 jobs were threatened at Swan Hunter. They could read about it in a special *Daily Mirror* 'Money' supplement that had appeared.

'They've brought back the pride to a city ravaged by recession. Under manager Kevin Keegan, Newcastle have blitzed their way to the Premier League. And it's not just the hearts of their fanatical supporters that are being lifted by the triumphant Magpies – their pockets are being lined as well. All over the city, businesses are reaping the benefits of Newcastle's return to the big time and, with the promise of massive television exposure the following season, the city is convinced it can attract investors from all over the world to help bring back the boom times.'

All this because of the exploits of a football team and, of course, Kevin Keegan.

How did it happen so quickly, this supercharged, Keegan-guided rush into a Premier League, which desperately needed teams with flair and imagination in its over-stocked larder? Did the new manager really have the imagination and vision his assistant Terry McDermott spoke so admiringly of, or was it through some extraordinary powers of persuasion that he got the message across to his players? It was no good trying to say Keegan had some secret telepathic powers, but what he had proved in his first full season as a manager was that he could do a job others had failed at so miserably.

Martin Peters, who had been an England squad member with Keegan under Sir Alf Ramsey, but who never actually played on the pitch with him, believes Keegan had one vital bonus in his contract which other managers did not have.

'Kevin came to the Newcastle job knowing he was secure financially. He hadn't needed the job, so could relax a bit more in a situation where other managers couldn't. He could afford to be more laid back and accept the odd bad run. By being relaxed, he could give his all to the job and not be paralysed with fear about the future. In the end, Kevin did a magnificent job. I always thought he could make a good manager; he was so self-disciplined and hard working as a Liverpool player. Success in his first full season! Kevin never believed in wasting time.'

It was probably because Keegan felt he had spent too much time on the golf course, that he was persuaded by Newcastle in the first place to take the manager's job. He had been quoted as saying that being employed as a manager was not for him. He gave tactful excuses, he made the odd succinct observation, and he told the odd celebrity he met on the golf course he wouldn't dream of taking up the challenge.

Both his daughters, Laura Jane and Sarah, had become teenagers by the time he thought it right to put his Marbella golf clubs away and hit the trail to his old stamping ground at St James's Park, where he had retired in triumph in 1984 after helping Newcastle win promotion to the First Division.

He was announced dramatically as manager at a Newcastle press conference on 5 February 1992. This time there was no Arthur Cox to hover over him. Keegan was boss, facing a task others would have found doubly daunting. Sixty-year-old Sir John Hall, Newcastle's racehorse-owning chairman, appeared to enjoy the conference enormously, looking regal at these types of function, without being overbearing or putting people down.

He had never claimed to be a football expert, but his passion for Newcastle United Football Club, a club debt-ridden and seemingly ebbing away into the lower berths of the Football League, was gaining momentum. Sir John had made a considerable fortune for himself as the founder of the Metro Centre, the largest shopping and shipping centre in Europe. The arrival of Keegan, however, had not been simple.

The new manager's predecessor had been Osvaldo Ardiles, the much-loved 'Ossie' of White Hart Lane and Argentina's 1978 World Cup winning team. Ardiles had arrived at St James's Park after a two-year spell in management at Swindon Town. Despite his undoubted intelligence and tactical knowledge of the game, which he used to influence the Newcastle squad, it failed to click into a winning team. The 'sinking Tyne ship' sank deeper, and the supporters demanded Ossie should be sent to the River Plate, well away from Tyne and Wear. But Sir John Hall had brought Ardiles to St James's Park to keep the club in the Second Division, and he was reluctant to dismiss him. He liked Ardiles – his charm, his good South American manners and his sound knowledge of legal affairs, having qualified as a solicitor during his Tottenham Hotspur playing days. An exclusive article in a Sunday national newspaper quoted Sir John as saying Ardiles would not be leaving the club, and that was that.

However, the results had not been encouraging, so there would have to be a change. Ironically, Newcastle's first match in the 1993/4 season would be against Tottenham Hotspur, who had just appointed Ardiles as manager.

To say Sir John Hall brought Kevin Keegan to Newcastle, would be overstating the case. When Keegan did arrive on his doorstep, Sir John showed an abundant flair for making the Tyneside hero welcome, by standing beside the player and holding up a black and white scarf with 'Newcastle United' inscribed across it in large capital letters. It made a good picture for the newspapers, but in truth Sir John was acting as front man in the photograph, since all along he'd been part of a *fait accompli* involving his own son, Douglas, and the jovial Chief Executive of the club, Freddie Fletcher.

There was only one man Keegan wanted to help him run the team at St James's Park, his old Liverpool and Newcastle playing colleague, fellow racecourse punter and snooker opponent, Terry McDermott. This appointment was about the only stipulation Keegan made, and Sir John was wise enough to tell his new manager to get away fast and get his man on the phone, before McDermott was snapped up. Not that there had been much danger of that. McDermott had more or less settled into a life of gentle retirement playing golf, snooker and tennis, and having fun out of the firing line of professional football.

The game had brought McDermott 25 England caps, a place in Ron Greenwood's 1982 World Cup squad, and numerous medals under Bob Paisley's guidance – the most important one of all, coming in the European Cup Final in Rome where he scored the first goal for Liverpool against Borussia Moenchengladbach. Though normally totally controlled when in possession of the ball, he gave the impression of running like a clothes line hung with flapping towels in a high wind. McDermott was so loose and easy on the ball, that opponents were deceived when they went in to challenge him; his arms dangling free at his sides, no extravagant pumping action, no enforced exaggeration, just free and easy. But now Keegan was on the phone at St James's Park ringing the Merseysider he called his 'buffer'.

Would he like the job of helping Keegan save their old club, Newcastle United, from relegation? It took only five seconds for McDermott to say 'Yes'.

'I would have come in and helped make the tea if necessary,' said McDermott.

McDermott was hired, much to Keegan's delight. It was going to be hard enough to get the sinking ship back to port, but getting one's messages across to virtual strangers in the dressing room after being out of the game for so long was going to be a nightmare unless he and McDermott persisted and got their 'We shall not go down' message across straight away.

Newcastle's first match under Keegan received the same pomp and Geordie ceremony as his playing days with the club. Keegan duly emerged from the dug-out, waved his arms in

20

acknowledgement at the hero worship he was receiving, and watched his team beat Bristol City 3–0. There were enough rusty players in the Newcastle set-up to make the new arrival feel totally comfortable. He noticed them, when probably the fans didn't, since they were too absorbed by their team winning under the new 'Messiah'. As McDermott said, his new gaffer didn't sit back once the players had trudged off the St James's Park pitch that February afternoon.

Some of the players in his squad felt that there was much to applaud about their new boss, especially when it came to training methods. It was here that Keegan's absence from the front-line did show up on cold, early spring mornings at Durham. Mick Quinn, transferred to Newcastle from Portsmouth in 1989, a year after the departure of Paul Gascoigne to Tottenham Hotspur, had scored 32 goals in 45 matches and was a hardened old pro who had been around the football League scene since the days when his new boss was playing for Hamburg. He had travelled far and served many clubs, and was, like McDermott, an irreverent scouser when situations needed it. He had seen managers come and go, not only at Newcastle, and didn't have to be told about the running of football clubs and all the pitfalls which lay underneath an employer's political jousting. He had been a Derby County apprentice, then a striker with increasingly regular slots in the first teams of Wigan Athletic, Stockport County, Oldham Athletic and then Portsmouth, with whom he had stayed for four seasons.

At St James's Park, Quinn promptly began rattling the ball into opposing nets, much to the delight of the Geordie crowd. However, his natural instincts in the opposition's penalty box had become rather toothless by the time Messrs Keegan and McDermott arrived at the club. Quinn moved on to Coventry the following season, where he quickly began shooting goals again as voraciously as he had done back in his first months on Tyneside. When he left, he didn't have too favourable a view of the Keegan roadshow, especially his training methods, which he thought were badly organized.

An opening victory against Bristol City under Keegan was all very well, but the manager knew with the uncanny vision gained from his first boss at Liverpool, Bill Shankly, that Newcastle United were labouring like a tug boat on its last legs – there was a great deal of tugging, but little sign of real progress through the water. Keegan's policy was to get down to work immediately, although he decided that a full-scale workout at the club training ground at Durham Castle after the Bristol match, accompanied by a Don Revie-style dossier teach-in followed by a Bill Shankly pep talk, was probably not a good idea. But it would be back to work the following Monday on the training pitch, trying to put right a few obvious faults that had been apparent on the Saturday.

McDermott noticed Keegan's determination. He had seen so much of it at Liverpool, and twice now with Newcastle, where he played first against Keegan in the 1974 FA Cup Final, and then with him during the promotion season in 1984.

'Wherever Keegan is, things seem to happen now. Other people might have three- and five-year plans, but with Kevin even next month might be too far ahead for him. It's always *now*.'

The time for action had come early on in his first season at Newcastle, with time trickling away and relegation threatening like red-hot cinders piled on the manager's dug-out. If he did not get new players, Newcastle would be going down despite the glossiness of the rescue plan to save a club £6.5 million in debt that had been second from the bottom of the old Second Division when he arrived. Keegan wanted new players now. Otherwise, he could see little hope of the once-proud Magpies holding on to their flimsy status in the Second Division. There was something titanic about Keegan's attitude, and the Newcastle staff couldn't have failed to notice it, from the chairman through to the humblest apprentice.

Even so, the money for transfers that Keegan expected, was not forthcoming. Not for the first time in his long career as a footballer, and now manager, had he felt like walking out, convinced his own judgements were right. McDermott felt the Keegan pressure-cooker getting hotter and hotter. As a player, Keegan had walked out on Bill Shankly and Don Revie, though only briefly on both occasions. But doing so had demanded some pluck even though both decisions seemed impetuous and misjudged. In Shankly's case, his own Dad told him off, while with Don Revie, Frank McGhee, among many leading sports columnists tut-tutted, 'Who does Kevin Keegan think he is?'

Now a situation over buying new players had brought matters to a head. Would the little man be off to his family, horses and golf so soon after emerging out of the shadows of self-imposed exile on a distant Spanish green? Since Keegan had an open-ended contract with the club, it wouldn't be too difficult to walk out, as the club was loath to act now, and he would be powerless to prevent disaster. In this defiant mood, he continued to have rows with a defensive Sir John.

The Keegan arrival may have been euphoric, but the hunting horns which had greeted the new boss on his arrival at St James's Park were now muted. It was clear that Newcastle were still struggling. It was a wonderful public relations job, and there was no better pro in the business than Joseph Kevin Keegan, but Newcastle's actual results hardly promised salvation. When Keegan sat in his office, he brooded momentarily in the tradition of US President Harry S. Truman, and the 'buck stops here'. Sir John Hall was not afraid either to take the buck, but the club's £6.5 million debt was not a foundation for going out and buying expensive footballers. Keegan had his reasons, and good ones too, for needing better players, but there were limits to what a once carefree club could do during times of recession. The buck was certainly knocking on the door of Sir John's office, as the club's 'split board' refused to allow Keegan his new recruitment policy.

Matters got so bad that Keegan and McDermott decided in private that there was a 'lost cause' or 'split board' operating at St James's Park. Whatever they said from the dug-out on Saturday afternoons had lost all meaning, because the team was below the standard Keegan required.

Before the home match against Swindon on 14 March, Keegan and McDermott attended Thursday training, picked the side, then left St James's Park on the Friday night, seemingly forever.

'Well, that's it. Bugger it,' spluttered Keegan. 'These things happen, it could have been all for the good, but it wasn't.'

As the car accelerated onto a northern motorway, the two pals, the 'Gaffer' and the 'Buffer,' could have raised two fingers and said, 'Show us your medals then!', as England's former captain had gained a clutch of League and European medals with Liverpool and Hamburg, and McDermott's career with Liverpool bagged five League titles and three European Cup medals. They needed no credentials as players, but the dampening feeling of an unfinished task left to mildew in someone else's inexperienced hands began to grind its way into the pair's thoughts. They had been in management for a very short time. Leaving so soon hurt.

Sir John and his son, Douglas, were anxious that Keegan's impetuous behaviour did not cut the cord between themselves and Newcastle United. Sir John had been a bit hasty in his euphoric messages to the media after the first victory under Keegan. One victory does not win a campaign, and Sir John might have held back in hailing the winning of three points.

'This has put the smile back on the faces of our financial backers [a £10 million rescue scheme to save the club was in the offing]. When we lost to Oxford United, the money for the rescue plan disappeared. We ran some projections through the computer and this victory confirmed that the club could not exist if we were relegated. Now I'm confident we can survive.'

Sir John spoke too eagerly and too prematurely, having had Keegan presented to the world as Mr Salvation, and there should have been moves to encourage the new boss with a morale-boosting casket of cash to buy the odd player. So you couldn't exactly blame Keegan and his assistant for feeling the chairman's door had been slammed in their faces. Obviously there was a cashflow problem at the club, but other companies were managing to hang on by their fingernails during months and months of mad, mad recession under the Chancellor of the Exchequer, Norman Lamont. Keegan felt Newcastle were in a position to buy players. So when the team started losing again under his command with players he considered not up to the job,

Keegan decided he wouldn't add to the thinly-rationed grey hairs which had slipped into his own trimmed fortyish coiffure, and would walk out now. He would take his old Buffer along with him, and they would vent their frustrations, perhaps on a snooker table in McDermott's home-spun neighbourhood on Merseyside.

They were on the M6 together, on the Carlisle Road and heading towards Liverpool when McDermott made a singular and very important decision. 'We're going back,' he said. No hanging around, it was back to St James's Park. Somehow, via a mobile phone in a Hexham lay-by, the departing Buffer persuaded Keegan to give notice to his bosses that he was on the way back for a chat.

Perhaps Keegan remembered the incident, early in his Liverpool career, when Shankly had refused to believe the new Scunthorpe arrival had a painful leg injury and told him to report for the team bus for the trip to Stoke. He had walked out then, angry that Shankly had thought he was exaggerating his ailment, but it was Joe Keegan, rather more abruptly than McDermott, who had sent him back to 'Shanks' straight away. 'You've got a contract, son,' he said.

McDermott could have said the same. Both himself and Keegan were under an obligation to Newcastle to save the club's neck. Running off wouldn't solve anything. If Keegan had been impetuous, it was McDermott who made the move to get them back on duty. Was it also the memory of a night when McDermott failed to turn up for the Football Writers' Association annual dinner in London in 1980 because, as the story goes, he had gone to the races? McDermott knew that by walking out on that dinner he had let himself down in eyes of his manager, Bob Paisley, who had looked white with rage when he accepted the Footballer of the Year trophy on behalf of his player.

It wasn't quite so simple – this brief retreat, and then back to a cosy chat and reformed reunion with Sir John and the 'split' Newcastle board. You can bet there were some 'effings and blindings' over various phones, as there usually are in football when managers, chairmen and directors are not getting their way. The game was not made for gentle vicars, as Sir John must have realized when he came in from his stately home, at Wynard in Durham, to take up the club chairmanship. Even though Keegan and McDermott did take charge of the Swindon match, which Newcastle won 3–1 through goals by David Kelly, Gavin Peacock and Mick Quinn, there was no mood of celebration. Keegan was seen by a Newcastle supporter drawing away from the car park. He was on his way to his Hampshire home to oil his fax machine and await developments concerning his plea for new players.

Who had been the most disillusioned so far: the chairman, the players, or the new management team? The incoming manager was raw, whatever his considerable admiration society might have said about the great 'vision' seeing him through the difficult opening rounds. Raw, chilly mornings sometimes turned to freezing ones on Tyneside, and at the Durham training headquarters, players didn't always have patience with the superlatives heaped on a small man trudging around a bit of muddy grass. Although Keegan, with the support of McDermott tried to convey his own attitudes and tactical savvy into the minds of his troops, the response on Saturday afternoons was not encouraging.

The legendary former Tottenham hero, Danny Blanchflower, also knew a great deal about the game but when appointed manager of Chelsea by chairman and admirer, Brian Mears, most of his ideas simply flowed over the heads of his playing staff, with the exception of Ray Wilkins and a few others who were prepared to listen. Keegan was equally enthusiastic, and those who didn't respond to what he had to say made him impatient. He didn't like seeing his tactical plans hitting a brick wall on Saturday afternoons. Keegan had gone into the job certainly expecting more help from his chairman, and the club in general, although, as he put it, 'the top of the club hadn't been right for 40 or 50 years'. He believed he could do the job, but not even Moses should have been expected to save a tottering Second Division side from the plunge at such a late stage in the season.

What Keegan needed was tanks, not pop-guns. It was a difficult time for Sir John, left brooding about Keegan, the club rel-egation issue and club debts on his beautiful country estate where Tyneside was only a painful illusion a long way away. Keegan's sudden exit with McDermott must have surprised him, as previous ones had surprised Shankly and Revie. Although Keegan was not exactly welcomed back, the sudden departure did force the issue into the open so that, in good time, Sir John and the club agreed to find the money to purchase new players.

The month of April 1992, however, proved a dreadful and near fatal time for Keegan and McDermott following their brief exodus the previous month. Starting on 30 March with a 6–2 thrashing at Wolverhampton, Newcastle lost four more match-es against Tranmere Rovers, Ipswich Town, Millwall and Derby County. If any intruder wanted to make digs about the Keegan–McDermott management team being 'raw', they were entitled at that point. Just how close Newcastle came to taking the plunge into the Third Division and probable extinction can be seen from these results, which tended to be forgotten during the time of euphoria a year later at St James's Park. Keegan and McDermott knew they had to rebuild the team, but would they still have one to rebuild the following season? As the pair took their places in the Newcastle dug-out at Fratton Park, Ports-mouth on 25 April for the penultimate League match of the sea-son, Keegan had every right to feel he should pop home to Jean and the girls after the match at their nearby Romsey home – and stay there. It seemed a hopeless cause, despite his determination to save the club from the drop.

Amazingly, and somewhat dramatically Newcastle managed to win 1–0 through a goal by David Kelly, Newcastle's second highest goalscorer that season with 11 and a Republic of Ireland striker who had sprung to considerable fame as an opportunist with his first League club, Walsall. Unhappy spells with West Ham, where he was barracked by ill-disposed Upton Park fans, and Leicester City preceded his move to Newcastle the season of Keegan's arrival. His goal, against a side that had lost to Liverpool in a replayed FA Cup semi-final and had been going steadily towards promotion under manager Jim Smith, was the most vital scored by a Newcastle player during Keegan's short spell in charge. If ever Keegan felt like going off to kiss the Blarney Stone, now was the time.

When Keegan went home, he hung on to a five-bar Hampshire gate, pinching himself but still not believing the team had won. Two of the signings Keegan had made were immediately in the action – 'Easy Rider' Oldham defender, Brian Kilcline, who had captained Coventry in the 1987 FA Cup final, and Kevin Sheedy, the goalscoring Republic of Ireland midfielder on a free transfer from Everton. Both Kilcline and Sheedy played their part in what would prove a time of elevation for Newcastle during their crucial final two matches, but perhaps the most gutsy performer was Gavin Peacock. The Kentish born midfielder had played with the number eight shirt throughout a turbulent season under Ardiles following stints at Queen's Park Rangers, Gillingham and Bournemouth before joining Newcastle in 1990. He finished with 16 of Newcastle's 66 League goals, three of them penalties, the last one claimed in the game at Filbert Street against the play-off representatives, Leicester City.

Peacock's goal in the 2–1 victory was followed by an own goal from Leicester's Steve Walsh to guarantee safety for Newcastle on an afternoon at Filbert Street in which after the match, rival fans skirmished around the press area, picking fights. The welcome from the Leicester fans had been as abrasive as it could be for the noisy Geordie contingent. Keegan's views on crowd violence were well known, having himself been kicked and threatened by Welsh fans at Ninian Park, his eyes smartened by tear gas fumes in Turin when England fans went on the rampage, and later being roughed up by three youths while sleeping in his own Range Rover. It sickened him, and he was always quick to say so, without diving too much into the sociology books to discover the causes of hooliganism as studied by sheltered university types.

The afternoon had not been a convivial one. At least Newcastle did manage to cling on to their Second Division status in 1992, which was after all what the incoming manager had been brought in to do. He had got the battered ship 'Magpie' back to port. So the Newcastle board could go off on holiday now and celebrate, ironically, the club's return to the First Division, as the old Second would now be called.

Kevin Keegan made off to Spain, and the chances of him returning looked bleak. The money to buy new players had only gone so far. Keegan still wanted to strengthen his staff, but he had only received long looks from Sir John Hall and the board. Some tense talks had got under way again.

Meanwhile, back in Spain with Jean and his daughters, Keegan was enjoying the same old Costa ambience; the same rushing Sol-laced traffic running free and sometimes fatally along the motorway beyond earshot from Casa Keegan; the same chatty days playing golf at the Rio Real Club where he had made firm friends among the caddies on the course. Although he had only been a manager for a short time, Keegan was nevertheless in need of relaxation after weeks of nerve-racking emotion in the dug-out, and weeks of unsettled negotiation at St James's Park. One caddy at the club was overjoyed at the very mention of Keegan's name.

'Señor, that Kevin is good at everything he does. I have played with him here many times. I know his handicap is officially five, but I can tell you he can get that down to two or one. He is good enough to be a professional and he has the professional touch – practice, practice, practice every day'.

Up at his sumptuous residence, Keegan dug in his heels and waited for Newcastle's reaction to his continuing at St James's Park on his terms. The Los Monteros hotel, with its plush chalets, tennis court and poolside palm trees was a good place to relax. Eventually it was Sir John's son, Douglas, who flew from Newcastle airport to Malaga and then on to Marbella, with the club's blessing and a deal which would make Keegan club manager on Tyneside for considerably longer than the short, and ultimately successful period, he and McDermott had put in since February. It was late May when Freddie Fletcher and vice chairman Freddie Shepherd arrived, summer waiting to unleash its airless, blinding light along the Costa del Sol, with the seventh Rio green bordering Casa Keegan already lush and tropical.

Keegan was often on the course but put his second sporting passion aside for four days as he sat down to business with Hall, Shepherd and Fletcher. Hall, once described by Patrick Collins, the *Mail on Sunday* columnist, as a chain-smoking Ian Rush lookalike, was also chairman of the family firm Cameron Hall Developments.

Keegan was delighted and relieved by Douglas Hall's new contract deal. It emphasized priority would be given for a £2 million transfer fund, which Keegan had intended on, at the end of the season if further progress between the club and manager was to be maintained. Keegan's insistence on a written guarantee was granted, and the fact he was able to spend £1.5 million on new players during the following season meant that the team would be challenging for promotion. Douglas Hall did not hum and haw or mumble out any 'mañana' excuses. He was anxious to get Keegan back to St James's Park as quickly as possible after the end-of-season break. Fletcher and Douglas Hall were the ones who had brought Keegan to St James's Park in the first place. They wanted the Mighty Atom back to push Newcastle United into the Premier League, and both of them knew that given the resources, Keegan could do it.

Keegan didn't seem to waver too long over the three-year £120,000 deal which he would sign later at St James's Park, and was delighted at the invitation by Sir John to move into a house on the Wynard estate. It would help him settle during those early days on Tyneside, when Keegan felt uprooted from the family home and stud farm in the New Forest where he had become a familiar, squirrel-like figure in green wellies, hopping over five-bar gates to look at his prized nags. But somehow the Wellingtons hadn't suited his image, unlike football boots that were divinely created for him. Hence, the determination to bring to an end the board room upheavals at St James's Park during early summer.

If Terry McDermott had felt pessimistic about his own future at St James's Park, the meeting on the Costa, and Keegan's agreement to sign the new deal, helped erase any speculation in his own mind about what it would be like going back to playing snooker and attending the races full-time again as a comfortably retired footballer. Three months of soccer under Keegan had given McDermott the 'taste' again. He wanted to be in on what could be a challenging season for the Magpies. Then the phone rang, and Keegan delivered the good news. The pair would be working together again, and hopefully they could get ahead with their plans, of which there were many. McDermott was also given a three-year contract, and to say he was 'over the moon' could not have escaped even the most junior of Tyneside reporters.

'It looked bleak last week and there seemed to be no way out. Now it's sorted and we are both delighted. I'm ecstatic about going back to Newcastle, and I believe the club have the best man for the job in Kevin.'

McDermott had every excuse on that day, 21 May 1992, to raise a glass of cheer. Keegan hurried out his own statement as a relieved Douglas Hall's Newcastle delegation took time off in the sun-drenched life of Marbella to celebrate. Having Keegan and McDermott around to run the Newcastle show for the following season was a coup, despite the upheavals of the previous weeks. Keegan's words from the Costa del Sol were eagerly digested by the Geordie supporters rooted as ever to every soccer paragraph on the pages of the *Journal and Evening Chronicle*. The big splash was all they needed as an excuse to raise another pint of Newcastle Brown Ale. The club sponsors must have purred as well. The Messiah's words, all the way up from the Rio's seventh green, sounded sincere and optimistic.

'I wanted to come back if everything was right. Things had been happening at St James's Park (the boardroom upheavals) which had nothing to do with me, but now all the uncertainty has been lifted. I'm cutting short my stay in Spain to fly to Newcastle on Tuesday and begin work. My heart has always been with Newcastle, and what has happened now is good for the club, good for the fans, and good for Kevin Keegan. All the differences have been removed and I'm happy. I'll be moving my family to the north, lock, stock and barrel.'

Sir John Hall, whose exchanges with Kevin Keegan had threatened to sabotage their relationship, now felt the need to extend yet another welcoming hand.

'Kevin fully understands our financial position now. We will help him in every way we can to overcome the problems. His reputation will greatly assist us in these endeavours. What we need next season is a promotion push for the Premier League.'

Without saying so in print, Sir John was so anxious to retain Keegan at that stage that even if money could not be found for new transfer deals from club financiers, he would dip into his own pocket to help out – which he did with the arrival of Andy Cole at Newcastle the following March. The optimism expressed by both chairman and manager on that May day certainly had a great bearing on the triumphs and celebrations to come. There was an almost cyclonic rush of challenging air on Tyneside as Keegan rushed in to take over as manager. He had already made his mind up about how the job had to be done. The phone, office or mobile, was rarely out of his hand, and his battle cry for action could well have mimicked the great New Orleans jazz pianist, Jellyroll Morton.

'Hullo Tyneside. Give me Dr Soccer. He's got what I need. Know he has.'

The prescription Keegan needed was for new players, and again like his old mentor, Bill Shankly, Keegan showed he had a hidden flair for bringing in exceptional talent. Keegan could spot a 'good 'un', sometimes even if the good 'un was beginning to feel he was a failed good 'un after months in the wilderness. Signing for Kevin Keegan changed all that.

Compared to the precipitous events surrounding the first, and so nearly final, weeks of Kevin Keegan's managerial appointment at St James's Park, the following season, so triumphant and fulfilling at the end, was remarkably trouble-free. Cheered by his new three-year contract, and having Terry McDermott on deck again to help with the navigation, Keegan, in his own typical way, got down to work on the hull of a nearly burnt-out Newcastle ship.

There were a number of reasons why the team rose so magnificently to the challenge. While the players themselves and the professional first-team coach, Derek Fazackerley – a very shrewd tactician promoted by Keegan – deserved all the Geordie praises poured upon them, at the end of the day the manager's contribution on the bridge was of paramount importance. Here was a former professional footballer who had come 'out of the cold', so to speak, to take over an ailing Second Division club and was now transforming it into a smoothly running cruiser. This had happened not within weeks of the start of the new season, but within minutes of the kick-off of the opening match against Southend United on 15 August, when one of the manager's signings from Sunderland, the ubiquitous, hardworking Paul Bracewell, scored for Newcastle.

Keegan was shrewd with his signings once he had obtained the money to buy new talent. One of his most significant purchases was bringing Robert Lee up from the South after years of striking goals for Charlton Athletic. Lee, who cost £700,000, made his League debut ironically for Charlton in the 1983/84 season, which was Keegan's last in senior football at Newcastle. Cynics said Lee and family would never settle on Tyneside. But as the season got into full swing, Lee's goalscoring powers, which had seen him score 25 goals in his two previous seasons with Charlton, began to show themselves once more. The manager was also being written about. After a visit to Newcastle's training ground, Brough Scott wrote a piece in the *Independent on Sunday*.

'While it may be true that Kevin Keegan never intended to take up football management, here he is in his element. The mane of hair may be greyer these days and the muscled torso a bit slacker, but here again is the little inspirational dynamo whose fearless self-belief lifted him from an unpromising Scunthorpe apprentice to the very top of the European game.'

Newcastle United under Keegan were carrying all before them and continued to do so, winning their matches and opening up an enviable lead at the top of the First Division.

'We haven't changed anything massive in the way we play,'

Keegan said. 'There is no way you can go so quickly from the bottom to the top. We have pushed Gavin Peacock forward, and have tried to play more in the opponent's half. But you can't make a system and say "play that way". You've got to suit the players in your team.'

Keegan was never far away from the white telephones at the training centre office – the liaison link with the aircraft carrier based over at St James's Park – and all the pressures prevailing around the chairman's inner sanctum.

'The club is still £6.5 million in debt. I wouldn't want that problem,' Keegan vouched.

'But I know one thing. If we get gates of 28,000 it helps. For too long, people have talked of this being an unlucky place. They even added a second Magpie outside the ground to stop people thinking "one for sorrow". We are saying out loud we will be in the Premier League, that nothing will be bigger than this club.'

Keegan's was not an idle boast and the early season bounce a puff of Tyneside wind. The season progressed not as a wild sprint, which would run out of steam, but methodically, like the schoolboy cross-country runner Keegan once prided himself on being. Sprinting had never been Keegan's forte, but he certainly enjoyed the way Newcastle romped away with their opening run of eleven opening wins.

Lee Clark, the shaven-headed midfielder, quick on his hooves and mean to opposing goalkeepers in the box, received the greatest praise early on. The 19-year-old out-and-out Geordie, born in Wallsend and admired for his skills as a schoolboy by Paul Gascoigne, didn't waste time in creating havoc in rival defences. He was so sure of himself, so confident when the black and white chips were down, that clubs like Southend United, who fought back to equalize in the first match of the season after being 0–2 down, couldn't be certain it would stay that way with Clark around. Clark duly scored Newcastle's winner in that match, and in the second, a 2–1 win at Derby, the same player capped an inspired performance against the promotion favourites by beating four men and smashing in a shot from 20 yards. The winning continued for Keegan on 26 September as

Robert Lee showed up for his first match for Newcastle at Peterborough and made the only goal of the game to stretch Newcastle's victorious bonanza to eight games.

Three more victories against Brentford, Tranmere and Sunderland – the last, a 'pulsating derby clash' according to the *Daily Express*, was decided by a free-kick from Liam O'Brien, earning Kevin Keegan's team a 2–1 victory, their first at Roker Park for 36 years – had put the League leaders into an invincible mood. So who would have expected the twelfth and thirteenth matches at Grimsby and Leicester to go sour?

Newcastle's run of victories ended on 23 October at Grimsby through a goal by Jim Dobbin in injury time. Then the boat began to rock again as the *Daily Express* reported Leicester's 2–1 victory at Filbert Street a week later: 'This was not United's best of the season. Even another Liam O'Brien goal could not earn a point.'

It was time for that well-known Keegan fizz and sting again. The team were determined to do better at Birmingham on 4 November, winning a best-of-five-goals thriller through an own goal by Trevor Matthewson. An entertaining 0–0 home draw against Swindon, with the visiting player–manager, Glenn Hoddle the star, was followed by four consecutive wins against Charlton, Watford, Cambridge and Notts County, before things came unstuck against Barnsley on 13 December, a goal by Brendan O'Connell bringing Newcastle their third League defeat.

By Christmas, Keegan and his backroom team were still confident of holding on to their lead, despite Millwall taking a point, which should have been three, at St James's Park. Newcastle had equalized with a highly dubious penalty on the hour, when a linesman spotted an obscure heading offence.

Boxing Day was fiesta time with a 30,000 capacity crowd at St James's Park, including the Keegan family, relishing David Kelly's two goals in a 2–1 win against Wolves. Once again, the ruthless advance was checked by Oxford United's 4–2 win at the Manor Ground, Newcastle's biggest defeat of the season. Keegan didn't panic but there was still a long way to go until the promotion positions were decided in May.

Two wins against Bristol City and Peterborough, and three draws against Southend, Luton and Derby in January preceded Newcastle's first defeat in 1993. It occurred on 9 February at Fratton Park, when goals by Guy Whittingham, his 33rd of the season, and Welsh international defender Kit Symons caused morale to sag on the Gallowgate terraces. Two goalless draws against West Ham at Upton Park, and bottom-placed Bristol Rovers at home (managed temporarily by Keegan's old admirer, Malcolm Allison) did not help to boost confidence.

Goals had been scarce of late, but the *Daily Express* reported an end to the famine on 28 February at Tranmere when two goals by Lee and one by Clark, gave Newcastle their tenth away victory of the season. Brentford were annihilated 5–1 at St James's Park in March, but then butterflies began to catch up with Keegan. When Lee's old team, Charlton, took a point away from St James's Park in a 2–2 draw, Newcastle no longer could regard winning the First Division championship as a formality.

The pressure had been there, but Keegan had responded by looking almost dapper in jacket and tie on match days, which proved a calming influence on his tracksuited companions mouthing instructions in the Newcastle dug-out. When things went against his team, as they did against Swindon, Keegan would take off his jacket and stand in his shirt sleeves and patterned coloured tie, looking more like a Doncaster horse auctioneer on show day.

When he boiled over, it was with good reason, and the Swindon game – which Chris Tait, editor of the Newcastle supporters' bible, *The Mag*, described as '90 minutes of grievous bodily harm…Swindon couldn't score unless they dived or made use of an arm' – was just one occasion when Keegan found himself looking for answers. For one, he couldn't understand the attitude of Glenn Hoddle's team. They were supposed to play good football, as they had shown at St James's Park earlier in the season, but this was something different.

It was mid-March, the season was getting on, and Newcastle had been losing valuable points at the top. West Ham, Portsmouth and Swindon were beginning to close in on the chase. So Keegan's response was to do something he normally shied away from – to seek out the referee and enquire why he had not blown for a free-kick against Steve White for hand-ball instead of awarding the fatal corner from which Colin Calderwood scored. The referee was 20-year-old Graham Pall, the youngest referee on the football league's books. His response was to slam his dressing room door in Keegan's face. The manager was hurt, but decided not to take the matter on.

'I've already been fined by the FA this season for speaking out, and I'd like to build up my bank balance before I say anything.'

Many media reporters present were certain Keegan wasn't over-reacting to what clearly seemed a wrong decision. Neil Harman wrote in the *Daily Mail*, 'It would be fair to suggest that most in the County Ground, bar those that matter, would testify on oath that White took control of a pass with his arm when brushing Lee Clark's challenge aside. The corner Swindon were awarded brought about the winning goal.'

This incident is mentioned because it showed once again Keegan's in-built determination to seek out what he thought was a grave injustice to his players. He had generally played fair on the pitch, but when he became a victim of what he presumed to be injustice, he would complain. In deciding not to continue to pester the stubborn Mr Pall after being rudely shown the door, Keegan had displayed good sense for one so fresh to football management.

However, this impetuous action was still enough to make Keegan an object of doubt in his critics' notebook. There was a feeling accompanying the heavy April showers, that Newcastle United could be outsprinted at the finish, and left to battle for a Premier League place in the unwelcoming play-offs. Keegan, it was said, was showing signs of cracking up. On 24 April, Portsmouth (who would again miss out on promotion) beat Wolves to go top of the First Division. Tony Francis, writing in the *Sunday Times*, was there to describe this short-term southern monopoly.

'So accustomed have we grown to the sight of Newcastle at the forefront, that the destination of the First Division seemed hardly worth discussing. Now, after seven-and-a-half months of North East monopoly, a club from the opposite end of the country has taken charge.'

For sure, but not for long. With Keegan, McDermott and Fazackerley bailing out the St James's Park dug-out in torrential rain the next day, Newcastle's single-goal win through Steve Summer's thrilling shot over the Sunderland wall, corrected a setback that Stephen Bierley in the *Guardian* wrote, was as 'all Geordies fully expected, only temporary'. By then, Newcastle had some relatively unsung heroes in defence: Barry Venison, Keegan's Player of the Year, goalkeeper Pav Srnicek, a Czech international, Steve Howey, and Kevin Scott. He praised the fans for their continued support as Newcastle scaled their final peak, winning their last three matches at Grimsby, and at home to Oxford United and Leicester City.

'I was delighted by the way we battled hard against Sunderland and bounced back to the top of the First Division. It had been a very dangerous fixture for us.'

Keegan, for a moment, presumed Lee Clark drowned at sea at the Sunderland match, but the grinning player emerged eventually from a large puddle. There was still time for a bit of humour and the 30,364 crowd saw the funny side of it.

During the post-match celebrations at Blundell Park, the manager looked triumphant, but he also looked as if he had been under considerable pressure. The grey hairs were shining and the lines around the eyes were caught by some cruel lenses. Yet he was fresh as a Tyneside daisy the next day, as the club's main sponsors, Newcastle Breweries, reported the start of a staggering increase in beer sales, and a jump in demand for Newcastle Brown Ale in 40 countries around the world!

Keegan waited around just long enough for the final 7–1 annihilation of Leicester City before pushing off on holiday with the family to Disney World in Florida, and then to a beach in Barbados rather more secluded than Cleethorpes. He moved so quickly that he had no time to pick up his Barclays League First Division Manager of the Season award down at the Savoy Hotel in London.

The next Premier League season could wait, but for those left behind it was a good time to reflect. Keegan's name started to be bandied about in the press as a successor to Graham Taylor, who was having a wretched time as England manager. However, Keegan was more concerned at relaxing, having not only rekindled Newcastle's fortunes in his first full season as manager, but also in the admiring words of one of their former managers, Jack Charlton, 'Keegan ignited the entire North East at a time when it was desperately needed.'

Two of Keegan's closest confidants, Arthur Cox and Mick Channon were not at all surprised by the speed of their friend's success, or his qualifications to be a future England manager.

Cox, the present Derby County manager, and boss at Newcastle during Keegan's last season as a player, said, 'Right at the start when Keegan was made Newcastle manager, I predicted he would succeed. It's in his nature. Outwardly, he gives the impression of looking relaxed and confident. But inside Kevin is a cold, hard professional. Mark my words, he's a bad, bad loser. And I should know – because Kevin is the only person in football I've ever had a close relationship with.

'The Newcastle success,' Cox felt, 'was only the tip of the iceberg. I'm sure he's ready-made to take over from Graham Taylor – without gaining Premier League experience. Kevin's got that Pied Piper touch. People respond to his enthusiasm and knowledge as a former world-class player.'

Channon, Keegan's horse trainer-friend, broke away from supervising early morning gallops at his Lambourne stables to say, 'Kevin takes a distant view of horse racing these days in the same way I take a distant view of the soccer scene. But I've seen and heard enough to know his right to the international job is a racing certainty, a foregone conclusion.'

On 23 June, it was announced that Keegan had purchased Peter Beardsley, a former favourite in the North East, who he described simply as 'the best player in the country'. A paltry £1.5 million had been paid for someone whose skill could add thousands to the gate, and help win titles.

2
EARLY DAYS IN DONCASTER

Kevin Keegan's childhood as a Geordie miner's son living in backstreet slums at 25 Spring Gardens in central Doncaster, was bound to be seized upon by national newspapers ever eager to print a rags-to-riches story. Keegan's almost instant rise to fame with Liverpool made him an irresistible subject for the odd pose in a derelict South Yorkshire alleyway equipped with the perennial perm, flaired jeans and a football trapped by a polished casual shoe.

George Best's rapidly crowned successor could afford to laugh at how smooth such transitions could be – when the early life he remembered had been far more corrugated and harsh as a member of a five-strong family living on the bread-line. Joseph Kevin Keegan had been born at Elm Place, Armthorpe, a mining village outside Doncaster on 14 February 1951. Father Joe worked down the pit as an employee of Markham Main colliery, now closed down, but visible from the road through its gaunt blue lift shaft towers looking almost Martian in the pale evening light. Joe promptly moved his wife Doris, daughter Mary, two years older than Kevin, and the new baby to a Coronation Street-style terraced house near Doncaster central station.

The 1950s may have been a time for recharging the batteries for a nation emerging from the ravages of the Second World War after the morale boosting Coronation of Queen Elizabeth II, but the Keegans lived in conditions another miner's son, D.H. Lawrence, wrote of as existing pre-First World War.

There was an outside lavatory in a ramshackle garden, and a detached out-house where the family washed in a tin bath and where, day after day, Doris Keegan hovered over endless chores.

Joe Keegan, who suffered from chronic bronchitis, was a hard man but no harder than many of his fellow miners brought up in even worse conditions in their childhoods. Kevin's grandfather, Frank, had been a well-known pit hero after helping to save 30 men and a pit pony while on duty at the West Stanley colliery in February 1909. Joe had moved south to Yorkshire after being unable to get regular work on the Durham seams. Such scratching around for employment was not exactly a hero's reward for a former Chindit sergeant who had served in one of the toughest Second World War infantry zones in Burma. But Joe took his return to civvy street philosophically. If life was harsh for the Keegan family, then it was also harsh for many of their friends and other neighbouring families. As for young Kevin, it often took a good clip around his ear to keep him in line, because Joe's eldest son (Mike arrived seven years later) was inclined to be mischievous as a young lad in those grimy back-streets. His own memories of his misdemeanours and subsequent punishment administered by Dad remain fairly well-stocked.

Joe Keegan was not always out of trouble himself in the chatter-box atmosphere of 25 Spring Gardens, being something of a local ale drinker (though not an alcoholic) and a gambler; he often sauntered to the betting shop with Kevin being tugged along by the hand to visit the gee-gees. Such enjoyable pastimes linked to the hope and turf often got the Geordie miner into trouble. Doris avenged one drinking bout when, after Joe had stumbled home and had fallen into a deep Burmese jungle nap, she, with a flash of inspiration geared to revenging gross bad manners, blacked the snow white hair which had adorned Joe's head from early manhood with shoe polish, leaving his moustache snowy white as usual. He was still hungover on the 25-minute bus drive to work the following morning. A friend failed to recognize him, saying he knew Joe, but not this black-haired stranger calling himself Keegan. Joe was not amused, nor by the length of time his hair took to return to its original colour.

Such unrehearsed domestic happiness enabled the Keegan family to retain a degree of outward stoic humour in Yorkshire slum conditions, which for many resident families were lifelong drudgery. Doris Keegan ran the three-bedroomed household with a dedication of a part-time working housewife living on her wits and shrewdness in the face of a husband not always fully alert, and who sometimes failed to deliver the correct house-keeping money. Doris grew much more alert about numbers when Joe taught her how to play dominoes. They incidentally became one of the best domino pairs in Doncaster.

Their wee Kevin, however, was taking some time to become Doncaster's future soccer superstar. The trouble was his height, which showed little sign of raising the lad to a level that his friends were reaching. Kevin was wee to say the least, and although he kicked the ball endlessly against the expensive doors of the Co-op Funeral Service opposite the Keegan's with his friend David Anderson, son of the Co-op manager Stan, the exercise failed to act as a boost to growth. Like Diego Maradona, who could not be kept away from his pet football, almost drowning when he fell down a manhole in Buenos Aires with his prized leather, Kevin kept booting his own ball, given him by his Uncle Frank, against those grim doors guarding the dead. Whilst the Keegan house in Doncaster has long been demolished, the Funeral Co-op still remains in service, a souvenir of Keegan's early determination to become as good a footballer as his boy-hood gods. The mortuary doors were polished but firmly shut when the author walked past on his way to the remnants of Spring Gardens at the same time as the Newcastle manager was taking a well-deserved holiday in Barbados at the end of his tri-umphant 1992/93 season. As twin reminders of the much younger Keegan's obsession with kicking a football, the doors offered a memento to the daily savagery. Sometimes they were left open by mistake, allowing Keegan and his friend, David, to get a quick glimpse of the corpses laid out on slabs, courtesy of Mr Anderson. It might have been somewhat ghoulish, but if fit-ted the pattern of rough, working-class life.

Joe Keegan was a member of the local Liberal Club, and a

Catholic married to Doris, a Protestant. There seems to have been no internal upheavals about choices of schools when young Kevin was sent to Catholic St Francis Xavier Primary school at Balby Bridge. The Keegans had moved to a 1930s council house at Waverly Avenue, Balby, two-and-a-quarter miles away from Spring Gardens. In far more open country, there was a huge slice of sporting green called the Bullring, where Joe's elder son could indulge in his favourite pastime of playing endless soccer, with a few weeks of hitting cricket balls thrown in for good measure in the summer. Sometimes, Kevin used his younger brother as a goalpost, which wasn't popular with Mike. The Bullring was a god-send because it didn't matter how many boys turned up to play, they simply slotted into a game in progress without any objections or orders to get lost. Dave Rix, who later worked with Keegan at Pegler Brass Works as a junior clerk, remembers playing football with Kevin.

'There were forty-a-side on the pitch and coats for goals. You could always see Kevin going hell for leather in the middle of the traffic jam where the ball was supposed to be. In rain or shine, Kevin was always there playing his heart out.'

St Francis Xavier Junior School was attended by an average of 300 pupils from two parishes, a 'cosy little school' according to Keegan and much built-over three decades later. The view from Roberts Road outside still reveals a scene, which dwarfish Keegan must have witnessed daily on his way to get a bus home – a row of red-terraced houses exactly the same as they were then, except for the odd protruding saucer-shaped satellite television aerial. Carl Dunkley, who was appointed headmaster at the beginning of the 1980s, revealed the sad news that one of his predecessors, Sister Mary Oliver had died in the summer of 1993. It was Sister Oliver who first noticed that Kevin Keegan had a gift for soccer when she had seen him scurrying around in the playground or playing for his school team. It must have clicked in her mind, because she wrote in his school report, 'Kevin's football must be encouraged'.

Sister Oliver and two other nuns who taught were keen that their boys could play as much football as possible after class, though the sports field now used by the school after being reclaimed from land owned by British Rail, was not in use then. Somehow the caretaker found a vacant vegetable patch for the boys to play on, and the chirpy, sometimes cheeky Kevin Keegan obviously came to Sister Oliver's notice through his mastery of a half-laced-up ball. Her analysis would become so famous that it brought an invitation to appear on 'This is Your Life' with Eamonn Andrews in 1979, when a selection of Doncaster family and friends and work-mates appeared. That Sister Oliver had the foresight and perception to notice the emerging qualities of a future England captain, was enough to make her famous. But she had many other qualities as a headmistress and teacher, and is remembered at school for her kindness and guidance shown to not always the most genteel of South Yorkshire pupils. Kevin Keegan was always grateful for those remarks she made about his football.

'She was like an angel to us, interested in everything we did and always quick to encourage us.'

Kevin Keegan could be a difficult customer, however, when it came to making the cheeky miner's son buckle down to his schoolwork. He was football daft with little time to think about the challenges of English, Maths and History. He wanted to get out into the fresh air even when it was sleeting across the gently rolling urban landscape littered with untidy waste dumps, work-yards, and the odd postage stamp of putrid weeds, where a football could be kicked about without permanently damaging anyone's knees on broken glass. It is fairly easy to imagine what Kevin Keegan was like in class. He was the one who chalked up silly jokes on the blackboard and pranged a nearby girl pupil with an elastic band. When Carl Dunkley took the author around Keegan's school, some of the classrooms, in which he sat and misbehaved, were still there. Although, there was no sign of a joker like Kevin wearing the same blue shirt and grey slacks and blowing raspberries from the rear desks, it was not difficult to imagine him being there in one of those cosy little classrooms, with the odd stuffed weasel or fox on display by the teacher's desk. Keegan could be a pain in the classroom for Mrs Cecilia

Wrennall, his form mistress, who wrote on his report: 'Kevin has done good work during the year, but his tests were disappointing. He is an exhibitionist and will do much better when he loses this trait.'

There was the small hut area, linked by a passageway from the rest of the school where Keegan's Class Four was based, and which could become like an iceberg in mid-winter with a coal fire lit by a teacher in the mornings for warmth. Keegan, with his noted energy, once badly cut his tongue colliding with another pupil. The injury was so bad, in fact, that Keegan's longish tongue was severed and he had to take it with him to hospital in a handkerchief where it was sewn on again successfully. Not that Kevin Keegan, OBE was a dunce at St Francis; on the contrary he had topped the class at several lessons. Yet he was always playing football around the clock. He slept with his football close to his bed ready for instant transportation to Town Fields, a Doncaster recreation area crammed with 15 football pitches and 30 spindly goalposts. After coming up with a winner on a horse, Joe Keegan had bought his son his first pair of football boots – a £2 low-heeled pair obtained from a sports shop run by a former Doncaster Rovers player, Ray Harrison. Keegan polished them, smelt them, worshipped them. These boots were sacrosanct in his young life committed to kicking a ball around the flat wastelands of Doncaster, South Yorkshire.

Keegan fancied himself as a goalkeeper at first, but like many young recruits to a profession which had often been nicknamed 'daft' or 'mad', his lack of inches would let him down under the crossbar. He might have been springy, stocky and brave as a gladiator in his own penalty area, but when it came to reaching up to divert wickedly in-swinging crosses over his crossbar, he was often a loser. Keegan's growing determination to succeed as a budding Gordon Banks was only thwarted through the height problem, and given another few inches he would certainly have made the grade 'between the sticks'. At least Doris Keegan welcomed his move into midfield and attacking roles. He had the habit of coming home caked in mud from goalmouth diving in the past (Mum referred to her son as being 'sludged up to the eyeballs'). Keegan was still very much a goalkeeper when at junior school, representing a mixed team from St Francis and a neighbouring school, St Peter's at Town Fields at weekends, although he managed to knuckle down to his lessons long enough to pass his 11-plus examination. Unlike many more sheltered boys of his own age group in the early 1960s, Keegan had already discovered ways of adding to his small pocket money allowance. Ingenious methods of earning the odd coin were born, of an early age, when he and his market friends, Dave Anderson and Maurice Freedman devised money-making schemes when roaming Doncaster Market, which was one of the busiest sections of a large agricultural and mining area. Discarded wooden tomato boxes were handy to chop up back in Spring Gardens and sell at tuppence a bundle.

After Dave had knocked the smaller Kevin around after some firewood industrial dispute, the outraged Keegan rushed home to his father with a tearful tale to tell on Dave. Joe said, 'Hit him back, and don't come in here crying.' The message sunk deeper than the speaker might have imagined. It sunk so deep that Kevin Keegan would carry his Dad's reply all the way into adulthood, which goes some way to explaining the incident referred to at Wembley in 1974 when he hit Billy Bremner in a Charity Shield match after being intimidated, and was sent off. When Dave started bullying Keegan again, he received a good hiding from Keegan junior, which made his father laugh, because he had been watching from a window. Secretly, Joe Keegan was pleased that his tot was fighting back.

Another scheme to raise money by Keegan and his pals was at the Glasgow Paddocks, a large horse-auction area three miles from the St Leger racecourse, where Kevin and his friends could earn up to half a crown cleaning punters' expensive cars. When the time came for the Paddocks to be demolished, the car cleaners were mortified. It meant the end of a good weekly income, and Keegan and his partners were shown sitting on their redundant buckets by the local newspaper. Not for the last time, Kevin Keegan gave a chirpy press conference to a willing junior reporter, who was impressed by his subject's powers of elocution, though given in a somewhat broad South Yorkshire accent. It was being thwarted from getting a newspaper delivery job at the age of seven, though, which really fired Keegan into a state which dominated his later life. He felt utterly shot down when the female newsagent told him he was too small for the job since he wasn't tall enough to reach the letter boxes despite carrying a box around with him. When the woman turned him down, asking him to come back in a couple of years (by which time he had left the area), he felt he had been slapped across the mouth. It was the same when he had to give up playing in goal. Size was everything in Keegan's case. Doris Keegan, now a widow living outside Doncaster, remembered the almost ruthless way he took to building up his own physique.

'Our Kevin was a very puny lad, always dashing off to the youth club to do weight-training exercises to build up his body. But he was always generous and big-hearted. Even as a youngster, when I gave him a few coppers to spend on himself, he would come home with a present for me.'

Mum Doris was happy to receive her tiny gifts, and also seeing her son building his frame up like some of the budding boxers who used to work out at Bruce Woodcock's gym in the town, or the wrestlers working out at the Doncaster Corn Exchange. At first Doris, who had put her considerable energies into looking after the welfare of a mining family, didn't think a great deal about her eldest son turning into a famous sportsman.

'Don't know where Kevin got the talent – there's no sporting blood in our family at all. It always was football with Kevin. I was more than worried about it too. But it was better than going down the mines. I guess it was worth all those broken windows and the hours spent chasing after him to get him to come in.'

Apart from the obsession with football, Keegan did some boxing and sparring, and was pretty nimble on his pins and mean with his fists, but nothing to make Bruce Woodcock go off to his pub and start talking about Kevin as the new, wee, white Doncaster hope. Woodcock had been a big white Doncaster hope after the war, winning the British heavyweight title in style and being put up by some tongue-in-cheek speculators as a future Limey opponent for Joe Louis. But Woodcock was not like Tommy Far in his prime, and when he did fight a mean Yank named Tami Mauriello in New York, nobody had bothered to tell the Doncaster lad that American pugilists from Manhattan did not always abide by the Queensbury Rules. He was cruelly headbutted before the fight was stopped.

Woodcock, however, was still a popular legend in a town which enjoyed its Friday nights at the boxing ring or watching the wrestlers at the Corn Exchange. Kevin Keegan's school days were based firmly around the town's sporting programme, which included watching Doncaster Rovers play at their Belle Vue stadium opposite the local racecourse. There was certainly no lack of vibrant atmosphere in the old, smoky, sporting hall of Doncaster in the late 1950s and early 1960s. Keegan was not the only participant to get himself hurt, either by a mule of a young left-back with spikes for kneecaps, or an angelic-looking local boxer with lead in his gloves. Brian Glover, the Bobby Charlton lookalike schoolmaster in Ken Leach's film 'Kes', remembers being scarred for life in a contest in Donny (Doncaster) against Les Kellet, the Clown Prince of the ring from Bradford, in a televised bout on ITV World of Sport. There were cheers for Kellet, boos for Glover, whose *nom de guerre* was Leor Arras from Barnsley.

'I acknowledged the boos. Looked as villainous as I could. Sneered into the camera. You can bet it was because it was on telly that some bright spark had wrapped the ropes, not with the usual bandages, but with coloured plastic. It would look much better on the camera. Bouts were going really well. Punters up in the air. Les puts me in a headlock. Runs my mug down the top rope. Punters loved it. I didn't. The edge of the plastic cut through my top lip like a knife through butter. Bled like a pig I did. Ruined referee Kent Walton's DJ. I've still got the scar, runs parallel to my top lip. Unfortunately, its a bit puckered, the scar is, at one end, and if I'm not careful, I can easily nick it when shaving. When I do nick it, and I do quite often, it bleeds quite heavily – hence the bog role. Bloody Donny!'

This was Kevin Keegan's home township booing poor Brian

Glover all the way to the station as they did rival right-backs at Belle Vue on Saturday afternoons. Donny heroes like Alick Jeffrey had become almost as famous in the 1950s as Busby Babe representatives, Duncan Edwards and Eddie Colman. But for two broken legs, Jeffrey would have become a regular member of the England team after the Munich air disaster, but the injuries destroyed his international ambitions. Keegan watched him fairly regularly after crawling under a fence at Belle Vue to gain entrance to the lean terracing.

'Jeffrey was ten years ahead of everyone else on the pitch at a time when he was supposedly finished. He had a great shot to go with is other skills.'

Keegan's freebies at Belle Vue later worried his conscience to such a degree he once offered to pay the club for all the times he had scrambled under their fence.

Keegan moved on to St Peter's Secondary school, at Cantley where the discipline was far more severe than at St Francis Xavier's, and where the new boy found himself regularly in trouble for clowning about. One of the masters had taught at Borstal and was a mean swisher with the cane. Keegan once earned twelve strokes instead of six for putting what used to be called blotting paper in his pants as protection. The master was not fooled. Keegan's skills as a brilliant mimic showed to the full at St Peter's, but not always with the approval of the teaching staff. When he came back on a visit to his old haunts in Doncaster after he'd become well known, he amused his old pals by doing his Charlie Chaplin impression wearing a Saville Row striped-blue suit, bowler and walking stick. However, doing it in classtime didn't make him popular with his housemaster, who also ran the sports programme.

Buckling down to the far harder disciplinary codes of St Peter's Secondary before taking his 'O'-level exams, didn't suit Kevin Keegan's outgoing nature. Some of his masters believed the budding footballer was being cheeky just for the sake of it – his swollen knuckles, after a good rapping from a blackboard eraser by a teacher were proof of the feeling of mistrust between teacher and pupil. When Keegan did take his 'O'-levels, his choice of art as a subject proved to be inspired because nobody had realized before, least of all Keegan, that he had some previously hidden talent for painting and drawing. He thoroughly enjoyed splashing the paint down with a Jackson Pollock bravado on large pieces of white paper. In fact, he grew proud of his colourful images, and became such a dedicated member of the St Peter's art class that he might well have gone on to become an art student who had played professional football for a short time, like Keith Bell (Rochdale) and Harry Clarke (Sunderland), both of whom attended the Royal College of Art in South Kensington.

Keegan did achieve two 'O'-levels when he was fifteen, in history and art. Neither of these qualifications was guaranteed to get Keegan very far in business or commerce, but these stuffy professions were not for him anyway. Keegan had firmly made up his mind that he wanted to become a professional footballer, although any luck he craved for to help get him a foot in the soccer trade door cruelly deserted him time and again.

Since his removal from the St Peter's goal because of his height disadvantage, Keegan had shown up well in midfield, taking much larger players on and often hitting the ball against their shins to get the benefit of a quick rebound. Joe Keegan often used to turn up to watch, wearing his Sunday suit, because being a miner, he liked to look his best away from the sooty coalface. Keegan always said his father was among those he owed most, for encouraging him to make the grade in football, the others being Bob Nellis, a future chairman of Doncaster Rugby League Club, who helped get the youngster a trial at Scunthorpe; Scunthorpe's manager, Ron Ashman, of course; and Bill Shankly. Keegan had shown moody signs of casting aside any idea of becoming a professional footballer after being turned down first by Coventry City, managed by Jimmy Hill at the time, and then Doncaster Rovers, quick to give their local recruit a brisk nod towards one of their Belle Vue exits after the youngster turned up for a trial. Coventry had gone to the length of asking permission from the headmaster of St Peter's to have a look at the Keegan lad's promise. The head allowed Keegan to travel to the West Midlands for a trial, but the youth team manager, Graham Hill, eventually turned down the shy visitor from Doncaster, for being too small physically.

'My late father had done his best to dissuade me from concentrating entirely on becoming a professional footballer, urging me to learn a trade or obtain qualifications that could stand me in good stead if I failed to make the grade. But so confident was I, that I ignored his advice. Advice, I would give any aspiring youngster knowing the failure rate of clubs. But after being turned down by Coventry and Doncaster Rovers, my home town club, I began to have my doubts. However, Dad, despite his caution had faith and encouraged me to persevere. He had come along to watch me play. Unlike some misguided fathers, he didn't run along the touchline yelling out a constant stream of advice, trying to play my game for me. He realized I had to do it all on my own.'

Keegan's early career as a player was overshadowed by a rival, Kevin Johnson from Bentley West End School. Like Keegan, Johnson was on the small side, but far more skilful. When Johnson was signed by Sheffield Wednesday, his career looked to be zooming ahead with a future cut out for him at a glamorous club like Manchester United or Leeds. Like so many players of his kind, though, Johnson failed to make the grade, and when Keegan once met him waiting outside Anfield for a chance to see Liverpool play Newcastle, Johnson admitted to his old Doncaster pal, he was not in the Rolls Royce League, being a representative of Hartlepool United in the North East.

Keegan was certainly not born with a magic wand in his hand where a career in football was concerned. He joined Enfield House, a central Doncaster youth club team, and took some mighty batterings from some very tough opponents who used their boots, elbows, kneecaps, craniums, and the odd tooth to make their rugged messages known. The pint-sized Keegan was often sent spinning to the ground, before getting up and spitting out the odd thimble of blood from a cut mouth. This was when Keegan started his weight-training in earnest, although nothing like as seriously as some of the larger fellows who wanted to become venerable giants in some pretty rough areas of Doncaster.

Before becoming a full-time professional, Keegan took a job for a short period as a stores clerk at Pegler Brass Works in Doncaster. Unlike the less accommodating 1990s, there were all kinds of jobs available for school-leavers in the mid-1960s. Unable to make the grade just yet as a footballer in a country passionately in love with soccer following the 1966 World Cup win, Keegan turned up on the shop floor one morning. His job involved making inventories of mops and brooms which were loaned out at regular intervals to the staff. Not very inspiring work, but for Keegan the job at least brought in a useful weekly wage to take home before settling down to a weekend playing or watching soccer. Keegan was shy on the shop floor, sometimes making a large detour on his rounds to avoid the attentions of factory girls drawn to his boyish good looks.

These days the Pegler factory in St Catherine's Avenue, Doncaster, is more modernized, with a smart front reception area. However, the tall broom handle-shaped chimney at the other end of the works, with Pegler inscribed in white paint, is a reminder of Kevin Keegan OBE's only working job outside professional football.

Boredom often struck him square in the midriff when his thoughts began wandering to the great outside beyond the factory gates and the sports he had so enjoyed while a secondary school boy. Apart from his constant obsession with football, Keegan had done well as a cross-country runner, finishing fifth in the Doncaster Schools Championships, while no young South Yorkshire man would have dared not to played cricket in the summer. Keegan captained the St Peter's cricket side, but never remotely reached the class where his masters might brood on the arrival of a new Sir Leonard Hutton or Geoffrey Boycott.

Joe Keegan regarded his son's tenacity and dedication on the sporting fields of Donny with a great amount of personal satisfaction. It helped compensate for his own declining health in which his miner's illness could reek havoc with his lungs. Doris had taken him away once to the Welsh seaside to try and recuperate from a severe bout of illness – but Joe would never be free of the disease brought on by continuous work below ground. He did, however, live to 71 years of age, passing away in December 1976, seven months before Keegan's greatest triumph in Rome.

Harry Holland, who ran the Pegler reserve side for whom Keegan turned out at weekends, remembers the influence Joe had over his son when he was a modest clerk.

'Whenever Kevin played he had to get permission from his Dad. If his Dad said jump, Kevin jumped. It was as simple as that. Joe Keegan was one of the old school.'

Holland, a florid-faced, friendly man, has been a clerical worker at Pegler (founded in 1899 as a manufacturers of plumbing and piping materials) for almost all Keegan's life span.

'When Kevin joined the firm, I had been around for some time and must have seemed quite old to him then. But I ran the reserve team, and was happy to get him a game. Kevin wanted to do better naturally, although the first team were doing well and winning trophies in the Bentley League. They wouldn't change a winning team – so Kevin only got a few games before he went off to Scunthorpe.'

Even Keegan thought these rugged Pegler first-teamers took their football 'a little too seriously'.

'That was probably why they didn't think I was good enough for them. It seemed to be their whole lives, whereas to me it was just good fun, although their attitude gave me an insight into what professional football would be like.'

Holland was a former Royal Army Service Corps conscript clerk, who had almost blown himself up lighting a mobile boiler on manoervres for the British Army on the Rhine. While he had learnt to abide by military discipline in the early 1950s on the battleground forests of West Germany, Keegan was of the next generation – more cheeky, less ready to tolerate the overlording comments of one's 'superiors'. He scampered around the working aisles at Pegler kicking a rolled-up piece of newspaper, which didn't go down too well with the establishment based beyond the shop floor area.

'Kevin used to enjoy going out training on Tuesdays. He

looked far happier on the soccer pitch than checking stock and order in central stores.'

There were times when the emerging 16-year-old with an eye for the girls on Cleethorpes seafront, found some of his giggling female staff members a bit too suffocating with their devotion. This was the era of the 'Beatles'; the factory girls' crushes were firmly centred on John, Paul, George and Ringo whose portraits they pasted all over their rooms back home, but they didn't mind giving the eye to a Donny boy, especially that skinny little Kevin in stores.

'I think Kevin only made the Pegler first-team twice,' recounts Holland. 'Not surprising really. Bentley League was tough, you played against miners' teams, got kicked all over t'place. It was hard, very hard. And Kevin was only 16, still small.'

You couldn't blame the first teamers for taking their football seriously, given their factory routine, austere Donny surroundings, and their restriction to annual holidays in Cleethorpes, Skegness and Blackpool. Playing for the Pegler firsts acted as a morale-boosting drug for Kevin – although the young Keegan didn't see it that way. He thought the players were 'stuck-up', but he missed the point at the time. It wasn't until he went back as a Liverpool player to join some of his work-mates in a few council pitch fund-raising kickabouts that he acknowledged the sheer passion which can enflame players in the lower orders. Harry Holland had that passion, but he was already getting on, in Keegan's view; already an old man 'whose fitness did not match his enthusiasm'. Meanwhile Holland had made up his mind Kevin Keegan would never make the big time in football. With two years to go before retirement, and 43 years in the service of Pegler behind him, Holland still remains amazed it did happen.

'Not for a million years did I envisage Kevin becoming a footballer who would play for Liverpool, Hamburg (becoming European Footballer of the Year) Southampton and Newcastle; captain England and become a successful Newcastle manager. Not in a million years! You could have taken me out and offered me all kinds of bets, I wouldn't have wanted to know. I just thought Kevin would make his way as a fairly good player in local football.'

Similarly Keegan's friend, the bespectacled Pegler clerk, Dave Rix, hardly imagined Keegan's golf would improve into semi-professional standard on the world's links. 'We used to go out and play a little golf together. Kevin was mad keen, but was not very good at the time. I had a handicap of 42 and used to beat him.' The links used by Keegan and Rix were far more primitive than the almost mecca-like plans Doncaster Council Planning committee drew up the year Keegan won his first illustrious pennant as Newcastle United's manager in 1993.

In the council's own words, and ones obviously highly enticing for their most famous footballing, golf-crazy son: 'It's a project which will create a championship golf course to be part of the PGA European tour and give our borough a facility which will be the envy of the golfing world.'

'We didn't have any posh gear – just took a club each, out there in wind and rain, and it wasn't gin and tonic in the clubhouse but on to football and more wind and rain and some big bugger trying his best to give you an early dinner choking in mud,' Rix recalled.

Both Holland and Rix could remember vividly the time when Keegan was recommended to Scunthorpe United by a 'larger than life' Bob Nellis, who had caught sight of Keegan playing for Pegler reserves on Saturday morning, Enfield House Youth Club on Saturday afternoons and for the Lonsdale hotel, a public house near the racecourse, on Sunday afternoons. Keegan's zippy running along the wings could hardly be missed by any observing local scout out walking his dog in the Doncaster area. However, Nellis, who worked for a furniture and drapery firm in central Doncaster not far from Spring Gardens, decided Third Division Scunthorpe might be on to a good thing for young Kevin. Rix said, 'Nellis used to drive young Kevin 25 miles to Scunthorpe for trials with intermediate teams on Saturday mornings. That meant missing our reserve games – he kept quiet about those games, no bragging about them.' Nellis was a player himself, playing Sunday League soccer for his Lonsdale companions' team in Woodfield Social.

Nellis acted with amazing grace for a player who was continually taunted and by-passed by his Lonsdale rival. After a match, he surprised Keegan by enquiring whether his opponent was interested in taking part for Scunthorpe, and the Pegler clerk readily agreed.

'I jumped at the opportunity,' says Keegan. 'Sure, enough, it proved a case of third time lucky after Doncaster Rovers and Coventry, and I joined 'The Irons'.'

The middle man in the move was Jeff Barker, chief scout of Scunthorpe, who had asked to be alerted by Nellis of any budding talent in the Donny area. Keegan had signed for Scunthorpe as an apprentice-professional on 2 January 1968, under the wing of manager Ron Ashman and the trainer Jack Brownsword. It took four or five trial matches to convince the Scunthorpe backroom team that Keegan had a future in League football, before they invited him to sign on at the princely sum of £7 a week. Keegan did himself a financial disservice, because after paying £4 for his digs in Scunthorpe, it only allowed him £3 spending money. So he had to go carefully, budgeting his spending. Not that the Yorkshire town built around the Old Show Ground resembled Paris for a night out on the town, but Keegan made the most of the fish and chip bar. During the close seasons, it was back to Mum and Dad in Waverley Avenue, Doncaster.

Keegan soon learnt that a footballer's life in the Third and Fourth Divisions (Scunthorpe were then in the Third, soon to be Fourth) was far less affluent than being a white collar worker at Pegler Brass Works. He had earned £4 or £5 a week when he worked there as a 16-year-old, but could raise his salary to £8 by working overtime. As time passed, Keegan did make financial progress at the Old Show Room Ground, his earnings rising from £7 to £30 a week by the time he signed for Liverpool.

The new Scunthorpe signing was, of course, overjoyed when he put his signature down on paper at the Old Show Ground, which used to be a show-jumping arena at the turn of the century. His decision did not go down at all well at Pegler Brass

Works. Harry Holland remembers the reaction of Fred Leatherland, the stores boss.

'Fred was none too pleased. He told Kevin he had no future in football. "You'll not make the grade, lad," he said gruffly. And when Kevin did leave, he told him he needn't come back to the firm if he failed in football. Fred was a bit like that. But he might have had a point. When Kevin joined Scunthorpe, he had shoulders, no legs and was often used as a ventriloquist's doll by opposing players. But after some hard work, he left for Livepool with an impressive physique.'

Keegan's manager, Ron Ashman, is still a popular, legendary hero in Norfolk, having taken part in that romantic FA Cup run as a member of the Third Divison Norwich City side which reached the semi-final in 1959 before losing to Luton Town. Norwich's present chairman, Robert Chase, remembers watching Ashman's side as a boy, the lights of the coaches returning the victorious City supporters home, turning the dark waters of the Broads into a sparkling fairyland.

Keegan discovered quickly that Ashman was no Fred Leatherhead.

'He was a sensitive man who cared about people. It made him many friends. No manager could have been so considerate. But it may have held his career back in a hard game. Ron always did what was best for me – bringing me into the first team at 17 and dropping me for games against very physical, fierce-tackling sides to avoid the risk of my being kicked out of football. I was still very frail and also hadn't learnt to jump as though competing in the Horse of the Year Show on the Old Show Ground. When I was 19, he gave me my first taste of responsibility by appointing me captain in preference to older and more experienced men in the side. Whenever I got disheartened, there was Jack Brownsword, our trainer, another father-figure to keep my spirits up.'

It was while at Scunthorpe that Keegan ran into the girl he would marry as a Liverpool hero – Jean Woodhouse, a bright, blonde schoolgirl studying for her 'A'-levels at Percy Jackson Grammar School. The young professional footballer had spied

Jean and her friend Wendy Devlin letting out frenzied squeals, as they were flung round and round on the swings at the Leger Fair. Everyone was in a good mood after seeing Lester Piggot on the famous Nijinsky win the 1970 St Leger to achieve racing's triple crown.

Keegan and his friend, Phil Niles, took the two girls to a local pub, and after a drink or two the boys dropped the girls off near their home in Keegan's Cortina, bought partly through the sale of his first car, a Morris 1100. That seemed to be it, a meeting almost forgotten. But the future bride and bridegroom did meet again at the Top Rank Christmas dance at Doncaster. The sound of beating jive and raised youthful voices laced by intoxicating Yuletide cocktails hardly made the meeting conducive to finding out more about each other's backgrounds – especially as Kevin and Phil had arrived with two other girls. Like so many romantic liaisons, the link was highly tenuous at first, with another of Jean's friends, Ann Skidmore, declaring in the pub the next night, in that haughty way some young girls use to disguise their nervousness, that she fancied Kev more than Phil. Jean, who would later pass her 'A'-levels in German and Economics, was far less choosy, saying she would talk to Kev and Phil – and take it from there. Keegan had gone to a great deal of trouble to disguise to his budding girlfriend the fact that he was a professional footballer. At first, he had been cagey about his car; he said it belonged to his Dad. It was simple. Big football names like Best had been seen to be leaders of an affluent life style and enjoying its perks on the way to a heavy hangover. Kevin didn't want to start sabotaging this romantic union by exploiting his own modest achievements as a public entertainer.

The crunch came when Jean, whose home was a fish and chip shop at Carcroft near Doncaster, decided to go ice skating and invited Kevin to go along with her. The game was up when Keegan said he couldn't go. Jean's uncomplicated Yorkshire outlook was incensed. Why was he dithering so much? He must have another date. It was then Keegan owned up to being a professional footballer employed by Scunthorpe United Football Club, which he could have done all along, because Jean was soon eagerly watching him play, even to the point of ticking him off when he swore too close to the touchline. Even later at Anfield, when you couldn't hear yourself speak, you could still hear Kev 'effing' and 'blinding' near the tunnel area. Jean would always love the action, and took along her black-and-white scarved daughters to matches at St James's Park when her Kev had become Newcastle United manager. She even confessed to a female scribe at Liverpool that she wore red knickers as a good luck symbol for Kevin on Liverpool match days. Love has no bounds – and even at the Old Show Ground, Keegan and his future bride managed for a very short time to imagine they were walking hand in hand beside the Seine rather than the peaty environs of the River Trent. When they began to be seen more and more together, Harry Holland cast his eyes approvingly towards the future Mrs Keegan.

'She weren't no model, but she was a lovely Yorkshire lass. She had met the right bloke. Kevin was always level-headed with both feet on the ground. He didn't go off night-clubbing or drinking heavily as a player. They made a good couple – and I enjoyed meeting up with them again on that "This is Your Life" show featuring Kevin in 1979. They brought along Laura Jane in a pram.'

The two moments of big-match glamour that Keegan savoured at Scunthorpe involved a League Cup match against Arsenal in his first season, and the proudest one of all when Scunthorpe knocked Sheffield Wednesday out of the FA Cup, winning 2–1 when Ashman' team were expected to be over-whelmed. Usually, the weekly attractions were far less glamorous, with the likes of Hartlepool, Workington Town and Newport visiting the Old Show Ground as Scunthorpe struggled to keep themselves respectably above the relegation zone.

Keegan got up to several pranks at the aptly named training ground at Quibell Park, which was a mini-bus ride from the Old Show Ground. But the great joker met his match with some hardened Fourth Division players like Ray Clemence's goal-keeping replacement, Jim Laverey, who had the idea of tough-ening his body up by diving onto the concrete surface of a car park. Derek Hemstead was the player who helped Keegan toughen up his own body by weight-training and constant supervision, not to mention cruel cross-country running. Mel Blythe, who won an FA Cup winners' medal playing for Southampton against Manchester United in 1976, lived in the digs next door.

However, Keegan's own days at the Old Show Ground were to be numbered. Rumours began to circulate in the local press about some of the top clubs being interested in him, among them Newcastle United, the club he would serve many years later. Keegan could only speculate, and wait for a call from Ron Ashman's office.

3
LIVERPOOL AND BILL SHANKLY

Kevin Keegan might never have become a Liverpool player but for an unusually short-sighted blunder by that wizard of talent spotting, Peter Taylor, when he was in charge at Derby County with Brian Clough. Among the many scouts who turned up regularly to watch Keegan perform as a Fourth Division player for Scunthorpe United at the Old Show Ground on windswept afternoons was a redoubtable, self-confident Baseball Ground spy, George Pycroft. He had a flair for rooting out talent in the most uncomfortable conditions.

Keegan, who was still a midfield player at the time, had heard rumours about Newcastle United, Sunderland, Leicester City, Sheffield Wednesday and Millwall being interested in his services. Arsenal had also asked if Keegan would go on a summer tour with them – but were refused. As Don Howe, Keegan's future England coach, recalls, 'If Kevin had gone, he might well have ended up at Highbury – and your story might have been quite different'. The local press often hinted a deal with a famous club was imminent, but Keegan found he was still playing in the Fourth Division the following week. Enter Pycroft, the eagle-eyed scout, employed by Derby to sniff out talent for them. He turned up at the Old Show Ground and immediately got that 'click, click' on his talent Geiger counter.

Keegan could play, and in Pycroft's opinion would make a worthy recruit at the Baseball Ground for Taylor and Clough. He rang Taylor nine months before Bill Shankly came in with his 'robbery with violence' snatch to take Keegan to Anfield for £35,000 – but Taylor sat back and did nothing about Pycroft's advice. He sensed Pycroft was 'over the moon' about Keegan, but still he decided to shelve the matter. When Clough heard about this much later from Pycroft, he wanted to know why!

Managers don't have a mandatory obligation to act on their scout's advice. Some of the time, such advice is wrong and a boy can be snapped up only to prove a failure, a costly one. Taylor put his head in the sand and stubbornly let Keegan get on with kicking a football around in the depths of the Fourth Division. Pycroft was edgy. He knew Derby had missed out on a future England international, but what was the use of grumbling. He had heard of other managers who had also made no move for Keegan. For instance, despite a phone call from Jack Brownsword, Scunthorpe's player-coach, who had rung Don Revie to say, 'If you want a good player, he'll give you 100% effort and will force his way into your team', the Leeds manager remained unimpressed. He did have the courtesy, though, to tell Keegan about his *faux pas* when he was England manager and Keegan his captain.

A distinct frost was forming between Taylor and Clough as Derby moved towards their 1972 Championship success. When Taylor suffered a reported heart attack and was convalescing at home, Clough brought in Pycroft to help him on the managerial side while his old playing colleague at Middlesborough recharged his batteries. Taylor had grown envious of all the attention his partner was getting on television and in the media columns, and hearing that Pycroft was setting up camp in the dressing room at the Baseball Ground, he became worried. So when Taylor came back, Pycroft moved out, but without the satisfaction of knowing Taylor had changed his mind about the lad at Scunthorpe.

Keegan doesn't seem to have heard of Derby's interest, or lack of it as it turned out. He was getting tired of playing Fourth Division football for modest wages, and had hinted to his friends he might pack in the game and go back to Pegler Brass Works reserves, so when the paternal Brownsword told him to stay put because he could become a First Division footballer within two months, Keegan was at first sceptical. He had heard so many rumours floating around during the past weeks, but he did what his coach suggested and soon the great day came. On 1 May 1971, Bill Shankly pounded in, and Kevin Keegan signed for Liverpool.

The kid from Doncaster owed Liverpool's interest to Andy Beattie, the former Scottish World Cup manager, a great friend and Preston North End playing colleague of Shankly's. Brownsword, as well as tipping off Revie about the midfielder, had rung Peter Robinson, Liverpool's secretary and future Chief Executive, who just happened to have been Scunthorpe's secretary on his way to Anfield.

'My knowing Jack, and being a former Scunthorpe secretary helped considerably in cementing the Keegan deal,' Robinson says.

The new grandstand was being built there when Keegan turned up for his medical and signing press call in his £800 plus, Cortina. In the past, the arrival of new stars on Merseyside to play for Liverpool or Everton (on the other side of the graffiti-smudged Stanley Park) hadn't always promoted a warm welcome, the odd scouser always intent on putting down any cockiness from a new arrival.

Tommy Lawton told the story of how he took a tram to Goodison Park to join Everton from Burnley and was confronted by the tram conductor.

'You Lawton?' he asked, recognizing Tommy's hair-greased head from a newspaper picture.

'Yes, I am Lawton,' Tommy answered.

'Then you'll never be as good as Dixie Dean.'

It was William Ralph Dean, surely Merseyside's greatest soccer idol and still the highest overall scorer with 60 goals in the 1927/28 season, who would present the Football Writers' Association Footballer of the Year award to Keegan in 1976.

'As an Evertonian, the only present I've enjoyed giving Liverpool players in the past is the ball in the back of their nets,' Dixie chuckled.

63

To the weather-beaten three or four press photographers who met the frail looking Scunthorpe midfield player that May morning at Anfield, there were few hints that Kevin Keegan would enjoy the hallowed successes reminiscent of such Anfield giants as Billy Liddell, Albert Stubbins, Ron Yeats, Roger Hunt, Ian St John and Ian Callaghan, who was still on the playing staff. Despite Bill Shankly's fussy one-off remarks about the new boy's abilities, there was hardly a stir from the visiting scribes and photographers. Shankly had hesitated, like Taylor and Revie, when first hearing about Keegan's talents from Beattie. But now, having taken the plunge, he wasted no time in promoting the new arrival as being worthy of the great challenge he expected his squad at Anfield to mount.

Many of the scribes had heard all this before. They were more interested in news about the Liverpool team facing Arsenal in the FA Cup Final at Wembley very shortly. Keegan wouldn't make headlines; an extended picture caption might do. Shankly had whipped Keegan away to the club surgery for a medical check, and though the Scunthorpe arrival's blood pressure was on the high side owing to all the excitement, the player passed the club's stringent medical check others had failed. Shankly was starry-eyed when he saw Keegan's physique.

'He looks like nothing dressed, but you should see him stripped off. He looks like a bloody tank!'

Shankly demanded his men – boys were not encouraged at Anfield – be 'tidy, clean and healthy' and above all to stay healthy and keep their bodies in shape by eating steaks, a somewhat dated idea now that modern players are primed on pasta, Italian-style. Shankly believed in physically strengthened torso development, a view which had followed him all the way from his PTI days during the war. He had noted that Keegan had built up his own physique with weights at Scunthorpe. 'The lad's exceptional,' he said. Shankly's interest in Keegan's body building was not new. Dennis Law recalled his experiences when Shankly was manager at Huddersfield.

'Shanks decided I needed building up. When I arrived at Huddersfield, I only weighed about eight stone and he knew

Above: The 1973 UEFA Cup final, first leg. Gunter Netzer can't stop Keegan scoring Liverpool's second goal in the 3-0 defeat of Borussia Munchengladbach at Anfield.

Left: Keegan and 'Crazy Horse' Emlyn Hughes after Liverpool's 3-0 FA Cup final triumph against Newcastle at Wembley in 1974.

Right: In the same match, a jubilant Keegan celebrates Liverpool's first goal with John Toshack, with whom he would form one of the most lethal striking partnerships in the history of the club.

Above: Suffering the ignominy of being sent off at Wembley during the 1974 Leeds v Liverpool FA Charity Shield match. Keegan tore off his shirt in disgust as the referee sent the Liverpool player to an early bath along with Billy Bremner.

Above: The one and only Bill Shankly.

Left: England manager Ron Greenwood offering some encouragement during an England training session.

Above: *Liverpool are 1975/76 Football League champions following their 3-1 win over Wolves on the last day of the season.*

Above and right: *Drama in Rome, May 1977. Despite the close attentions of Berti Vogts, Keegan was the star of the night, inspiring Liverpool to their first European Cup triumph. A foul by the Borussia Munchengladbach captain on Keegan eight minutes from time led to the penalty that sealed the match for the Reds. The final score was 3-1.*

Above: Outjumping Forest's Ian Bowyer during the 1980 European Cup final. Forest beat SV Hamburg 1-0.

Left: After a difficult start, Keegan eventually settled in at Hamburg, and was voted European Footballer of the Year in 1979 and 1980.

Left: *An aerial tussle with Johan Neeskens, England vs Holland at Wembley, February 1977. England lost 2-0 and, according to Keegan, '...were outclassed as badly as the 6-3 defeat by Hungary in 1953'.*

Right: *Goalkeeper Meszaros foils Keegan during a 1-1 draw between England and Hungary at Wembley in November 1981.*

Left: *Keegan and Trevor Brooking, two stalwarts of the England team in the seventies and early eighties.*

Right: In disagreement with referee Allan Gunn during a league match for Southampton against Spurs in October 1981. Graham Roberts is the Spurs player involved.

Left: Lawrie McMenemy had brought off the coup of the decade when he signed Keegan from Hamburg in August 1980. Attendances at The Dell soared as the 'Mighty Atom' helped to boost Southampton's fortunes.

Right: The England captain heads the second goal in his team's 4-0 thrashing of Northern Ireland in the 1982 Home International Championships.

Left: *The debacle in Oslo, September 1981. England's skipper with Norway's Hallvar Thoresen before England's embarrassing 2-1 defeat in a World Cup qualifier.*

Right: *England World Cup mascot 'Bulldog Bobby' and Keegan at the Abbey Road recording studios in February 1982.*

Above: Arriving at Spain's Bilbao Airport during the 1982 World Cup finals, with media attention focussed on Keegan's mysterious back injury.

Left: Keegan's World Cup lasted just 27 minutes as he came on as substitute in England's final match with Spain. Here he is swapping shirts with Antonio Camacho after a sterile 0-0 draw in Madrid.

that to survive in football you had to have a bit of strength. Shanks arranged with the woman who ran the cafe opposite our digs for me to be put on a diet of steak and milk. I didn't argue about that because I'd hardly eaten meat in my life before (Law's father was an Aberdeen trawlerman). Later on, he had me drinking Chinese tea without sugar or milk. It was diabolical. What a character Shanks was.'

One of Shanks recruits, who had earned much respect for his endeavours on the pitch at Anfield, was given the steak treatment to such a degree, that the effects clearly worried the manager, with or without chips. The steak-eater began to prowl around Anfield flexing his muscles and showing off his new found energy to such a degree, he almost upped and flipped his casuals in the direction of the Cavern Club across town. With uncommon speed, the steak-eater's girlfriend became pregnant When he heard all this, Shanks, a married man with a grown-up daughter, began to fret for what his steak diet might have done to the boy. When Shanks began to fret, everyone from Paisley and the boot room team down to the humblest boot polisher below decks heard about it in an NCO's tone of voice. One morning at Melwood, the steak-eater was running all over the pitch like Pele on Copacabana beach. Shanks turned to the benign Paisley and suddenly roared in his ear, 'Bob, we've created a wee monster!'

Shankly had been in charge at Liverpool for just over 12 years before Kevin Keegan turned up for duty. He had turned a mean-minded, complacent club, slumbering since the departure of Dan Welsh and Phil Taylor, into a vibrant force, once he had done his sums and brought in some new faces. When Liverpool were promoted to the First Division in the 1961/62 season, after dropping a mere point in their first eleven matches – a start, ironically, one of Shankly's favourite discoveries would emulate when he was manager of Newcastle in the autumn of 1992 – the Kop had to thank such heroes of the time as Jimmy Melia, Alan O'Court, and that great midfield man, Gordon Milne, bought from Shankly's old club, Preston North End, for £12,000 in 1960. While Shankly and his backroom staff, Bob Paisley,

Reuben Bennett, Joe Fagan and Albert Shelley concentrated on polishing the Liverpool 'system' to perfection, the team celebrated their return to the top league in 1962 by signing Ron Yeats, the towering centre-half from Dundee United for £30,000, and Ian St John from Motherwell for £37,500. However, this noteable Scottish pair who had helped Liverpool win the FA Cup in 1965 (St John scoring the winning goal) and the League Championship the season before, had left Anfield by the time the kid from Scunthorpe arrived. Others had gone too: dribblers including the greatest scoring hero of them all at Anfield, Roger Hunt, another England '66 representative and Liverpool's leading overall scorer with 245 goals between 1959 and 1969; and Tommy Lawson, the 'flying pig', had also given up his hallowed place to Ray Clemence in goal.

Keegan left the temporary Liverpool club office hut and plonked himself down on a dustbin lid. This was a wonderful gimmick, and the photographers moved in to snap the cheeky lad. He had imagination all right, and already Keegan was learning what to say to the media. Make them laugh, make them happy, they've got a job to do, a deadline to keep, and they'll come up with the right pictures and stories in the newspapers. But be nice, don't look as if you own the place. Keegan had a short message for the media before making his next move.

'Well, they are signing a load of rubbish.'

It sounded pure garbage, but the caption story fitted the scene perfectly. Keegan would now be watched by the Kop to see if he really was no better than a decaying tin of spuds. In the newspaper columns the next day, Keegan looked relaxed, almost pushy.

Shankly, anxious to get the signing over with, escorted the Scunthorpe arrival into the manager's office where Ron Ashman and Peter Robinson were waiting for the formalities of Keegan's signature. With the Cup final only a few days away, Robinson had a tight schedule, and the club secretary greeted Keegan in a friendly but business-like way, as if the youngster's mind would be made up in a matter of seconds. Shankly came straight to the point himself, longing to be out in the fresh air of Melwood telling the lads about his new discovery. He informed Keegan his salary would be £45 a week.

'Okay?' The manager half-turned away, expecting that Keegan would quietly accept before looking at Ron Ashman for a lift home to start putting his belongings together. But Keegan wasn't going to be rushed. The memory of Dad warning him not to 'sell myself cheap' came on strong. Keegan wavered, and a look of pure disbelief crossed Shankly's rugged face. He turned to Ashman and a fidgety Robinson for some sort of salvation which would tear this spot of mercenary arrogance off the shoulders of this young whipper-snapper. Then Shankly almost went into prowling orbit, trying to digest Keegan's words.

'Oh…I thought I would be getting more than that.'

Shankly hardened his jaw. Old professionals used to say that when Shankly hardened his jaw on the pitch, it was time to start 'fastening their thick shin pads'.

'That's upsetting,' replied Shankly. 'Don't forget young man, we're paying £35,000 for you.'

Then he unleashed a small sermon which Robinson, for one, would have liked cut. Shankly went on about the romance of a great club and what an honour it was merely to put on a Liverpool shirt. Ben Ashman had paled when Keegan stubbornly made his point. He could see a large sum of money, which Scunthorpe badly needed, being thrown away because of a youngster's brash foolishness.

'Think of the opportunity,' hummed Shankly, 'It's not what you get now that counts, it's what you get later.'

Keegan would, as the Kop regularly chanted, 'not be moved'. His salary back at Scunthorpe was £30, with an extra £8 for a win and £4 for a draw. Shankly's terms didn't seem so good on reflection. He would have to toil and sweat to get into Liverpool's first team. Would it be worth all the effort? He spoke again

'Yes, but I'm a bit disappointed with the terms, Mr Shankly, and I don't want you to feel I'm being cheeky but I'm nearly getting that much at Scunthorpe and they're Fourth Division. I must better myself.'

'Better myself'. It sounded a bit out of order, especially from such a shrimp who didn't know on which side his bread was properly buttered. Keegan looked into Shankly's piercing eyes expecting slaughter on Anfield, property. But Shanks climbed down, almost in a fatherly way.

'Alright, son, fifty pounds.'

Keegan couldn't wait to scribble out the first 'K' of his signature. He was a Liverpool player.

Shankly invited the new recruit down to London for the Cup final to sample one of those big occasions the lad might experience before a couple of birthdays had passed by. It was good that Keegan should be there in the stadium hearing incredible sounds wafting around the tunnel entrance and up in the stands where the players' families were seated going through all the agonies Cup finals brought to the less acclimatized. Keegan took Jean along to the game. They stayed at the Waldorf off the Aldwych, two sweet young things staying in separate rooms on different floors. Keegan ran into Roger Hunt, one of Liverpool's most popular players, now with Bolton Wanderers. Hunt made it his kindly duty to speak to the slightly gauche, young signing, who was wandering round in circles looking at the newspaper kiosk and postcard counter. Hunt wished Keegan much luck at Liverpool '…which is something I will never forget' Keegan said later. This was the same Hunt who had been one of his England heroes, watching the World Cup victory of 1966 on television. Hunt advised him to work hard at Anfield, which would enable him to get through and make the grade. Hunt must have spoken earlier to Shankly because he seemed to be aware of Keegan's talents.

Some of the senior members of the Liverpool party were looking for the bar for a stiffener before the journey towards Wembley. For Jean, the feeling was one of being alone in a big alien capital, as she was still only a schoolgirl and worried inwardly about how the Liverpool transfer would affect her friendship with Kev.

The couple watched the Final in summery conditions, while Arsenal chased their famous double under that shrewd tactician, Bertie Mee. That didn't mean Liverpool didn't feel they had a chance. They had some good players, including Tommy Smith and Ian Callaghan, who had both played in the 1965 final. Also on view for Arsenal were Ray Kennedy- Shankly's final signing for Liverpool before he departed from Anfield three years later, who had scored the winning goal against Tottenham to win the Championship for Arsenal earlier in the week, and who had also been awarded the Footballer of the Year award – and captain, Frank McLintock who almost had to drag his heroes onto the Wembley pitch to play Shankly's transitionary side. Two of Keegan's future team-mates, who would form such a brilliant partnership – John Toshack, the Welsh international striker bought for £110,000 from Cardiff City and Steve Heighway, a Warwick University graduate and Skelmsdale United product – were lured like their more senior partners into Arsenal's clinical web, which entrapped opposing players. Mee's goalscorers, John Radford and Kennedy were always in the hunt for a chance to strike at will on the break. Keegan tried to control his emotions as Heighway put Liverpool ahead with a wickedly-angled shot which confused goalkeeper Bob Wilson as it was drilled into the net at the near post, but Eddie Kelly, with a scrambled goal and Charlie George, with a venomous drive in extra-time, earned Arsenal the huge satisfaction of bringing both the Championship and FA Cup trophies back to Highbury. Shankly, with a few wisecracks, consoled some of the younger players like Brian Hall and Ray Clemence. Shankly looked out of the corner of a slightly moist eye to see the 20-year-old Keegan, head down, looking as if he had not only played, but felt responsible for the defeat himself. He looked more forlorn than the players themselves, who had at least got their medals safely in their sweaty hands. Shankly was succinct about Keegan's reactions.

'Kevin probably thinks that if he'd been playing we would have won, and we should have done.'

Liverpool, a 'nearly' team that season, had not produced goals, although the redoubtable defence had remained steady. Being knocked out by Leeds in the European Fairs Cup, runners-up in the FA Cup, and third behind Arsenal and Leeds in the Championship, wasn't good enough. Shankly gritted his teeth in that rock-like Ayrshire way and vowed to make his team return to their winning glory days of Anfield's recent past. He did not take long to make up his mind about Keegan. An end-of-season tour of Scandinavia gave Shankly and his boot room coaching team the ideal platform for future team building. Keegan was almost too lively in his haste to show what he could do in company with his more holiday-conscious team-mates. Keegan had fidgeted at the way some of their heads had gone down in the Final. He had suffered at the hands of that precocious North London youngster, Charlie George, who was so knackered at the end of full-time that he vomited on the pitch. But George showed Keegan a sample of what Keegan would show himself in future seasons – the will to pick himself up like the England World Cup players in 1966 on the same pitch, and go for the winning jugular.

Now Keegan had the ball at his own feet on a smooth piece of velvety Scandinavian soil. Switched by chance and a moment's inspiration by Shankly and the boot room boys into the role of defensive winger, à la Ian Callaghan, he wore his number eight shirt with pride, and was noted as a player of the future by the odd pipe-smoking local scribe. He even put away two zestful goals just to add to a very good first impression.

Would the Keegan story as future Liverpool hero become a reality? In the view of some of Shankly's confidants, he was still an average midfield player, who although he had considerable bounce and ambition, still needed a good kick up the arse at times when he forgot the Liverpool tradition of team–work and not giving the ball away under pressure. Keegan's time might well come, but a season or two in the Central League would rub off some of the Scunthorpe rawness.

Shankly, though, had other ideas. The new arrival was not for heavy screening. He would soon be exposed to the harsh, noisy, unremitting complexities of First Division football, though his few appearances in the Liverpool reserves at the end of the previous season had hardly caused an eruption in the columns of the Fourth Estate. Colin Malam, the *Sunday Telegraph's* football correspondent since 1973, and then working as a soccer reporter for the *Sun*, was marking readers' talent cards with new discoveries in a column, very appropriately named 'Action Man.'

'I had known of Keegan's talents at Scunthorpe, and now he was a Liverpool player, thought he would be highly suitable for a mention in a pre-season column. But the picture editor couldn't find a single picture of Kevin in the files, and had to alert the provinces for one. Strange, if you think the millions of portraits and action pictures taken since then.'

Malam alerted the large football readership in his paper to Keegan's fitness, dedication, goal hunger, and physical strength, despite his modest size. All were assets Bill Shankly had pondered over for more than a year before signing the Doncaster lad. This particular Action Man piece was read by regulars of The Park public house.

The first team had gone off on another pre-season tour, leaving Keegan to flex his body muscles under the care of the reserve team trainer, Ronnie Moran. Shankly's former right-back in the promotion team and a stickler for Anfield protocol which could be heard through a fog horn voice all the way from the training ground at Melwood to the stadium, Moran gave the cocksure Keegan a roasting at half-time for not playing 'like a Liverpool player'. Keegan was perplexed. But Moran didn't waste time, he told Keegan, in no uncertain terms he was dashing about the field and forgetting responsibilities in defence. Keegan had looked at himself as a 'free and easy' midfield player in the manner of Trevor Brooking for West Ham and England, without being obliged to run back and start booting the ball out of his own box.

But Moran was persistent. This was Anfield, and he wanted Keegan to play the Liverpool way, and he didn't mind shouting at Shanks's new signing to get his message across. In the end, Keegan played a far more disciplined game, the reserves beating Tranmere 2–1 and the winning goal, a penalty, coming when Keegan was chopped down in the opposition's penalty area. Another match, against New Brighton would convince Keegan's sergeant-major that Shanks's boy might be better used as an attacker. It was a brilliantly perceptive flash by Moran, who was to be a future caretaker manager at Liverpool between the departure of Kenny Dalglish and the arrival of Graeme Souness.

With Shankly back from the first team tour, Moran took the opportunity of blooding Keegan as an attacker against Southport. Keegan pumped home two goals to give the reserves another win. So impressive was this performance that Shankly decided to include him in the annual match between the first team and the Central League team at Melwood. This was done as an act of defiance towards the reserve team manager, whom he thought, wrongly, was anti-Keegan. The promoted first-teamer had a 'blinder', scoring three goals and whipping the heart out of the opposing defence, who he had played with only a day or two before.

Keegan got wind that Shankly might pick him for the first team against Nottingham Forest on the Saturday – a dream, kept at the back of his mind in case he was disappointed. He knew he had played well, but he didn't want to risk the disappointment of seeing his name on the reserve team football list again. When Shankly approached him the next day, he was almost mischievously sounding out the new recruit. He was testing his reaction, making him say something, a straight question which needed a straight answer. Many lads of the same age as Keegan might have plumped for reserve team duty because of their lack of First Division experience. But Keegan decided to be bolder.

'I didn't come here to play in your reserves.'

Shankly was impressed, 'Well, good son, off you go and have a cup of tea now.'

Keegan didn't have long to wait for the boss's answer. His name went up on the board, number seven.

The build-up to the actual match produced one or two nightmares. Keegan's family had planned a day out at Liverpool. Brother Mike, and his married sister Mary, would be coming along with Mum and Dad, and of course, Jean (by now the envy of her school). Keegan, in his nervous state, lost track of time and it was absurdly late when he left his digs in the Nook, Lilley Road, located in the Prescott Road area of the city, for the stadium in his sturdy Cortina. Two passengers, Mum and Jean, repressed their own anxieties, while Mike and Dad prayed that Liverpool's new number seven had a sound savvy of Merseyside navigation. He hadn't, and anyway the traffic was like Wembley on Cup final day. The route was blocked, but Keegan managed to propel the Cortina from one street to another, and arrived at the stadium gates 25 minutes late. Shankly was in a frenzy, not quite tearing his hair out but worried all the same. Keegan's late arrival had landed him into the lion's den, but a friendly one, since supporters out there on the terrace, ablaze with red and white scarves, were looking forward to catching sight of the new player, the little man with the George Harrison style hair. They had their autograph books sweating in their pockets, waiting until after the game when Keegan would emerge with or without a goal to his name. But those who had seen him play at Melwood knew instinctively he would score.

Keegan observed in his autobiography how he was glad he was late for duty, despite Shankly's telling off. He had allowed himself no time to work himself up into a frenzy of beginner's nerves. He pulled on his red strip, which was already laid out, and his 'winged' boots ready and laced for the Forest fray. Some of the older players gave him a gentle slap on the back, having hailed his late arrival with some mirth. It had been nice of Kev to turn up for the tea party. Shankly edged over and told Keegan to get out and 'enjoy himself', the usual quip. Keegan distantly heard the Scottish brogue before Tommy Smith summoned the troops and they were sucked out into an immense volume of sound. Unlike Wembley or Stamford Bridge, which are away from the pitch, the Anfield pitch is right there at your feet once the dressing room space is vacated. Keegan heard the sound, and it drowned everything – the Kop sound, the sound which was stored away until another match and then resurrected in even greater volume for the next.

Keegan sensed his boots pounding across the pitch, but heard nothing, only the sound – a colossal pounding in the ears. He thought of Jean and his parents, and wondered what they must be thinking. Of course, it didn't look like that from the press box. The new boy looked quite calm, quite in tune with the situation, as he made his debut alongside Toshack and the rest. He looked perky and in good shape; it might have been a routine Fourth Division game at the Old Show Ground. Keegan joined the other Liverpool players in a waved salute to every corner of the ground before the kick-off. Ray Clemence, another Old Show Ground favourite, didn't look nervous so why should Keegan? Somehow he knew it would be his afternoon and he would score. Many of the younger fans thought so too. Even before the kick-off certain latecomers in the press box less familiar with Liverpool's staff list were trying to remind themselves just who this Keegan was on the team sheet, especially as there were already chants of 'Kev-in Kee-gan' piping up around the ground.

He was Joseph Kevin Keegan, taking centre stage at Anfield. The challenge, he admitted was not beyond him.

'I believe I can live with any situation in which I find myself. If I were going into the ring with Muhammad Ali, I would honestly believe I deserved to be there. I wouldn't think about being knocked out, but only of winning. That is the person I am – not easily overawed. It explains how I was able to take in my stride the fact that I had just left Scunthorpe in the Fourth Division and was about to make my debut at Liverpool in the First Division on the first day of a new season.'

Cocksure? Well, not entirely because Kevin Keegan did find himself caught off guard by the representative of the Kop, 'a nice old fellow' who was allowed on the pitch by the police as part of a ritual welcome to a Liverpool newcomer. Keegan got a full whiff of the pre-match boozer's breath, and the roughness of an unshaven chin on his cheek as the Kopite snatched a quick kiss. The stadium burst out laughing and applauded as the 'representative' wobbled back to his standing space behind the goal. There were no more kisses, at least not for 12 minutes or so.

It was Peter Thompson who assisted in Keegan's first ever First Division goal, popping up on the right, instead of his customary left, and edging the ball away from a defender to John Toshack, who slipped a low cross to Keegan. Keegan failed to connect properly and the ball ricocheted off his boot between the goalkeeper, Jim Barron, and a spare Forest foot into the far corner of the net. Goals count, however they are scored, and Keegan's lucky dip immediately earned him the adoration of the crowd – though not the Forest defence, caught out by a lucky connection at the near post.

It was hail to the new arrival as Keegan jigged with joy, Peter Thompson and John Toshack searching him out to bestow their congratulations along with an arms aloft Liverpool team. Shankly might have said his daughter Jeanette would have hit the ball more crisply, but Keegan's first of 100 for Liverpool was probably the one he got most pleasure from, and with Jean and the family being there to see it, made the moment even better. It certainly boosted Keegan's confidence and he began to run all over the pitch, taking players on, feigning to go one way, and going the other. For a player considered relatively raw, he was doing things which some of the senior players judged afterwards to be exceptional. Keegan, used to the hard Fourth Division tackling, now had more space and caught up with the ball on sometimes hopeless missions.

During one Liverpool raid when he was making a nuisance of himself in the box, he was fouled, and Tommy Smith buried the penalty. Then it was Emlyn 'Emma' Hughes's turn, delighting the Kop with a third before that immensely gifted winger, Ian Storey-Moore scored a consolation goal for Forest.

Then it was back to the Nook for a quiet celebration and a life of increasing fame and celebration for a footballer that Shankly would say 'walked in here like a breath of fresh air'.

Keegan's debut in Liverpool's first team brought him virtually instant fame – inspired in some ways, unnerving in others – and he started winning football awards with great regularity. Some were valid, some bordered on the comic, though one of them, 'Merseyside Footballer of the Year', made him proud because it showed he had been accepted in a 'foreign' city. He had outpaced his more senior Liverpool colleagues. He was certainly flattered, his young ego swelling like a robin's redbreast when he learned he had been named the *Daily Mirror's* 'Monday Man'. Being 20 years old, and sporting that long trendy black hair, which when permed looked like a poodle's coat at Crufts, he looked the epitome of a modern footballer – smart white suit, flairs, and block heels.

Nobody enjoyed Keegan's explosive form, or the fame it brought him more than the manager. He had been the force behind the boy from Scunthorpe United and partly responsible for his leap from near obscurity to the regular headlines. Shankly had been the one who had returned home after Anfield matches to his patient wife, Nessie, talking about his new player becoming the greatest player in England. Keegan wasn't having any of it. Flattery was all very well, but even Shankly could go over the top sometimes.

'Go on boss, that's what you tell everyone.'

Shankly refused to retract. 'No, no, I'm right. I'm not saying you'll be as good as Denis Law, but you are going to be one of the greatest players in Britain.'

Keegan savoured such remarks from his manager, which would profit him financially when Shankly started doubling his salary on a regular basis. The manager had respected Keegan's determination to be awarded a decent salary when he arrived, and these pay rises were his way of showing how he appreciated Keegan's marvellous early seasons for Liverpool.

'Many people helped me on my way, but only one person made me. That was Shanks . As soon as I joined up with him, I started to become a player. He was perfect for me, because I'm the type who likes to strive for a personal target, and Shanks would set them for me. He worked it all out after a month of watching me play for Liverpool. He knew where I fitted in, what I was going to do, and what he had to do to get the best out of me.'

There was, however, the odd occasion when manager and budding superstar fell out. One came early on at Liverpool after Keegan had bought a new car, a Capri, to replace his old Cortina. This replacement was to cause the owner a sudden loss of pride. A painful injury to a bone in his left foot forced Keegan to miss a match. Shankly, with his distaste for players who had the cheek to pull out unless they had a broken leg, made a meal of moaning about Keegan's affliction. The injury was one of those mysterious ones with a club specialist diagnosing a touch of tennis elbow in the left foot. Shankly couldn't stand it – he hinted Keegan was skiving. Shankly would have been throttled in his Preston days had he tried to drop out for such dubious reasons. It was no good. Keegan would have to travel on the team coach with the rest of the players, who were due to meet Stoke City. The impression Shankly gave was of a high-ranking policeman summoning Keegan up as a military deserter. Not for the last time, Keegan decided to run off home, because it enraged him to think his boss believed he was 'cheating'. But when Keegan duly arrived in Doncaster, it was only to be reprimanded by his own father for doing a bunk while the Liverpool team travelled to the Victoria Ground.

'You're on a contract with Liverpool. Get back there,' said Joe Keegan.

Keegan did go back, his remorse at having walked out before the match reduced by the fact he had chosen to make a stand. He was no cheat. That was certain.

Shankly put an end to what could have become an escalating spell of tension by not bringing the matter up when they next met. The injury was later found to be caused by Keegan's Cortina clutch, which was stiff enough to strain an elephant's foot. But it healed, and Keegan was soon back in action again. It was a relief when all the walking he had put into rehabilitation, down cobbled streets and through rows of crumbling, vacated slums, had toughened up the foot. It was walks like these which brought Keegan into contact with the harsh realities of Liverpool city life. The poverty and the ugliness was at the same time populated by a stubborn, humorous scouse breed, many of whom filled the Kop to capacity on Saturday afternoons. Keegan remained devoted to this section of fans, until they turned against him after he left for Hamburg.

'I can't even think of playing for another club. Where else can you find supporters and an atmosphere like Liverpool Football Club?'

A cautious Sir Alf Ramsey did not hesitate to blood Keegan in his England Under-23 team against Scotland the following February at Derby. Keegan was winning caps on his way to becoming a senior player. Hysteria, however, has a habit of dying down and Keegan soon found that opening game against Forest was a one-off, the new hero would now have to be absorbed into the team. He would have to work, he would have to toil week in, week out, on the training ground at Melwood under the inquisitive gaze of Shankly, Paisley, Fagan and Moran, the reserve team manager. He actually enjoyed Shankly's three-a-side, all-out 30 minute matches which would have winded a cheetah in the bush. Like Oliver Twist he did crave for more, but was not punished for it. In fact, his stock grew, much to the approval of player witnesses such as Ian Ross.

Ross went to Shankly, who liked to hear opinions from his team members if they were positive, or funny enough to make the hallowed boss chuckle like an uphill tractor changing gears.

'He's a hell of a hard boy to tab, boss,' Ross said, looking respectfully at a Scotsman many Kopites thought of as 'God'.

'You dinna have to tell me that, lad.' Shankly turned his head somewhat quizzically at Ross.

'He's twisting and turning all the time, he's so quick and you never know what he'll do next.'

Shankly knew all this, but nevertheless relayed Ross's enthusiasm to his coaching staff. It was what they all knew already and, confirmed Liverpool had on its books one of the most exciting prospects in their history.

Keegan scored nine League goals that season and appeared regularly enough in the first team to show the fans they might have another Billy Liddell to worship in the future. Despite Keegan's scurryings and darting offensive runs at opposing defences, Liverpool had once again to accept the end of another season devoid of trophies. Derby County, with Clough and Taylor still in full command despite the obvious frailties of their union, won the Football League championship by one point from the FA Cup winners, Leeds, while Keegan got his first taste of Cup failure when Leeds knocked Liverpool out of the Cup, and Bayern Munich dispatched the team from Europe with two goals by England's 1970 scoring rottweiler, Gerd Müller. The team Keegan would serve so well during the next tremendous season was clicking, but not as sweetly as Shankly, or Keegan would have wished. During one 0–0 stalemate at Stamford Bridge late in the 1971/72 season, the football skills of Alan Hudson, in Chelsea's midfield, completely overshadowed Keegan's South-West London debut. He found himself being repeatedly pushed back towards his own goalkeeper Clemence's sandy green pudding of a goal area. Shankly's team that afternoon may have been careful not to lose, but in mean mood they were about to achieve just the reverse. Ray Clemence showed more authority in goal; Chris Lawler and Alec Lindsay were trustworthy full-backs; and Larry Lloyd and captain Tommy Smith, with his sinister Charles Bronson 'Magnificent Seven' looks, made formidable barriers at the back. Emlyn Hughes had joined Liverpool from Blackpool for £65,000; Ian Callaghan's role in the mid-1960s had been as a shrewd right-wing tormentor; Peter Thompson was raiding on the left, and Brian Hall, Keegan, John Toshack and Steve Heighway shared attacking roles. Hudson's memory of Keegan's arrival provided some interesting contrasts. Unlike Keegan, Chelsea's enigmatic midfielder allowed his career to turn on and off like the twinkling lights of a disco as his injury-handicapped career advanced, sometimes backfiring during spells with Chelsea, Arsenal and Stoke City.

The flair-up between Keegan and his captain Tommy Smith became almost folklore on Merseyside. Two dudes on the ranch brought together in inevitable confrontation: the Mexican-moustached local boy, known as the 'Iron Man', and the saddle-happy kid from Doncaster with a six-shooter reputation. A Hollywood film script might well have adapted the story into a 'Big Country' saga, with Shanks playing 'Big Daddy' and Bob Paisley his benign brother. Like many confrontations which bring those with more authority and experience in contact with ambitious new dudes, the drama became wildly exaggerated. A dressing-room upheaval between 'Smidge' and the Kid, which worked out in the most salubrious way in the end, had both parties falling into each other's arms in mutual hero worship when Smith set up both Keegan's goals in the 1974 FA Cup final.

The feud reached a peak, according to Keegan's autobiography, when the pair had to be separated during one training session at Melwood. Larry Lloyd moved in to what amounted to a Keegan rescue act, the Doncaster kid wheezing out of the corner of his mouth, 'Keep hold of me, for God's sake. Don't let go of me.'

Keegan recalled he did not get on with Smith during his early days at Anfield. He was the hard man Shankly used to tell to go out and 'shake a rival team's bones'. The newcomer was greeted with an avalanche of publicity, and suggestions that the next George Best had arrived at the gates of Liverpool Football Club. It was not very much to the club captain's liking. But Keegan was not a party freak, though he trained until his guts were tied in knots. He was a stickler for his own discipline, did much charity work, and devoted his Thursdays to looking after handicapped children. He went to bed early before matches, for he genuinely loved the game with a passion which sometimes confused his captain who might have thought he was thinking only of his own welfare.

Putting the matter into perspective Smith, who now writes regularly for the *Liverpool Post and Echo* laughed off suggestions that he really had it in for Keegan.

'I was certainly a big-headed bugger at the time. If a member of our team didn't stick the ball in the net with an easy chance, I was the first to come down on him. I liked to win. It was in my nature. Always had been. I remember giving Kevin a bollocking once. In a game where we played Newcastle, Malcolm Macdonald scored three against us, and Kevin kept trying to help us out at the back. That wasn't his game. Afterwards, I told Malcolm it was the last time he would score against us. I can't remember his doing so again, and he certainly didn't in the 1974 Cup final when it was our Kevin who got two from my passes. I didn't have to bollock him then. Kevin probably found the Liverpool life very different from his Doncaster background when he came to us. On Merseyside, you've got to be a bit harder. I'm a scouse, and was very outspoken at the time. Liked to go out for a drink and a bit of dancing after a match, but made sure I was a steady influence as captain. I had been with the club for some time when Kevin arrived. I joined the ground staff as a kid and I used to clean the 'furniture'. Some of the older pros were rough and gruff which must have influenced me. But we all got on. Kevin wasn't a goody-goody, but he worked very hard on his self-discipline and training. He was quiet, but not boring. I remember when he first came into the side. We were looking for a goalscorer because although we were not conceding goals, we weren't scoring them either. Kevin changed all that. He was amazing, he had the ability of turning the slightest chance into a goal.'

Keegan, after initially thinking Liverpool's Iron Man was the club bully, altered his opinion considerably, as he got to know 'Smidge' better.

'He began to understand that pressure from other people had pushed me up to where I was, and it was not any conscious effort on my part to show that I was a cut above everyone else at the club. My attitude toward Smidge changed, though I always answered him back when I thought he was wrong. I grew to respect him enormously as a player. He was a great captain, never selfish, always battling for the boys and not just for himself. He always ensured that everyone had a fair share of the rewards that came the team's way. As a player, Smith was always known as a hard man. This was a fallacy. He had one season in which he was over-zealous with opposing players and getting a reputation for it. He then spent the rest of his career being a very good player without getting the credit for it.'

Keegan and Smidge would have their dream farewell as members of the Liverpool side when Smith scored Liverpool's second goal with a near-post header in the 1977 European Cup Final in Rome. The way Keegan hugged Smith after the Liverpool number four had buried the ball in the back of the net, certainly pushed any previous tension into history.

Keegan's early career included other problems. Jean hadn't settled easily into the Liverpool ambience of her own living quarters and a part-time job as an optician. Keegan's growing fame was a natural hazard. Jean joined Keegan in making an almost mandatory pop record which sunk deep into the River Mersey with the progress of time. It was better they got engaged, and even married, like so many of the other Liverpool players, although the altar was not reached for three years after Keegan had joined Liverpool. The future bridegroom was still making his way in the game, and he was in no hurry to walk down the aisle.

Then there were the fans, the Anfield worshippers, who supplied the oxygen on match day. After the Pegler factory and Scunthorpe, they were Keegan's morale-boosters, pushing him on during the bad times. Some of the fans turned against him at Anfield after he left for Hamburg. Tommy Smith thought it was by not being exactly honest about why he had left.

'Kevin is not a greedy person, and has done a great deal of good work in his time, but when he went to Hamburg, he should have said he was going to make his pot of gold. Instead, he said he was going to improve his football. The fans didn't believe him. They felt their hero wasn't telling them the real reason.'

Keegan still had plenty of time to enjoy the fame on Merseyside as Liverpool progressed towards more trophy triumphs. He was the player the Kop rolled up to see despite the cruel remark George Best later made behind his back, that 'Kevin Keegan isn't fit to clean my boots.'

Shankly strengthened his midfield in the close season by buying Peter Cormack from Nottingham Forest and was in no doubt why his team emerged so powerfully to outwit their rivals, Leeds, Arsenal and Derby.

'We played to our strengths. We pressurized everyone and made them run. It might take you 80 minutes to win but don't get frustrated because 90 minutes is a long time.'

Nobody did more for Liverpool than Keegan who kept pressing for a winning goal. He put away nine League goals in the 1972/73 season and made many more for Toshack and Heighway. This was a time of nail-biting in the dug-outs for in nine matches that season, Liverpool chose the last ten minutes to claim the victor's spoils. Not everything was gilded. Liverpool were knocked out of the League Cup by Spurs and the FA Cup by Manchester City, after a Maine Road replay. But Shankly refused to let heads go down in the dressing room. There was still everything to play for. Keegan's regular goal-assists matched his ability to find opposing nets, as he soon proved when Liverpool began to turn the screw in the championship stakes. A 3–2 win at Anfield after West Ham had led at half-time, showed Liverpool's new emerging superstar at his most lethal. The normally unflappable Bobby Moore lost so much concentration that he was booked. Keegan had set up John Toshack's first half, headed goal and scored the second himself before Emlyn Hughes won an exciting match. Both Keegan and Hughes were singled out in press reports as contenders for places in Alf Ramsey's World Cup team for the crucial qualifying match against Poland, in October at Wembley. But Ramsey did not read or act upon such advice. Neither played in a match that was drawn, and cost England a place in the 1974 World Cup finals – a calamitous state of affairs which led to Sir Alf's dismissal seven months later. Keegan was far too preoccupied with Shankly and his own boss's business to fully comprehend the full, devastating meaning of England's elimination. An England team did not appear in the finals until 1982 in Spain when Keegan was a senior player himself, and considered over the top by many cynics.

Beating Ron Greenwood's cultured West Ham, still led by Bobby Moore, was always a bonus and to achieve the double that season proved satisfying to Shankly. Keegan showed once again in front of a discriminating East End congregation what a wonderful prospect he was. With Tommy Smith back in the fold after recovering from injuries sustained in a car crash, Liverpool turned West Ham over with a goal of symphonic beauty which West Ham would have been hard-pressed to challenge, even in the days of Moore, Peters and Byrne in the 1960s.

A new arrival in the Liverpool side, local boy Phil Thompson, passed the ball square to Heighway midway inside the West Ham half and the Republic of Ireland winger duly sprinted towards the by-line, pulling the ball back for Keegan to head into the home net. No nonsense, no fuss, a strike delivered with cold steel. It seemed so routine Keegan was scarcely hugged by his team-mates, but it was a goal worthy of another Liverpool win as they pounded on towards the title, leaving their great rivals Leeds United to contemplate their own plight in losing not only this race, but also going down to Ian Porterfield's lucky goal for Sunderland in the FA Cup final.

Keegan could not have had a more useful opportunity to promote his talents to an audience than in the run-in to the UEFA Cup final. His contribution as they beat three German teams, Eintracht Frankfurt, Dynamo Berlin and Dynamo Dresden, as well as the Greek side AEK Athens on the way to the semi-final, was phenomenal although he would never have claimed so. The semi-final threw them against a Tottenham Hotspur side who already had a good record in Europe, and it was a shame in the minds of patriots that the UEFA final could not have been between two English clubs that year. For Liverpool, their main ambition was to get their name on a European trophy for the first time, and they approached the first leg against Spurs at Anfield in the same way as they would have prepared for a meeting with Real Madrid or Ajax of Amsterdam.

Ironically, it was the loyal full-back Alec Lindsay who gave Liverpool a flimsy one-goal lead to take to White Hart Lane, where Keegan, for all his efforts to score a decisive second goal, felt his spirits sag as Martin Peters scored four minutes into the second half to level the aggregate 1–1. But this Liverpool team showed they could battle on the back of supreme fitness and unceasing pace. Steve Heighway went dancing off two minutes later to shock Spurs with a breakaway goal and although the redoubtable World Cup hero, Peters, scored again to make the score 2–2 on aggregate, Liverpool squeezed into the final against Borussia Moenchengladbach by way of their precious Heighway goal. Liverpool were in their second European final under Shankly (the first being lost in 1966 in the European Cup Winners' Cup against Borussia Dortmund). Keegan and the team celebrated joyfully on the way home, although the task of winning their first League Championship since 1966 was still a major priority – a triumph which was won with a final total of 60 points, the runners-up, Arsenal on 57 and third-placed Leeds with 53.

Keegan, who had by now grown his bristly black sideburns, was all wound up for the first leg of the final at Anfield on 9 May 1973, ready for the most compelling challenge of his career so far. However, the adrenalin evaporated when the match was abandoned after 27 minutes when torrential rain flooded Anfield. The teams assembled again the following night, but already Shankly had done his homework after seeing how vulnerable Borussia had looked in the air during the brief moments of play possible. He chose John Toshack to fill the centre-forward berth instead of Brian Hall, and the move soon benefited Keegan who could hardly contain his joy when he headed in Toshack's perfectly square nod-on to give Liverpool the lead after 20 minutes. With the Moenchengladbach defence in a state of jitters whenever Toshack received the ball in the air, a penalty was conceded by the Germans from Lindsay's cross. Keegan was delegated to take it. The Kopites looked towards the Borussia net when Keegan emerged to deliver an executioner's shot from the spot. But the Borussia goalkeeper managed to save it, and Keegan ran back into the action modestly sanguine about the imperfection of his attempt. Penalties were to be scored, and he knew it, but he was hardly crestfallen. Before half-time, Keegan had struck again following another linking move with Toshack, to give Liverpool a two-goal lead, surely a winning platform for the return, especially as Larry Lloyd used his bulk and height to head in Keegan's corner to make the final victory 3–0.

It was soon after Lloyd's goal that Keegan and his team-mates were nonplussed when Heighway conceded a penalty, but Ray Clemence became the centre of adoring Kop attention when he leapt to his right to save Heynckes' full-blooded shot from the spot. Keegan and his team-mates, not to mention a more cautious Shankly and his boot room team, were optimistic they could hold onto the lead since Liverpool had not conceded four goals in one match throughout that season. Although everyone connected with Anfield knew this highly talented German team, inspired by the mercurial midfield talents of Gunter Netzer would come at them like wolfhounds in the return match.

Rhine warning bells linked to pre-match butterflies in their Ruhr dressing room, proved a salutary lesson that no lead is sacrosanct in football, as Keegan would wryly recall. Liverpool were trailing by two first-half goals from the elusive Jupp Heynckes, as Netzer and his colleagues put more pressure on Ray Clemence's goal. There were strong signs that Liverpool were going to finish up second-best again. They had support backed up by a large section of soldiers of the British Army of the Rhine, who kept singing, 'You'll Never Walk Alone'. As the crowd got behind the English side and Netzer's grip in midfield weakened, Liverpool got back into the game and hung on to win the trophy 3–2 on aggregate. The fun began the moment the final whistle sounded. The Kop fans raced onto the pitch to hoist their heroes into the air. Where was Keegan? Where was the Mighty Atom to whom Liverpool owed so much for their stupendous first victory in Europe? He was up there on a utility bridge of burly scouse shoulders being run round the Borussia stadium. He loved it. And why not? He was struggling to keep his balance as men and boys he did not know from Adam conveyed him round the pitch. There was Shankly, somewhere between the dressing room and the pitch, a Liverpool scarf around his neck, celebrating and hugging anyone who wanted his strong-armed grip.

Somehow Keegan made it back to the dressing rooms, and later to the team hotel, where the press corps joined in the celebrations which went on until dawn. Colin Malam remembers, 'There was something special about the occasion – Liverpool's first victory in Europe, yes, but it also showed what a special bond there was at Anfield. The sheer joy of hanging on and winning that match unleashed a great surge of relief. For Keegan, it was a wonderful night. He was certainly on his way to being a superstar by then. Europe had woken up to the fact.'

Keegan's most successful season so far had brought him to the attention of not only the footballing public but people outside the game who sometimes listened to radio commentaries and began to pick up the names of footballers. Bryon Butler, a long-serving member of the BBC radio soccer commentary team and a distinguished author, remembered how the name Keegan began to stick in his mind after outside broadcasts, because he used it so often. Butler's admiration of the player began to grow with every commentary he did of Liverpool games.

Keegan's growing national charisma as a future England captain, was observed with a certain caution by commentators within the game as experienced as Butler. The example of George Best showed how fickle success could be. Best had that very season temporarily retired his wayward genius from the game in a Christmas bust-up at Old Trafford, which had seen Frank O'Farrell shown the door as manager in favour of Tommy Docherty. The fact that Best's natural genius had been lost in a riot of drunken pleasure, was a warning to any budding footballer.

Keegan was altogether different from the handsome Best. Keegan had spent years creating his own credo – hours of toil and sweat and being badgered by Shankly and his team on freezing days at Melwood. The players were required not to wear warm tracksuits but match kit because that's what they wore on match days. Best could put on his strip, yawn and go out on to the Old Trafford pitch to deliver performances of divine magic. He may have had a raging hangover or been out all night at a party in a suburb of Manchester, but his natural gift and precociousness could see him through. Keegan wasn't like that. He played his football life by the Shankly book, healthy, clean and tidy. He played in a team and teamwork was his code. Yet his strong character prevented anyone from taking advantage of him.

'It was the character on the park rather than the ability you noticed first, the authority and dedication to discipline,' Bryon Butler recalls. 'There was something about the guy not of the common herd. He had a quick mind, quick feet, he was a sparkler. Keegan lacked the ball skills of such post-war immortals as Wilf Mannion, Jimmy Logie, Len Shackleton, John White, Rodney Marsh, Stan Bowles and Alex Young and he was the first to admit it. He did have leadership qualities and could link brilliantly with his Liverpool team-mates.

'You always felt Keegan was going to do something extra-special. He was such a strong character, a general. He grew in stature in spite of being a little man, and deservedly became a superstar of the English game.'

What Keegan lacked, according to Billy Wright, a former England captain, was an ability to conceal his true sprinting capacity. Wright told David Miller of *The Times*, 'No matter how fast Stanley Matthews did anything, he was always under control and had something to spare. George Best had it. Kevin Keegan didn't. When Keegan was moving at top speed, you could see he was flat out.'

Such reservations, however, did not stop Ramsey from selecting Keegan for his senior squad in 1973. Mick Channon, who had become a great friend of Keegan, knew all about Ramsey's process of not being rushed and putting players into the fold too soon. Even Ramsey, who had said that Martin Peters was ten years in advance of his time, came out at one of the press conferences he dreaded, by saying Keegan reminded him of Geoff Hurst.

The 'Mighty Atom', as the Kop had affectionately nicknamed their Doncaster pirate, was in Ramsey's opinion, well worth comparison with the 1966 World Cup final hat-trick hero, because, like Geoff, 'he was one of the few players in recent years to realize the value of using the whole width of the pitch'. Keegan was unsparing with his devotion to teamwork; even more, to be fair, than Hurst – who remained the essential goalscorer despite his willingness as a former wing-half to help out at the back or go looking for the ball when it was being screened by mean rivals. Ramsey liked Keegan, he liked his attitude, but he was going to make him bide his time.

Tony Pawson, in his book *The Goalscorers* got to the nub of Keegan's essential qualities he had witnessed from the press box.

'Keegan' s manner is quiet, but he has the steel that the

goalscorer needs.' After being spirited away from Scunthorpe by Bill Shankly, Keegan said of himself, 'Ambition, that's what drives me. I'll run until I succeed. I'm relieved when it's Saturday, you know. It's pressure all week, but I react opposite to most. When I get out there on the field it's a relief. All the talking is OK, but I think this is what I'm here for – to play.'

Keegan was aware of the aggression within him that had to be controlled.

'I must improve my temperament. If someone kicks me I must curb my desire to kick him back.'

The outstanding success had been with Liverpool, rather than England where he had had no Toshack to steer chances to him. Keegan was always lifted by the atmosphere of the Kop, as Jackie Milburn used to be by Newcastle crowds.

Pawson noted how level-headed Keegan was. 'Hero worship brought its worries as well as its benefits.'

'The only thing I feared in life [Keegan says] was missing an open goal in front of the Kop supporters. I would rather die than to have that happen. It's funny. Empty the Kop and it doesn't look anything. Yet when its full you feel there's a million people there. When they start singing "You'll Never Walk Alone" it made my eyes water. Sometimes I've actually been crying while I'm playing. I hope one day to get the pressure George Best got. Or Bobby Moore. I don't envy anyone who's got it, but those who have and start grumbling about it are fools.' Pawson compared the dark-haired Keegan's qualities with those of a blond inside forward of an earlier generation – Wilf Mannion, the hero of the youthful Don Revie. Mannion had played 357 games for Middlesbrough and gained 26 England caps, averaging about a goal every three games. Like Keegan he was an unselfish player making openings for others by his brave and tireless play.'

By the early summer of 1973 after Liverpool's UEFA Cup triumph, the Kop supporters had every reason to believe they had a performer who would achieve more than golden boy Mannion ever did. Although the Keegan–Toshack partnership became more and more celebrated as a regular scoring duo, their goal flow was still unable to check Leeds' awesome advance towards the 1973/74 League Championship title.

Keegan's two full international appearances under Ramsey in 1973 were not conspicuous successes, and caused a certain chill between player and manager. Both matches were World Cup qualifying games against Wales – internationals Keegan did not relish because the home countries, players he came up against knew his style of play better than any other players in the world.

Of Keegan's sending off in an Under-23 match on 1 June 1972 against East Germany in Leipzig Ramsey said, 'I was very sorry for the player. He had been kicked severely.' This somewhat underestimated the treatment Keegan got from the men behind the 'Iron Curtain'.

'I had been chopped nine or ten times in the first half with no protection from the referee. I was chopped yet again early in the second half by Klaus Decker, retaliated, and was sent off.'

Such a rare occurence of Keegan blowing his top against some clumsy East German bullies was shelves by people in high places (an FA Disciplinary Committee taking no further action).

Keegan's name kept on cropping up in Ramsey's thoughts during his regular train journeys from Ipswich to Liverpool Street – he couldn't avoid hearing about Keegan, or noticing him on his Saturday 'watching matches'. Ramsey had already praised Keegan in print. But Keegan was forced to wait by Liverpool. He was among some famous World Cup names, including Bobby Moore and Gordon Banks, for the full England squad to play against Yugoslavia, but being late September, Liverpool had a League Cup replay coming up, one which required Keegan for domestic duty. Shankly reluctantly withdrew Keegan from the party, telling the disappointed player his chance would come again. Ramsey would see to that. Keegan was sceptical. Ramsey had been known to look elsewhere for players, but having always a good intake of men from Anfield of squad players like Roger Hunt, Peter Thompson, Tommy Smith, Ian Callaghan and Gordon Milne, he respected Liverpool's excuse. Keegan's next call-up took only two months in coming when on 7 November 1972, his name was included in a 16-man squad to play Wales in a World Cup qualifying match at Ninian Park. Ramsey's new boy made his way with typical alacrity to the team headquarters to be met with an atmosphere which was like the first day at school.

Keegan was 'new' to the remaining veterens who had played in the 1966 World Cup, like Moore, Banks and Ball, and some of the later arrivals like Martin Chivers and the court jester, Rodney Marsh. He arrived with a bit of a chip on his shoulder He was an outsider, a player who had emerged from the obscure, hacking unsubtleties of Fourth Division football to become an instant wonder kid on Merseyside. But Bobby Moore, for one, didn't let him down.

'Bobby Moore put himself out to help Keegan and pass on his advice. Moore did not stay in a clique, neither was he a captain who would dive off to his room. He remained with the team and had a knack of smoothing things over if players hurt each other's feelings. He had an aura about him. He did not have to shout, but just whisper, and people would listen.'

Moore took Keegan aside and gave him advice about the pitfalls he might experience outside the game, pitfalls Moore unfortunately would suffer from in later life, like greedy hangers-on and dodgy business deals.

When Ramsey did name the team, Keegan was selected to play alongside Rodney Marsh and Martin Chivers. It was a new experiment by the manager, which unfortunately backfired. Although England did manage a 1–0 win, Keegan couldn't blend with the elusive Marsh, while any hope that he might find a target-man, with a flair for nod-downs, like Toshack, disappeared with Chivers. The threesome did not click together and to cap it all, Keegan missed a fairly easy chance of scoring.

'It came late in the game at Ninian Park,' Keegan recalls. I moved in on Gary Sprake, decided not to chip the ball over him, but take it past. He seemed to get ahead of my thinking. When I looked he had every nook and cranny of the goalmouth filled. I tried to place it through his legs, but Gary had 'conned' me into doing this.' Sprake, by coincidence, had lost his place in the great Leeds side to David Harvey.

Ramsey selected Keegan for the second qualifying match

against Wales at Wembley, but in the words of Keegan, 'I flopped' and he was out for the duration. A goalless draw hardly suited England, and helped bring about their abrupt dismissal from the 1974 finals. Many critics thought, 'What's up with Ramsey? He doesn't let you play the way you do at Liverpool' – but it was precisely the opposite. Ramsey wanted Keegan to play the Liverpool way. The trouble was that Shankly's boy didn't have some of his other team-mates around him who knew the Liverpool way, and Keegan found himself wandering off forlornly to the wing, hoping for a pass.

'Alf was criticized for not selecting me again, but in fairness, it was a risk he could not repeat. He had tried me twice and I flopped. He was intent on trying to qualify for the World Cup. In a way, I felt like an intruder. The spirit of 1966 and 1970 was still around the squad, even though most of the old faces had gone. When a new face appears, it means that an old face has disappeared. It also happens at club level. You have a successful side, but every time someone new arrives one of your old friends goes. Although you might not resent the newcomer, you cannot help thinking about your old colleague.'

Ramsey did stand by players of whom Keegan was critical. One was Peter Storey with the 'cold eyes' who, when the pair met during matches between Liverpool and Arsenal, 'would try to stop me [Keegan] in any way he could, which he was good at'. Keegan rated Storey as being inferior to Norman Hunter, but he did have the qualities Ramsey wanted – the ability to win the ball like a Nobby Stiles and give it to a colleague who could do something with it. Storey knew his limitations. So it was Keegan out, Storey in, again.

Keegan, was of the opinion that Sir Alf Ramsey did not sound like a football manager. 'Most certainly, we will attack the opposition', or 'Most certainly, this is our strongest squad'. There was an air about him that suggested he might think himself a cut above the players. Nothing could be further from the truth. Ramsey was a player's manager. But he went, all the same, in May 1974 during the same week Keegan scored two goals in the FA Cup final. Ramsey was treated shabbily, it was thought, by many of those devoted players who turned up in force for his farewell. What had been a gloriously captivating era of English football was, however, now sadly tarnished.

Bill Shankly tended to think of foreign teams as distractions from the real and all-abiding purpose of Liverpool's mission in life – winning the League Championship. But Keegan already had the foreign 'itch' in his system, having witnessed how well Borussia Moenchengladbach and Red Star could play, but he kept his feelings muted. The boss had an uncanny flair for hearing what was going on around the Anfield camp. In his earliest days at Anfield, Keegan learnt that even the slightest lapse on match day, like a show of too much affection for a watching wife through a kiss, could be construed as an act of gross disobedience by the hard-jawed, grizzled paragon of Liverpool Football Club.

By the spring of 1974, Liverpool supporters were preparing for another noisy assault on the twin towers of Wembley, with the Geordies of Newcastle United lined up as opposition. Liverpool's run had not been without the odd moments of discomfort. Doncaster Rovers, the representatives from Keegan's birthplace, had been leading 2–1 in their third round tie with 20 minutes to go. It was one of Doncaster's favourite sporting heroes who duly equalized for Liverpool, forcing a replay which Liverpool not too surprisingly won. Of Keegan's equalizer in the first match, Shankly told him, 'That's probably the most important goal you'll ever score. Not only will it give the people of Doncaster the chance to see you play, it might also win us the Cup.'

Three years before he had been a tense spectator – now he was at the top. Revered by the Kop, Keegan was being hailed as a great new England prospect in the build-up towards the 1976 European Championships and the World Cup in Argentina two years later. There was a special zip in the way Keegan went about his training. He couldn't wait to turn the screw in a Newcastle defence which had looked dreadfully vulnerable for an hour in the semi-final against Burnley. His team-mates watched him tie up his laces with a determined look in his eye. 'Do it for Shanks, do it for Shanks,' the challenge kept repeating in his brain.

A new-style Liverpool saw Emlyn Hughes and Phil Thompson take over as centre-backs in place of the injured Larry Lloyd and Tommy Smith moving to right-back in place of Chris Lawlor. Smith looked back on the occasion with mixed feelings, especially with regard to a disagreement with Newcastle's Alan Kennedy before the match.

'It was a wonder we didn't come to blows in the tunnel before the match. I felt sore at Alan Kennedy for saying I was getting too old for the job. Kevin, of course, couldn't wait to get on with the game.'

When the teams did emerge into the grey weather, the noise level threatened to break all other records at a Wembley final. Shankly walked ahead of the Liverpool team beside the Newcastle manager, Joe Harvey, who had won the FA Cup twice in 1951 and 1952 as a player for the club. He could boast of Newcastle's five previous visits to Wembley in which they were unbeaten.

Keegan had the scent of victory in his nostrils from the opening whistle. All the energy he had build-up since he watched Liverpool lose to Arsenal on a far hotter day three years before was put into this match as he helped string passes together with Peter Cormack, Ian Callaghan and Brian Hall in midfield, while linking up front with Toshack and the elusive Steve Heighway. Shankly had noticed Newcastle's vulnerability to accurate one-two's outside their penalty area when the teams had met in a League game at St James's Park. So Liverpool used a continental cat-and-mouse style game to wear down Newcastle's suspect defence, which was without the influential David Craig through injury.

Liverpool had been unlucky just after half-time when a marvellous effort by the left-back, Alec Lindsay was ruled offside, a linesman spotting Keegan as the offender. Liverpool were adamant the decision was unjust and went out for the kill, their well-known strengths wearing down the toiling Newcastle defenders, with Lindsay emerging time and again as a constructive extra attacker. As for Keegan, according to a *Sunday Telegraph* reporter, 'Little Keegan darted all over the green plain at Wembley with the speed of a cheetah. Once he eluded Terry McDermott (his future colleague at Anfield, and second in command on the manager's bench at Newcastle) near the by-line but his centre was brilliantly taken by Ian McFaul.'

Keegan's first goal in the 57th minute, a net-breaking half-volley, came after the wily Tommy Smith had set him up following Heighway's cross. Keegan was hugged by almost the entire Liverpool team, nobody had deserved a goal more than the Liverpool No. 7. Every time Keegan touched the ball, he put an extra thousand pounds on his value and won another thousand schoolboy hearts. He was on the hunt, and Newcastle would surely fall again, as they did to a brilliant goal in the 75th minute. Cormack found Toshack, who headed the ball on to Heighway. The Republic of Ireland winger raced through the Newcastle defence and slipped the ball past McFaul.

Newcastle were in disarray, and Macdonald's lamentable volley from close range almost went clean out of the stadium, and just about summed up their approach to their first defeat at Wembley in six visits. By now our schoolboy hero was enjoying himself, scampering around and bemusing the opposition with what would have been called in boxing 'a flurry of last round jabs'. He was looking for another goal just to seal Liverpools' triumph for Shanks, who was about to retire. Keegan got his second goal just before the final whistle, driving the ball in from close range from another Tommy Smith cross.

At the end of the match, Shankly was whisked away for television and newspaper interviews, but not before he joined Keegan and his merry dancing red team in front of the Liverpool fans singing 'You'll Never Walk Alone'.

'You won the Cup,' Shanks said simply, then walked away towards the tunnel, wearing a red and white scarf.

Meanwhile, Keegan stood holding the FA Cup, a portrait which would appear all over the national press the next day and win him the adoration of the city of Liverpool when the team returned for the victory celebrations.

4
LIVERPOOL IN EUROPE

*T*he close relationship between Shankly and Keegan, in which both Shankly's fatherly devotion and Keegan's sense of duty to Shankly were rarely disguised, came to an end that summer when Shankly retired. Now the 23-year-old superstar was about to embark on a career with Shankly's replacement, Bob Paisley, and in rapid succession, three England managers – Joe Mercer, the temporary stop-gap before the arrival of Don Revie, and then Ron Greenwood. For Shankly, Keegan had fitted brilliantly into his team philosophy of never giving the ball away.

'We devised a system of play which minimized the risk of injuries. The team played in sections of the field, like a relay. We didn't want players running the length of the field, stretching themselves unnecessarily. So while there was room for individuals within our system (Keegan for one), the work was shared out.'

Shankly didn't have to be reminded about his super snip from Scunthorpe; he had plenty of time now to reflect on Keegan's achievements at Anfield and what he remembered pleased him.

'Kevin is like a whippet, like a weasel after rats – always biting and snapping at your legs. He reminds me of Denis Law when he was 16. He's got everything: fantastic ability, two good feet, he is energetic and courageous and he has the will to win. Keegan's a perfect size, a fully-fledged middleweight – the greatest fighter of them all.' So spoke Shankly the boxing fan.

When Joe Mercer stepped in to run the England team for

seven matches while the FA were making up their minds about whom to appoint as Ramsey's successor, Keegan was asked to join the party for the three-match summer tour of East Germany, Bulgaria and Yugoslavia. His own clownish high jinks and good humour were well-equipped to go with Mercer's appreciation of fun and laughter while on tour.

The England party were in a relaxed mood when they set off with the old bow-legged Joe, who was in constant pain from a back problem. Mercer knew the game inside-out. He had a long, outstanding career at Everton, where he won a League Championship medal, and with Arsenal after the war where he won two more League championship medals, and an FA Cup winner's medal. He also gained England caps as wing-half, alongside some of the greats of the time – Stanley Matthews, Tommy Lawton, and Stan Cullis – before managing the successful Manchester City side in partnership with a very different type of character, the flamboyant coach, Malcolm Allison.

Joe wanted the England team to play well, but also to relax and enjoy the trip. This philosophy seemed to take hold immediately. The players, in their colourful shirts and pop-star spangles and glossy rings, looked as if they had just emerged from a holiday in Tahiti with Joe the squire courier and the bouncy Ted Croker in his blazer looking like a junior Embassy attaché, called in to assist in case of any problems. Talented players like Tony Currie, Frank Worthington, Keegan, Mick Channon, Ray Clemence and Dave Watson could indulge in high jinks, yet still perform well when they were on the pitch, beating East Germany and Bulgaria before flying to Belgrade for their most difficult fixture against Yugoslavia. The Yugoslavs had been a constant thorn in England's tours of the past, so Keegan and company approached the game with understandable caution. Then an incident involving Liverpool's favourite son in Belgrade changed the whole nature of the tour, and ended with a bruised Keegan reflecting that foreign policemen at foreign airports should always be treated with grave caution. Some of the witnesses, who saw Keegan being taken away and roughed up by members of the Yugoslave secret police, were full of sympathy, but Ted Croker needed all the diplomatic skills in his capacity as secretary of the FA to sort out a most delicate matter. He and Mercer, in great pain again and wincing with every stride, had seen Keegan being physically 'beaten up' and they could barely contain their feelings.

Croker noticed Keegan being marched away by the police to an interrogation room where, according to Croker, the police 'roughed him up'. Apparently the edgy Yugoslav police had been under the misconception that Keegan was deliberately causing a disturbance by mucking about on the luggage conveyor belt. Croker went to the headquarters where Keegan had been searched, abused and physically insulted, and began waving Keegan's passport in the air. He demanded Keegan left with him. It was touch and go until the police grudgingly agreed and Keegan was escorted away by a protective Croker. The rest of the England squad were anxious to get out of Belgrade after this incident. But it was Mercer, despite being unable to move comfortably because of his back ailment, whose appearance at a players' meeting later helped to quell a major diplomatic row, plus a great deal of bad feeling between the two football associations. As he often showed, Mercer was full of good sense, and was wise, courteous, kind and always had the time to listen to other people's funny stories on the subject of football.

'We can all go home, no problems. Kevin won't be able to come with us. He'll probably have to stay behind to answer charges. The only way we can get him out is by sticking together on the field. It's their country off the field, but they can't stop us on it.'

England played Yugoslavia the next day and the victim of Serb aggression followed up Mick Channon's goal with a diving header to make the final score 2–2. After an official FA complaint was delivered , Keegan was allowed to leave with the rest of the England party, and yet another potential scandal ended before it had really begun. Keegan's great friend, Mick Channon, told how three heavies manhandled Keegan out of the baggage area with his arms behind his back, a rather painful way of escorting someone who was innocent. Channon found out later that Keegan had been punched and generally done over, just because he was trying to get one of his bags.

'Nobody was drunk, there had been absolutely no trouble, but Kevin had suffered because of police-state methods. You can't reason or talk to them.' Then up came Joe saying, 'Listen lads the only way you can show these people up is to get out there and give their team a bloody good hiding.'

Mercer's seven-match spell had at least uncovered one gem for the incoming manager, Don Revie. Kevin Keegan's enthusiasm and known abilities would fit very nicely into the new manager's plans to lead England to the next European championships in Yugoslavia and the 1978 World Cup in Argentina. The 1973 World Cup disaster had been put aside. Now it was time for Keegan and Revie's 'New Army' to go out and show the doubters that England had a team to respect. Keegan had time for a quiet holiday before joining up with the first of his new managers, Bob Paisley, at Melwood in preparation for the FA Charity Shield match against Leeds United. This was an occasion regarded as low-key on the fixture list by the backroom boys, but being Leeds versus Liverpool, it would always be a competitive game. There was also the added attraction of both sides being under new management, Brian Clough having taken over a difficult task from another legendary leader, Don Revie. With Shanks (leading Liverpool out for the last time at Wembley) and Revie no longer in charge, Paisley and Clough took to their appointed chairs under the Royal box, and awaited a contest which although it would never be a tranquil afternoon, with a full season ahead and another formidable League, Cup and European programme, it was unlikely that anyone would get a nasty injury, or an irritating suspension. That was how it appeared as the game progressed. Keegan, enjoying the space and freedom out wide, taxed Leeds with his darting runs, and the men in white got themselves into a dreadful tangle at times, with Norman Hunter dumping Steve Heighway on the grass as a reminder that this was, after all, for real. Iron Man, Tommy Smith complied with this doctrine when he was booked for a thundering tackle from behind on Allan Clarke. Keegan was behind Liverpool's opening goal after 19 minutes, sending in a shot which Harvey could only block, before Phil Boersma, another new face in the Liverpool side, whipped the rebound into the net. The Leeds equalizer came from Trevor Cherry in the 71st minute, from Paul Reaney's flighted cross. But the actual game of football had lost all its *raison d'être* by then, Keegan and Billy Bremner having been sent off for fighting by the Bolton referee, Bob Matthewson. It was not as if this unsavoury event had came totally out of the blue. There had been some further rustic challenges thrown in, including one gruesome tackle by Johnny Giles, one of the most creative and respected players in the game, for which he was booked. The Bremner–Keegan firestorm proved a shock, however. When at last Mr Matthewson had managed to get the names of Keegan and Bremner into his notebook and dismissed them with a regal wave of the arm, the stadium became a riot of booing and ill feeling. Bremner and Keegan unwisely tore off their shirts, and made their own way to the stadium tunnel.

Keegan's dismissal was a shock, Bremner's less so. The Scot had just spent a hard summer leading Scotland in the World Cup Finals in West Germany – a trip under manager Willie Ormond which had been far from disappointing. Scotland emerged unbeaten in their group, but were nevertheless eliminated after a goalless draw in a crucial match against Yugoslavia. Bremner had missed an open goal against an off-colour Brazil which would have seen Scotland safely through to the quarter-finals. An over-excited Prime Minister, Harold Wilson, watching the game after his arrival by helicopter, had hoped he could help fan Tartan glory along the Rhine.

The disappointment stuck for Bremner – and with his old mentor, Revie, replaced by someone who his Elland Road teammates regarded as 'cocky', the Bremner kettle was bound to boil over at some stage. Keegan's animosity was more difficult to define, but the experience of being roughed up by the Yugoslavian police may well have disturbed his equally sound mind, and Shanks's departure had certainly hurt. He was busy, opening garden fetes, and supermarkets as part of his lifestyle outside football which earned him a reported bonus of £30,000 a year. He whizzed around in a Datsun sports car, helped move himself from his old digs at The Nook in Liverpool to a converted, luxury Welsh farmhouse. He had been busy, unlike other more spoilt footballers, never failing to turn up for an opening if he could help it. This had been a very short close season for Shanks's wizard, and the strain was getting through to him. The sending off incident, referred to as 'Wembley's disgrace' in the national and provincial press, simply exacerbated this problem.

The stress caused by guilt, shame and understandable indignation had certainly caught up with Keegan when this reporter discovered him near a team coach in the Wembley tunnel after the game. Other colleagues had rushed down for quotes after goalkeeper Harvey's penalty miss for Leeds had meant Liverpool winning the Charity Shield. Keegan stood still, muttering a few words like 'disgrace' and 'I was victimized', words which were almost inaudible with the clamour going on in the dressing room area. It was amazing. May's Cup Final hero had become Wembley's victim and Shanks's wonder boy image had been torn away in one moment of ludicrous irascibility. Keegan was only human, but he would be better advised to face the consequences like a gritty, more-hardened Bremner was doing, flinging in a few Stirling mutterings to fill a few reporters' notebooks. Keegan did go back to face the press interrogation and also his own worried father, who had arrived outraged by what he saw as an act of gross injustice towards his son. Joe Keegan took on a more paternal role however, having vacated his seat in the stand with Jean, and Keegan's brother Mike after the sending off – he spent the rest of the match brooding over the incident back stage until catching up with his son. He told Keegan not to worry, the incident was over, knowing of course it had only just begun – and repercussions would follow. It was then that Billy Bremner put his head round the Liverpool dressing-room door, a brave act under the circumstances. Facing him was an almost-naked Keegan and his Dad, the ex-miner and jungle fighter. Bremner was full of remorse. The Stirling kid said simply, 'Sorry'. Keegan replied, 'It's alright.' Well, that was that –

until Dad suddenly exploded, perhaps thinking of other austere industrial times, when he felt equally ignored. 'Bugger off,' he said in an audible enough voice for the twin towers of Wembley to gather the echoes all the way from Markham Main colliery. It was a natural reaction, but as Keegan pointed out, it wasn't any good being annoyed with the Leeds man.

'I suppose it was natural to think Billy and I were at each other's throats after what happened, but I did not feel any animosity towards him and I know he did not feel any towards me.'

One witness to the sending off was Jack Taylor, who was FA guest of honour at the occasion after refereeing the World Cup Final in Munich. The Wolverhampton butcher thought: 'The dismissals had been fairly inevitable – seeing what large personalities both were at Wembley that afternoon, Billy just back from the World Cup himself, and Kevin, the scorer of two goals in the recent Cup Final. They came into contact, and you saw what happened.' The inevitable headlines in the press the next morning were missed by Keegan. He had a raging hangover, having taken out his woes sitting at the bar of a Doncaster nightclub, with the supportive owner Mick Wise. As with all such 'downs', the 'ups' were only just around the corner where who should arrive but a flustered Maurice Setters, a former West Bromwich Albion and Manchester United right-half, and England international, remembered as a fiery soul on the pitch with supercharged toe-caps. Bill Shankly had been ringing Setters, who was then manager of Doncaster Rovers, to say he needed Keegan to play in Billy McNeil's testimonial match in Glasgow on Monday. Keegan and Shanks had left the matter open at Wembley. Could Setters find Keegan, even allowing for the fact it was the dead of night?

Keegan didn't want to let Shanks down, but he felt he had on this occasion at Wembley. Shanks had led Liverpool out into the arena for the last time – his retirement afternoon. Keegan and Bremner had turned the moving afternoon into something else.

'I had too much respect for Shanks to refuse, and in any case, I was beginning to forget what had happened. I soon get over things. You have to keep bouncing back when everything gets the better of you. I'm constantly reminded that football is a great life, but I sometimes wonder how many people would be able to cope with the abuse and insults which accompany the glory.'

Clips of the sendings off were shown endlessly on television. But those who had been in the stadium did not have to be reminded of the uproar to come. Keegan remembered Johnny Giles taking a swing at him after the pair had crunched together in a tackle while Giles had the ball. Giles had been booked, despite Keegan's pleadings to Bob Matthewson that Giles actions had only been 'in the spur of the moment' . But disaster struck almost instantly when Bremner, seeking apparent revenge, took a dig at Keegan as he ran past. Ironically, the future manager of Doncaster Rovers might have cleared the danger zone had he not slipped, allowing an outraged Keegan to catch him up and aim a blow at him. Bremner took up the challenge of fisticuff's until the referee arrived like Clive of India inspecting a native regiment. Keegan thought Matthewson should have sent the pair off immediately, but as the television cameras showed, there was a long lecture about the two having early baths before the official finger went up. Funnily enough, it was the action of the two players in peeling off their shirts which outraged so many people.

Weaker and more evasive characters than Keegan might have found an excuse to pull out of the testimonial, to avoid the obvious press interest for one thing , and having himself exposed to every kind of ridicule going as the player who took a swing at Scotland's captain. Did he need to go through all that pressure after having gone through an awful afternoon in which he always thought, quite justifiably, that he had been provoked?

It was an apprehensive Kevin Keegan who turned up to play in the testimonial, but he need not have had any fears about Celtic warmth and hospitality coming from the 'Big Man', Jock Stein, Billy McNeill and a relieved Shankly. Stein gave Keegan a warm reception.

'I'm glad you came because these people up here want to see you play and it is in times of trouble that your true character shows itself.'

Stein could be quite formidable at times. Shankly's friend (who died of a heart attack immediately after managing the Scotland side's qualification for the 1986 World Cup Finals) could not have been more charming on this occasion and Keegan was able to enjoy the match as much as the large crowd.

Keegan had to put his match boots on the shelf after Parkhead when an FA Commission, under the chairmanship of Vernon Stokes, suspended Keegan and Bremner for eleven matches and fined them £500 each. With Sir Matt Busby a member of the commission, it was difficult to grumble about the severe sentence. Sir Matt stated that the action of the two players could have had a bad influence on English hooliganism – a valid point, but this was no consolation for the dejected Liverpool player making his way back to Merseyside with his manager Bob Paisley. The banned player told Paisley he would like a break from football and was allowed to take a breather from training to go on a golfing holiday in Bournemouth. Keegan's honesty over the disgrace of being sent-off stood him in good stead. As he said to Bremner when the verdict was announced, 'We're going to be made examples of, we're going to be made to pay for other people's sins, not just ours.' So when judgment came, Keegan was free to say as much as he pleased – which was mercifully free of self-pity and reproach for others. 'I feel bitter, I feel sad. But most of all I feel sorry for the upset this caused my Mum and Dad.' Keegan admitted his sense of outrage directed towards Bremner was 'stupid', but having admitted that, could there have been a more logical reason for it?

'I felt I had been made a fool of by the referee. I did not like that, but I accepted it, and I went off. I did not refuse to leave which would have been worse. Looking back, I could argue that the game had finished for me, it was quite natural for me to take off my shirt, but in the middle of Wembley, there was no reason for it.'

What all this drama did was to speed up Kevin's marriage to Jean Woodward, which the couple had proposed finding a date for the following year. But Joe Keegan's insistence that his son wed his girlfriend was the bargaining tool which Keegan Junior

used to persuade Dad to enter hospital for an immediate operation after he had been found to have a tumour. The wedding
took place at St Peter-in-Chains Roman Catholic Church,
Doncaster on 4 September 1974. Although it was a secret wedding attended only by family and close friends, the press did
eventually come to hear about it. Keegan looked decidedly
trendy in his white leather suit, check tie and shirt, and close-
cropped black hair, while Jean, resplendent in her long, white
wedding dress, looked astonished by the hefty peck she received
by the embarrassed superstar as the couple linked champagne
glasses during the wedding toast. The newly-weds had more
time to themselves by virtue of the FA punishment, but there was
also the strain of worrying about Joe's operation. Altogether,
1974 had proved quite a year of highs and lows for young
Keegan, but he was determined to get back on the pitch as quickly as he could. It was the only way he could show that he was
determined to regain his self-respect by scoring goals. He had
been fully fit, yet unable to play. Keegan had to wait until 12
October, when he converted a penalty in a 2–0 victory over
Middlesbrough in front of 52,590 fans at Anfield, who had been
impatient to see their hero back in the action.

But Paisley was starting to get things right. After seeing
through the first season after Shankly's departure with that
benign reservation the players found hard to adjust to, Paisley
came out of his shell at the start of the 1975/76 season. Relieved,
perhaps, that some of the modest changes he was making at
Anfield hadn't done any harm, Paisley gave lengthy runs in the
first team to the stylish Peter Cormack and the hard-tackling
Jimmy Case in midfield, with Ray Kennedy becoming productive as a left-sided midfield player, using his muscular strength
to move forward for many a strike at goal.

Keegan was pleased by the way Paisley got to grips with running the team. He had begun to accept Shanks departure – it was
no use crying over spilt Anfield milk, there was a new boss at
Anfield, and Paisley's general ship soon got hold of everyone at
the club. His method was to quietly will the staff to rally round
and help make Liverpool world-beaters. 'Once we got to know

the real Bob, our relationship with him was excellent and his confidence grew.' So did the confidence of other Shankly imports like Joey Jones, a left-back with piston legs the shape of tomahawks who became a folk hero almost as soon as he arrived from Wrexham, and Jimmy Case of the thundering long-range shots, and total commitment. David Fairclough was a goal-scoring super-sub nicknamed 'The Bionic Carrot' because of his glinting red hair under the floodlights; Phil Neil a right-back, admirably cool under pressure; and the racehorse lover, Terry McDermott, a scouser who linked them all, the action man with no time to read a book. Keegan's old enthusiasm came back, and needed to, because Liverpool would be badly stretched at the end of the season when they had to face what Paisley called 'three Cup finals' – two legs of the UEFA Cup Final against Bruges, and a vital League match against Wolves sandwiched between them, which would have a distinct bearing on Liverpool's chances of winning another League championship.

Liverpool had shown their mettle in the UEFA Cup semifinal against a redoubtable Barcelona side containing Johan Cruyff and Johan Neeskens , the Dutch 1974 World Cup stars. But a wonderfully executed move involving Keegan and his partner John Toshack ended with the Welshman putting Liverpool 1–0 ahead in the first leg in Barcelona, where the crowd showed their displeasure by throwing cushions onto the pitch in Catalonian disgust. Barcelona held Liverpool to a 1–1 draw in the return at Anfield, but Liverpool went through, and Keegan began to think about cup-winning medals again.

It was not surprising that Keegan's form for Liverpool during the 1974/75 season should have been below his normal high standards. His name had rarely been out of the newspapers, often for the wrong reasons, and it was fortunate that his wedding and FA Cup Final celebrations took pride of place in what otherwise could have been a forgettable year. Shankly's departure had also brought disruption to the Liverpool dressing room. His voice, his gestures, his Ayrshire quips to the press, and his total conviction in all matters had suddenly ceased to be. Bob Paisley had come somewhat reluctantly into the breach.

According to Graeme Souness later, he was never good at communicating with the players, but this was long before that particular glorious era. During his first months, though, Paisley struggled even more to get his messages across. What was more unkind to Paisley was that Shanks, the hovering ghost, wouldn't go away. He turned up for training at the hallowed Melwood in a residential part of Liverpool, his eyes roaming the far corners of the Liverpool FC training estate, not for pheasants but for the sight of his beloved Keegan doing a neat little twist and turn in a five-a-side. Nobody would have complained had Shanks worn a deerstalker's hat during the visits, which were regular, and hardly diplomatic. There had been a marked lack of zip about the team's form since Shanks had retired, and although the side finished runners-up to Derby County that season in the League Championship, it wasn't good enough for some of the Kop supporters.

Shankly was certainly not going to tie himself down to pruning roses. So it was goodbye to Nessie, and down to Melwood where his old deputy company commander was trying his Northumberland best to gee up the team. It was all very embarrassing, and Keegan, though he was devoted to Shanks, found it especially so.

'When we went to the Melwood training ground, Shanks would be there, quite rightly using the facilities. But would it not have been better to use them in the afternoons when Bob and the team were not there? The players would come into training and say, "Good morning, Boss" to Shanks and greet Bob Paisley with "Good morning, Bob". Poor Bob must have wondered what was happening. It was an embarrassing situation. It could be argued that the facilities should have been open to Shanks because he built them. They were the fruits of his hard work, his ideas, his successes. I just believe he should have used more discretion. I'll never forget Bob's first team meeting. He leant with his back against the wall of the dressing-room at Melwood, which seemed somewhat symbolic. "I never wanted this job in the first place," he had said. He might have pretended he wanted to be manager, but that was not Bob's style. When the real Bob came to light we discovered that he was not the head man we imagined him to be. He was no soft touch, but was instead a shy, modest man who always wanted to give credit to others.'

Keegan did think Shanks had been neglected by the club, although Peter Robinson, Club Secretary and later Chief Executive, couldn't have been expected always to nurse the retired boss along by inviting him to travel on the team's away trips, which Shankly thought the club should have done. Shankly had every reason to thank Robinson for the devoted way he had run the administrative side of the club while he was left to run the boot room. Robinson gave the impression of being a head manager at Claridges, his alert, bald good looks highly suited for wearing a morning suit and running a beady eye over the day's luncheon menu. Shankly's gripes went on until the club at last relented by asking him to attend the 1976 UEFA Cup Final as their guest. Shanks grumbled ungratefully: 'I accepted because I didn't want anyone to think I was petty, but it came too late.' He was by now a prickly old buffer, although the lads went on loving him until he died. But long before then, Paisley had earned his rightful throne. He allowed the system full reign, but brought in new blood as Liverpool looked again for another great team.

For Keegan, his early months under Paisley, and indeed under Revie's father-figure approach to managing England, were slow to ignite. He got on fine with both of them; it was natural that he should do, sharing north-country backgrounds and a lively mind when it came to football matters. But the star tended to brood more these days, and he was capable of having bad games. Liverpool suffered a few niggling defeats, including a League double at the hands of Arsenal. Their programme in the European Cup Winners' Cup, the only trophy winners' medal Keegan failed to collect while at Anfield, ended with a dismissal on the away-goals rule by the clever Hungarian side Ferencvaros, while FA Cup and League Cup jaunts were cut short by Ipswich and Wolves, respectively. Keegan's head was down.

His uncharacteristic lack of appetite for the game, which happens to all great athletes from time to time, appeared strange to his huge following. Keegan had another important date about the time that his suspension had been raging all over the newspapers – an England squad meeting with their new supremo, Revie. He began fussing from the start in a fatherly way, but Keegan was happy to acquiesce in this case to his new boss, especially as the first match under him was a 3–0 defeat of Czechoslovakia in a European Championship qualifying match at Wembley. Mick Channon, who had been one of the players retained by Revie from the Ramsey and Mercer days, thought Revie was going over the top when he told the players, on their first meeting: 'You will be punctual, you will call me boss.' Channon disliked this attitude. 'You are talking about internationals, not kids.'

The first meeting of 50 potential squad members for Revie's future teams assembled at a Manchester hotel after playing their normal Saturday afternoon matches. To hear the new boss ask them to go to bed early on a Saturday after their exertions, dumbfounded Channon.

'His point was that he wanted us to go back to our club managers, bright-eyed and bushy-tailed, as though an early night was in order – some chance.'

Apparently, Manchester discos did a roaring trade that night, although Revie wanted an early conference over the lengthy dossiers he had begun planting in his players' kit bags. For a while, Revie and Keegan seemed quite close, especially as Kevin was England captain. But other players found Revie's attitude suffocating, pedantic and insufferable – and paid for it. Frank Worthington went, then Alan Ball not long after. Alan Hudson, after his brilliant performance for England in a friendly against the world champions, West Germany, which Revie's team won 2–0, was also shown the international door.

'I [Channon] was asked to play a completely different role by Revie. He wanted me simply as a midfield kicker. When I didn't conform, I was out. Kevin also had trouble with him later on. It was a shame, because I played well against Germany, and so did Tony Currie'.

Keegan's problems with Revie came the following spring during the still lumbering annual Home International tournament. It started with an assassination threat handed to the Football Association before the England–Northern Ireland match in Belfast, with the threatened victim none other than the captain. Ted Croker handled the delicate situation. Should Kevin travel with the party? Scotland Yard advised that Keegan was 'at risk', but Keegan insisted on making the trip. He was captain, he was now an England regular in midfield, so never mind the politics. Keegan was not going to be run out of Belfast. The match, as it turned out, was goalless – but Keegan expected a more productive performance against Wales in midweek at Wembley before the arrival of the Tartan Army, the following Saturday. Keegan walked around chatting with Channon and his other team-mates while waiting for the routine team announcement at their hotel in the afternoon. Everything was routine on these occasions; the players began to hate the sight of hotel foyers, and anonymous men and women behind reception desks putting on shows of mind-boggling charm to arriving guests when, really, they didn't give a damn. But when Revie announced the team. Keegan was out. Revie's jaw was stoic; if he wanted a quiet ride in his fairly new post, this was certainly not the way to do it. Imagine Sir Alf dropping Bobby Moore at the height of his powers – Alf would have been savaged. But Alf never wanted to drop Moore, until Old Father Time and a bad mistake by his captain against Poland made it inevitable. Revie, however, could hardly have expected the reaction he got from Keegan. The Liverpool star packed up and went home.

Certainly Keegan's strengths as a human being – a refusal to be pushed around, even by his immediate boss – acted as a warning to Revie that he couldn't mess his players around in such an insensitive way. Keegan's lack of penetration against the Irish may have been an acceptable reason to drop the Liverpool wizard, but after what Keegan had gone through, and the tensions involved with making the trip, he hardly warranted being dropped. Channon was on the spot to see his friend in full retreat

'When Revie left out Kevin, he promptly got off the coach and headed for home. It certainly did the trick for Kevin. Once he was reinstated, he was never out of the side. For most players it would have gone against them with Revie, but not for Keegan. It definitely worked in his favour.'

Keegan was back in the side almost immediately – 'with a handshake and a let's be friends' from Revie before going up the Wembley tunnel to annihilate the Scots. The victory, in which Gerry Francis gave one of his most exciting performances for England, helped to play down Kevin's wounded feelings. Ted Croker professed to having been 'amazed' by Revie's decision, although the England manager handled his first major crisis 'well'. He rang Kevin and persuaded him to return on the promise of a place in the side against Scotland.

For Revie, the rift was mercifully over, but the captain's growing list of critics fussed around trying to keep the bonfires alight, while leading football writers also reserved their columns to lambast Keegan for staging his walk-out when Don needed all the support he could get.

But the criticism of Keegan was not entirely unwarranted or shorn of the voices of experience and knowledge. Keegan's squad protector and mentor, Bobby Moore, took Keegan to task in Jeff Powell's biography.

'He [Keegan] was an exciting player raising a question against himself. Because he wasn't picked for one match, he went running home to Liverpool. If you are going to be a great player you've got to take the kicks in the teeth. You're in top football for one thing, success. If you want an easy existence, then run away to Mum and stay there.'

What England's revered old captain said did make sense. It was perhaps fortunate for Keegan that Revie was so lacking in world-class players, and he needed the authoritative shoulder of his captain to see him through at times. Revie had been swept along with the many highs he had enjoyed over the years at Elland Road, but his dossiers began to turn opposition players into King Kongs who should be closed down at any cost and players were encouraged to read up on their homework. Many players said 'F--k it' and went over to a neighbour's to play cards. Channon called the dossiers 'mumbo-jumbo'.

111

There wasn't another FA Cup Final appearance at Wembley that year for Paisley's often irresistible team. Derby County had seen to that, while Burnley had triumphed after a replay against their expected superiors from Anfield in the League Cup. But there was plenty still to play for – Paisley's first championship for a start. First there was the opening leg of the UEFA Cup at Anfield to be won, followed by Liverpool's final League match at Wolves. A win would secure the championship for Liverpool. It was a cliff hanger all right, but Paisley didn't show a trace of nerves – the classic desert rat being used to such formidable obstacles before gaining a military victory.

So on to the first leg against Club Bruges. Liverpool were at their peak, and in splendid condition despite the tension building up with that ominous date at Molineux scheduled for the following Monday. The Anfield crowd urged their team on, confident that John Toshack and the rest would give Liverpool a comfortable lead to take to Belgium. Keegan was always on the lookout for a flick-on from Tosh, but he couldn't believe his eyes when a forlorn Ray Clemence trudged to the back of the net to retrieve the ball after Bruges had taken the lead. Keegan scurried away again, nagging and niggling, and it was inevitable that Liverpool would equalize before half-time. But instead of sitting back and defending their precious lead, Bruges went out to attack, and claimed another goal before half time to give Paisley and his back-up team some quandries to try and cure over the half-time tea. Paisley didn't haul Keegan off, but he substituted Toshack, much to the Welshman's frustration. It was a move geared to tactics rather than panic, and on came the iron man Jimmy Case to add extra weight to Liverpool's attack. Toshack's heading work might have been suddenly missed, but on the night the move worked. Liverpool came back in sensational style to win 3–2, with Keegan contributing a goal. The second leg lay thrillingly poised, but with the advantage to the Belgian team.

However, that nagging confrontation at Molineux had to be overcome first. Keegan and company knew that they had to beat Wolves because Queen's Park Rangers had a better goal-average which would have the London team the championship for the first time should Liverpool draw. Few would have begrudged Dave Sexton's team the title – they had a good side with some highly talented players, like Gerry Francis, Stan Bowles, Don Givens, skipper Frank McLintock and Dave Webb. They had entertained with many displays of positive football – but now came their worst hours as the radio commentary came on and they had to endure the agony of waiting. The champagne bottles at Loftus Road looked ripe for the popping at half-time with Liverpool trailing Wolves by a lone goal. Liverpool fought tooth and nail to get that equalizer as the strengths and determination indoctrinated into them by Paisley and the boot room kept them going. Their names were familiar – Clemence, Neal, Thompson, Hughes, Smith, Kennedy, Callaghan, Keegan, Heighway, Toshack, Case (sub: Fairclough) – but the scoreline wasn't. The title was going to London, surely. Then with 14 minutes to go, Keegan got on the end of a Toshack flick-on to bury to ball in the Wolves net (1–1). It was all or nothing now, as Rangers were still top of the League with a better goal difference. It was attack, attack, attack. There was Keegan scurrying away again, Shankly's weasel relentlessly tracking down prey. The Kopites looked at their watches – 'Lord, please be kind to us, bring us our winning goal, our salvation!' Five minutes remained when Toshack scored and his head was still aglow from being hugged by Red arms when Ray Kennedy emerged to confirm the title with a third goal.

This was a stunning moment for Paisley. For many seasons he had patiently sat back and listened to Shanks's dry one-liners which went along his team's successes. Winning the League had confirmed Bob Paisley as a manager to be reckoned with. He sat back like a veritable Cheshire cat and allowed the lads to let off steam. But not for long. That date with Bruges was beckoning, and for Keegan, it would prove one of the most satisfying nights of his career.

Under Peter Robinson's astute guidance, Liverpool Football Club made its way to the tranquil canal zones of Bruges, pleased as peacocks that they had become champions for the seventh time. Robinson and his administrative team's skills at getting Paisley and the team to a foreign station were unmatched. Bruges could not have offered a wider range of opposites to Merseysiders than the medieval merchant city, but the fans wandered around the local fish markets and shopping areas and Stella Artois taverns while Keegan and the lads prepared to tie up their laces again. It turned out to be a colossal night for UEFA football, for European football and above all for Liverpool who, despite weary legs, put on a magnificent rearguard defensive action to earn a 1–1 draw and ultimately claim the UEFA Cup for the second time. The Liverpool fans were forced to stifle their sagging emotions for only four minutes at the Olympia stadium when Lambert beat Ray Clemence with a penalty. It was four long minutes, but the memory of Kevin Keegan's goal in those vital, vibrant seconds will remain forever for those who were there. Maybe it was the sight of the Bruges goalkeeper stretching vainly to try and check Keegan's swerving shot which will stay in their thoughts, or the sight of Keegan submerged by a wave of red shirts, as team-mates rushed up to hug him.

The goal itself was savoured not only by Liverpool partizans but by neutrals watching with admiration from the posh VIP areas, such as some representatives of Real Madrid. Keegan's goal came early in the game, but its influence on the remaining part of the final was paramount as far as Liverpool was concerned. Tommy Smith, Phil Thompson, Emlyn Hughes, Phil Neal and others delegated to defend their team's right to claim the UEFA trophy were full of vigour and common sense, and Bruges found it hard to find an opening to score. Clemence was not without the odd need to stretch his long arms into the floodlights, but it all ended with Kev, the hero again, as goalscorer.

Paisley took it all in the laid back manner of a man about to go shopping. 'Liverpool have been geared to this sort of thing for 15 years – I only helped them along.' But it was not to be a tranquil for summer for Paisley despite all the glowing headlines which had greeted Paisley's feat in achieving the same success as Shankly in 1973 – in winning the Football League Championship and the UEFA Cup. Our Kev was off to that area of the world Shankly had often contemptuously eschewed as 'abroad'.

Gradually, the real facts leaked out. Real Madrid, past employers of Di Stefano, Puskas, Del Sol, Gento, Didi and Kopa, had taken a strong fancy to the boy from Doncaster and very much wanted him to grace their magical team at their somewhat fading palatial stadium, the Bernabeau in Madrid. There was nothing particularly new about the type of interest Real showed towards a gifted foreign player. They, and other wealthy clubs, had started importing foreign players with a vengeance since the 1974 World Cup – Barcelona, for example, signing the gifted Dutch international pair Johan Cruyff and Johan Neeskens to parade at the Nou Camp. The two camps had always been jealous of each other – Catalonian pride at odds with Castilian chest-beating – and having Keegan in their ranks as a budding World Cup star and England captain was a perk Real could not resist. But could Paisley resist? He didn't want to lose Keegan since Liverpool were going for another attempt on the grand slam – the magic double which had eluded them before and also, without being too greedy, the treble, with the European Cup to be fought for.

There was no denying it, Keegan was a cog you couldn't take away from Liverpool's system without severely damaging the entire works. There were replacements on the horizon, but Paisley had only one thing in mind – to carry through another brilliant campaign with Keegan on his staff. Being a kindly, rational person Kevin had made in known to the outside world that he would like to play abroad, and the idea of playing for such an illustrious club as Real Madrid really did intrigue him. So strong were his feelings on the matter that a special meeting was arranged between Keegan and the club chairman, John Smith, to discuss a delicate situation. Keegan put on his best suit and drove to Anfield for what could have been a showdown. It never happened. Keegan agreed to stay on one more season at Anfield and then move to Real or any other interested club abroad.

Keegan's successes at Anfield had tended to obscure some of the more dismal displays that the England side, under his cap-taincy, had been putting out under Revie since Czechoslovakia

115

and West Germany had been beaten convincingly at Wembley. There was nothing to suggest a tottering ship then, but gradually England began to rock and shudder as they went out of the European Championships through away defeats in Czechoslovakia and Portugal. Revie perpetually shook the dice, making wholesale changes to his team, so those long weekends began to be regarded as chores and a waste of time by the grumbling participants dragged away from their families. Revie had been hot with rage at the Football League's refusal to allow him the freedom to have his players together before European and World Cup matches – although Alan Hardaker, the crusty Football League Chairman, pronounced it wouldn't have made a shred of difference to England's performance if the league matches had been postponed. Worse was to follow in the World Cup, with England again on the skids as qualification became unlikely with a poor 2–1 victory against Finland at Wembley, which left Keegan and his players with their heads down and the crowd booing. Revie did take dramatic steps to chastise his players on their performance in that match, and apologized publically in the national press for England's poor showing. Revie was suspicious of the players' attitudes, though the way he sent them packing, such suspicion was a distraction from his own failings.

Even Keegan, whom he had struck up such a good rapport with early on, had become evasive by this time. On one occasion, Keegan took off with Mick Channon from one of Revie's weekend sessions at Hungerford health spa to attend the Devon and Exeter race meeting. It was all done in great secrecy, but Channon and Keegan were unlucky to be spotted by an alert local photographer with new binoculars who sent his prints to the press. The picture made a good splash, and Revie was hurt, giving the two musketeers a decidedly long look when he next spotted them. No disciplinary action was taken as Revie was short enough of goalscorers already, but he still brooded and he was hurt. Keegan got a telling off from Jean about the racing incident. 'I thought you were training for England, not at the Devon and Exeter,' she said.

One of Revie's faults, according to some of the players, concerned him spending too much time on England's commercial affairs, such as their famous, much-criticized ugly Admiral strip, which now looks as dated as a Blackpool cinema doorman's uniform, 1950s-style. It was fair enough that Revie would get his side an extra £200 bonus from the FA for a win, and £100 for a draw, but Revie's insatiable concern for the money-making side of England's football squad sometimes outweighed his own patriotic thoughts about assembling a winning team. Keegan was far more on the crest of Liverpool's winning wave than Admiral's and Don Revie's when the vital World Cup qualifying match against Italy came up on a mild November afternoon at the Olympic Stadium, Rome. Defeat for England would mean their chances of reaching the finals in Argentina two summers hence would be all but lost. The match itself naturally caused the maximum of attention in the English and Italian press. Although a Keegan-less England had defeated Italy 3–2 in New York in May, the England party was compared with the great team of 1948 with Stanley Matthews, Stan Moretensen, Tommy Lawton and Tom Finney who had been told by Walter Winterbottom to go out on the smouldering Turin park and give the Italians everything they had got and 'good luck gentlemen'. Revie required his players to 'clue themselves up' almost to the opening whistle on the information he had rounded up about some very talented Italian players: Bettega, Causio, Zoff and Antognoni. With Stan Bowles in the starting line-up, the team came out again thinking of 'those damned dossiers', as Channon called them, which 'were getting more publicity than the football'. The Rome match in November 1976 was one of England's worst exhibitions abroad since the war, but while the Italians did look a pretty good team, England were unlucky not to reach the 1978 finals. Revie did not help by choosing a lopsided team with a defender, Brian Greenhoff, looking plainly out of sorts in the middle of the pitch. The Italian crowd were particulary aggressive that afternoon, but one disturbing hint of trouble ahead for England occurred even before the kick-off when some of the less-experienced players, like Greenhoff, came out on to the green pitch with their heads down. The Italian players must

117

have noticed – they were cocky and eager to wreck Revie's dream, and the crowd soon noticed. They sensed England's mission had been carried out without an armed escort. They bayed for blood and as Greenhoff stuttered in midfield, the Italians began to strut around arrogantly. England were singularly disappointing, especially when it came to Channon and Bowles. The QPR man was so ignored once that he delighted the Rome crowd with a solo display of ball skills by a corner flag while awaiting for the game to resume. Bowles tried hard that afternoon to win the ball, but with only two men in midfield, Wilkins and Greenhoff, and with Keegan pushed back deep into defence, goal opportunities were rare. While Tom Finney had called England's 4–1 victory in Turin in 1948 'one of the greatest games of football I had the pleasure of playing in', Keegan would have said the opposite here in Rome, and to make matters worse, he was responsible for deflecting a fierce drive by Antognoni past Clemence for Italy's opening goal. Bettega's header from Causio's cross, which gave Italy their second goal, could not have been bettered by Keegan himself.

Liverpool's No. 7 vowed to show that Italian crowd one day what he could really achieve at the regal Olympic Stadium. The chance came almost six months later in fact, when Liverpool qualified to meet Borussia Moenchengladbach in the European Cup Final. The stadium selected for the May final was the same one where Revie's team had been humiliated. It was an event Keegan looked forward to with a special personal ambition – to prove he was a world-class performer, and not a poor leader of a mundane England team.

Keegan's last fling at Anfield could not have been more dramatic or emotionally turbulent as the Reds were driven along towards the treble. The 1976/77 season was to be his last for Liverpool, with Hamburg stepping to the front of the European club queue ahead of Real Madrid to sign Keegan for £500,000 – a record for any British player. The news upset many Kop fans, who thought Keegan was being disloyal by leaving the club which, after all, was his bread and butter, and had been his true platform to stardom. But the deal was sealed and it didn't matter what was said in Liverpool bars, or by rival players jealous of Keegan's continuing luck and success. It couldn't stop Liverpool grinding on that season with Keegan still playing his part as the canny poacher. In the League Championship, Keegan played a considerable part in helping Liverpool to win their record tenth title and claim 20 goals himself. Liverpool's away record hadn't been too impressive – on 19 December, they lost 1–5 to Aston Villa at Villa Park, a salutory lesson which warned Paisley and Keegan that all could be lost before anything was won. It needed responsible heads in the Liverpool side to keep the good Mersey tug chugging with three trophies to play for, cheeky West Bromwich Albion having knocked Liverpool out of the League Cup back in September. Keegan just went on pounding away at rival defences, seemingly oblivious that partners had been switched. He was so acquainted with the system that any changes during the match simply went on without anybody changing gear. Keegan adapted himself to a change of routine, and often took full advantage of it. If he didn't like it, Tommy Smith, the 32-year-old veteran who was often recalled because of injuries to Thompson or Callaghan, would give him a piece of his mind. Nobody felt incined to argue with Smith, who had been around for such a long time and knew Anfield inside out. He seemed to breathe Anfield, and didn't give a monkey's cuss for anything he thought was pompous or big-headed. Liverpool's invincibility at Anfield, linked to Keegan and Toshack's uncanny instincts for finding each other, saw Paisley's club move towards the title by the start of April. Grand Nationals often meant that League matches were switched to the morning so that both sets of playing staff and the crowd could jump into the nearest car, bus or convenient taxi to make their way to Aintree. On 3 April that year, the 11,300 crowd at Anfield sent the Kopites off to watch the first woman jockey to ride the National, Charlotte Brew from Coggeshill in Essex, on Charlie's Girl. Emlyn Hughes, Terry McDermott and Keegan, who had become progressively interested in the Sport of Kings through Keegan's friendship with the riding and race-horse owning England striker Mick Channon, joined the cheers for the local, much-loved Red Rum, winning his third National. 'Crazy Horse' Hughes and his Anfield party had a grin almost as wide as the victor's after the race. But even though in a betting mood, Hughes could hardly have forgotten the excitement of that 3–1 victory against Leeds United a few hours before. They must be firm favourites now to win the Championship. Things certainly looked bright from the point of view of their next challenge against FC Zurich in the European Cup semi-final the following Wednesday. The tension facing Liverpool was shown by Paisley. 'I don't even know the date of the Cup Final. Every game we play is just as important as it can be.'

Keegan's last match at Anfield in Liverpool colours on 14 May 1977 secured the necessary winning point in a 0–0 draw. With 55,688 people jammed into every corner of the stadium, the match was more a salute to the new League Champions, the FA Cup runners-up and the European Cup finalists. Keegan's departure from the pitch produced a necessary quote, almost too briskly, seeing this was supposed to be a celebration. But for the Kopites, Keegan's swansong tended to be absorbed by the celebrations that would greet the Liverpool treble. But the player was nevertheless moved.

Now Wembley was beckoning for the FA Cup Final, with a visit to Rome's Olympic stadium for the European Cup Final a few days afterwards. Paisley and the boot room boys prepared for both events without resorting to training overkill – the boys had played quite enough, already. The problem was to select the right team for Wembley, and they chose McDermott and Johnson instead of Callaghan and the in-form substitute, Fairclough. The news was not received too well in Liverpool, where David Fairclough had become almost a hero. Tommy Docherty had adopted a 4–2–4 formation with Macari, who had rejected a transfer to Anfield in preference to Old Trafford, and Sammy McIlroy in midfield with Steve Coppell and Gordon Hill playing wide as wingers.

Liverpool, sustained by their midfield trio of McDermott, Case and Kennedy, had looked thoroughly capable in the first half, of achieving their first-ever double, with Ray Kennedy relishing the prospect having been a member of the Arsenal side who beat Liverpool in 1971. Two scampering runs by Keegan, the first from a slide-rule-assisted pass from Kennedy, would surely have produced goals but for brilliant interceptions by Martin Buchan and Arthur Albiston. But the absence of Toshack hurt Liverpool more than they might have thought, especially as Johnson was plainly not invincible when it came to assisting Keegan and Heighway, in limbo on the left. The United players looked fairly shattered as they trudged back to the dressing room for their verbal pick-me-up from the Doc. But in the second period United markedly raised their game, pushing Liverpool's midfield back with some exhilarating runs. Their opening goal in the 50th minute had much to do with a backward mis-timed header by Keegan, which during its path in the wrong direction was conveniently headed on, tennis style, by Sammy McIlroy and Jimmy Greenhoff with a flick to Stuart Pearson who held off Joey Jones' challenge before booting the ball snugly past Ray Clemence.

Keegan wanted the ball. He waited patiently on the centre circle for the rejoicing United players to file back for the resumption of play. Pearson had been buried on the ground beneath Coppell and the United fans had been waiting for a moment like this since the days of Best, Charlton and Law, when they were almost spoilt by success. Keegan wanted so much to finish at Liverpool on the grand pedestal – the double would do nicely, the treble would be a bonus. Soon Jimmy Case brought the ball down on his thighs, gave a nifty little swivel of a hip, and belted the ball right-footed past Alex Stepney, who managed to get a palm to the passing ball but failed to check it. Keegan was the first to congratulate Case. United would find it hard to get out of that hole. But they did, again in the quickest possible time. Less than three minutes had gone since Case fired in his ferocious shot. Now it was United's turn to attack. Coppell passed the ball in his own half to Jimmy Nicoll who hoofed it up the field in the hopeful direction of Lou Macari who was being patrolled by 'Crazy Horse' Hughes. Macari proved that he could jump with the best of them for one of modest height and deflected the ball to Jimmy Greenhoff, not normally into indulging in heavy confrontations with Tommy Smith. On this occasion, however, Greenhoff found he had got the better of Smith. As the ball spun loose, Smith slipped, and an alert Macari was able to get in a snatched shot at Clemence's goal. The ball was destined nearer the corner flag than the goal until it struck Greenhoff on the chest and wafted into the air over Clemence and an appalled Phil Neal. Manchester United hung on to take the Cup and spoil Kevin and Jean's hopes of moving to Hamburg with the grand slam.

During February Holland's arrogant 2–0 win over England inspired by the departing Johan Cruyff had raised doubts in Keegan's mind. He had said early in his career with Liverpool he wanted to be another George Best or Bobby Moore. Now playing on the same pitch as the Dutch magician, everything he tried to do and attempt was nullified by Cruyff and the Dutch team's superb understanding. A watching Ted Croker called the Dutch performance 'one of the greatest team exhibitions I have ever seen. Cruyff proved he is one of the greatest footballers in the history of the game'. Keegan's final chance would come in Rome. The 'Eternal City' awaited Paisley and his team with a blaze of light which increased in intensity from the moment the first Vatican cat tiptoed towards a fishy dustbin at dawn.

Liverpool left England with a surging, accompanying army of some 25,000 fans, an extraordinarily large figure for any team to have at any time, even given this was Liverpool, the 1977 League Champions. The majority of the younger fans stripped to the waist and took advantage of cold beer bars near the Tiber (which were usually in dire need themselves of air-conditioning), but the whole episode passed by with none of the disastrous consequences of the Leeds riot at Parc des Princes at Paris two years before when a large section of the Elland Road fans rioted during the team's 2–0 defeat by Bayern Munich in the European Cup. The scousers used their own memorable trip as a way of showing they could behave in large flocks, inebriated, but happily savouring the unspeakable traffic noises of Rome as they lurched cans in hand across yet another bridge chanting,

'Kee–gun, Kee–gun' or 'Joey Joey Jones' or 'Give it to 'em, Bionic Carrot'.

It was a worrying time for Paisley, Fagan and Moran because John Toshack's chances of playing were looking slim following a recurrence of his injury. The Borussia Moenchengladbach camp had been telling their own accompanying press that the prospect of facing Toshack was giving them the 'jitters'. Better by far that Toshack didn't play at the Olympic stadium, because Keegan's value as a player seemed to diminish without him. This news reached the Liverpool camp and was digested inwardly by Keegan, who would have to adapt his game in the absence of his Welsh colleague. Besides, Toshack often said about their partnership: 'We wouldn't have been able to do without Steve Heighway's support. He was the one whose graft gave us so many openings week-in, week-out.'

Rome itself had become ablaze with red and white Liverpool banners. The green and white Rhineland opposition found it hard to compete, or captivate the Romans with their particular brand of humour, unlike the Scousers. The Liverpool fans had picked up the odd admiring ode from a Roman scribe during their wanderings round the city. The representative of *Il Messaggero* had written, 'The Liverpool fans don't devastate or pillage profane sanctuaries of churches, or pillage wine and salami from the shop shelves.' (It would be eight years before the Heysel stadium deaths, a disaster which made veterans of the football world wonder if the game had gone totally mad.) It was enough then to enjoy the boisterous behaviour of the scouser strippers along the Tiber, and the co-ordinated way in which they set off marching towards the Olympic stadium on the afternoon of the match. By then, the news had reached them that Toshack would be unable to play, let down by the injury which had kept him out of the FA Cup Final – much to the relief of the German contingent and to the near despair of the Welshman. Keegan wasn't feeling as nervous as some of the players, for what would be an evening's 'waltz' with his prime marker, West German international Bertie Vogts.

Paisley chose the side which had finished the FA Cup final,

with Ian Callaghan, the veteran from other glorious Kop epochs, included in place of David Johnson, who was substitute. Again the axe had fallen on David Fairclough. Paisley's plan was to play Steve Heighway up front as a roving pirate with Keegan tucked in just behind him, and a midfield quartet of McDermott, Kennedy, Callaghan and Case. Keegan was full of bounce and encouragement, since it was his very last game, and he had been swamped with good luck messages from Jean and his family, and all the other members of his contingent.

Paisley had been dining out on the story that the last time he had been in Rome was when he helped liberate it back in 1944 – with Tom Finney, of course. Paisley thought Keegan looked so fit, it would need a Panzer tank to stop him that evening. Keegan still looked ridiculously schoolboyish waiting for the presentations. Meanwhile, Bertie Vogts knew what he was going to do – mark Keegan all over the park. 'You'll Never Walk Alone' indeed!

The teams were as follows:

Liverpool: Clemence, Neal, Jones, Smith, Kennedy, Hughes, Keegan, Case, Heighway, Callaghan, McDermott.

Borussia Moenchengladbach: Kneiss, Vogts, Klinkhammer, Wittkamp, Bonhof, Wohlers (Hannes), Simonsen, Wimmer (Kulik), Stielike, Schaeffer, Heynckes.

The attendance in the stadium was 57,000, but the Liverpool fans certainly made the gathering seem double. Keegan was soon making a nuisance of himself along the Borussia right flank. 'There's no doubt the Germans are concerned about Keegan,' Barry Davies intoned early on in the game. 'I talked to the Borussia manager, Udo Lattek, who was not sure who was going to mark Keegan.' On a hard surface, with the temperature very high, it soon became clear who was watching over Keegan.

Borussia captain, Bertie Vogts, was assigned the job, one he would live to regret. Keegan was in one of those squat, muscular, elastic-band moods when trying to mark him proved intensely difficult. Keegan and Heighway at once began working tremendously hard to give width on the flanks, so allowing the heavily manned Liverpool midfield to take advantage of the space down the centre. If Toshack had played, the tactics would have been quite different, but in the circumstances, Paisley's plans looked highly appropriate. 'Keegan and Heighway are pulling their markers apart,' Davies purred to the viewers back home. 'Keegan is enjoying himself and rising to the occasion.'

But despite Liverpool's early authority which had their fans baying and chanting, the Germans assembled what might have been a devasting strike through a quick break. The shock of it momentarily silenced the fans – but not for long, for Keegan was even more determined to unshackle his German marker.

Liverpool's closest attempts in the first half came from their midfielders, Ray Kennedy producing an elastic save from the edgy Kneiss, and Jimmy Case having another chance desperately hacked away near the line. Keegan's value had not only been seen down his own left flank – he had done a tremendous amount of work in attacking zones outside the Borussia box. Davies praised Keegan for his first-half efforts. 'The only doubt in my mind is if he can keep up the work-rate in this humidity.'

It wasn't going to take a spot of humidity to weaken Kevin Keegan and, besides, he was determined to try and erase the embarrassment of that awful England display in the same stadium the previous November. The memory of that horror show drove him on as much as anything.

Liverpool took the lead in the 28th minute when Ian Callaghan sent Heighway away down the right, and the galloping winger sent McDermott clear to shoot past Kneiss into the far right-hand corner. Borussia's response after half-time could not have been more devastatingly conducted. Danish international, Alan Simonsen took advantage of a blunder by Case to shoot high into the right-hand top corner past a static Clemence to make it 1–1. The Germans were firmly back in contention and there was a nervous lump in many a scouse throat. When Uli Stielike burst through unchallenged, Clemence had to make the save of the match by blocking the future Real Madrid player's shot when a second German goal looked odds-on.

Keegan had promised that if Liverpool were to win, they would have to 'do the job properly, and do it in style'. It is what they began to do once the German storm had abated. This happened almost immediately, like a Roman shower. Two minutes after Stielike's attempt had failed, Liverpool won a corner which Heighway floated perfectly onto the head of the veteran himself, Tommy Smith, who bulleted the ball into the net.

Keegan continued to entice Bertie Vogts into obscure regions of the park, leaving gaps in the German defence. Vogts was plodding now. His tongue wasn't exactly hanging out, but the German looked dizzy. As Adrian Henri, the Liverpudlian poet, who was watching with his fellow Kopites, reflected: 'Kevin Keegan was everywhere that night, despite Vogts following a bootlace-length away. Next morning, the joke going round the Rome cafes was that, at the post-match party, every time Keegan got up to go to the bar, Vogts followed him.'

Eight minutes from the end of this Roman journey, Vogts would suffer the greatest indignity of all when he brought Keegan down near the penalty spot after another meandering run by the Liverpool player. Keegan might well have scored anyway, but the responsibility of taking the kick was given to Phil Neal who stroked the ball with unhurried fortitude past Kneiss.

Then the pandemonium began with the Liverpool supporters lighting their own verbal celebratory bonfires as referee Wartz blew the final whistle, and the European Cup was secure in Anfield's possession. Now Keegan could leave for the continent knowing his job was done. His own contribution to Liverpool's victory had been immense. There could be no doubters – even those who had said Keegan was a 'manufactured footballer' instead of an artist with natural gifts, had to bow to the obvious. Barry Davies promptly eulogized Keegan's part in the operation.

'Tonight, Keegan has given as good a performance as one has seen. Keegan had amply proved he was world class. What an end to the season and to his career at Liverpool.'

Everyone went to the Holiday Inn afterwards to celebrate with the winning side. It was more or less open house with scousers straying in from nearby cafes, to witness Paisley, a beaming Bill Shankly, Keegan and the large Liverpool party raising glasses of champagne in constant toasts, while one or two scribes were thrown into the swimming pool by a wickedly grinning goalscorer on his 599th appearance, Tommy Smith. Frank Keating remembered dancing the Gay Gordons with Bob Paisley while the author's memory was of Shankly stripping to the waist to put on a red Liverpool shirt. Jeff Powell had filed his piece hours before to the *Daily Mail* on what Paisley had called, 'The greatest night in the history of Liverpool Football Club'. Powell wrote, 'In a single brilliant performance, Keegan burst through the psychological block about man-to-man marking. Bertie Vogts, the most persistant shadow in world football, was run ragged. As a direct result, Borussia Moenchengladbach were steam-rollered to defeat.'

It was tough on Kevin Keegan having to bid so many farewells and take a few scouse kisses and backslaps on his return, with an England tour to South America imminent. Keegan needed to be there as captain for Don Revie, especially as Revie had told the Football Association he would miss the opening match against Brazil because he wanted to watch Italy play Finland in Helsinki – a result which would have a major bearing on England's World Cup qualification chances. Ted Croker thought the idea sounded sensible, and Revie's loyal assistant, Les Cocker, would look after the team in Brazil until Revie returned for the next match scheduled in Buenos Aires against Argentina. Keegan felt he had been riding roller coasters of late with so much excitement and tension leading up to his ultimate triumph in Rome. But he had been injured or battle fatigued in Rome, and that kept him out of England's match against the auld enemy at Wembley on 4 June, the day after he had broken the British transfer by signing for SV Hamburg for £500,000.

Trevor Brooking, who like Mick Channon had become a close associate of Keegan's, was also missing from Revie's line-up, and their absence hardly benefited an England side which was sunk by goals from Gordon McQueen and Keegan's Liverpool successor, Kenny Dalglish, Channon scoring with a late penalty for England. Scotland already felt they had the World Cup finals in the bag again, and what better than to celebrate their first victory against England for ten years. So much so, that their Tartan fans invaded the Wembley pitch afterwards, wrecked the goalposts, and hacked lumps out of the turf. Les Went, the Wembley stadium publicity man, was shocked. 'Disgusting, I've never seen anything like it here before.' The fixture was moved to midweek after that and gradually faded from the calendar.

England flew to Rio the day after the Scotland debacle unaware of the dramas and intrigues already working away at the very foundations of the Football Association at Lancaster Gate. Keegan and Brooking, who hadn't played at Wembley, did their best to cheer up the members of the losing team. Don Revie, it was thought, was making his way to Helsinki to watch Italy play Finland on the night England played Brazil in Rio.

Keegan and the team knew that a comfortable win by Italy would more or less see England fail to reach the 1978 finals – a bitter disappointment, particularly for Keegan, who had dearly wanted to follow Bobby Moore in captaining England in the World Cup finals. But it was no use letting the matter upset the system. Keegan made sure Cocker did not feel too much out of depth when he was in charge of the team in Rio de Janeiro where England, after their recent, much criticized failures against Holland and Scotland, restricted Zico and his colleagues to a barren night in a goalless draw. Cocker, the thorough-going Leeds number two, and Croker, the Cheltenham-based high-flying FA Secretary both agreed, on the way back from the stadium, that Don would be pleased that his team had played so 'creditably' on the night. In particular, young Trevor Francis had linked up well with Keegan, and was well worth keeping in the team for the second match in Argentina. Cocker even went so far as to tell Francis, the boy who had caused so much excitement in Birmingham when he appeared in the first team at the age of 16, not to go out in the sunshine and play tennis in Buenos Aires in case he got heat-stroke. That it was winter time in those parts didn't exactly matter – in Cocker, not Croker's view, South America was always hot, and crocodiles like Norman Hunter bit your legs off if they caught you. Francis was looking forward to

Right: In Newcastle colours alongside Geordie favourite, Peter Beardsley.

Below: Keegan strikes a poignant pose with a youthful Chris Waddle in an FA Cup tie against Liverpool in January 1984.

The many faces of Newcastle United.

Above left: *In a second division match against QPR in August 1982, Keegan and striking partner Imre Varadi cause panic in the Rangers' defence.*

Left: *Returning to Anfield for Newcastle's third round FA Cup tie against Liverpool in January 1984 – and an emotional reunion with the Kop.*

Above: *Anxious times in the home dugout as Newcastle manager Kevin Keegan sees his team go close against Glenn Hoddle's Swindon Town in a 1992/93 First Division promotion battle.*

Right: *Newcastle chairman Sir John Hall, with whom Keegan fell into dispute over the manager's demand for more money to buy new players.*

Above: Some of the players who helped Keegan's Newcastle reach the Premier League (from left to right, and below): Lee Clark, Robert Lee, David Kelly (subsequently sold to Wolves for £750,000), Barry Venison and Andy Cole.

Below: Discussing tactics with assistant Terry McDermott.

Below: *A return to the glory days on Tyneside. The Magpies celebrated winning the 1992/93 First Division title in style with an emphatic 7-1 victory over fellow promotion contenders Leicester City in their final home match of the season.*

Left: Kevin with wife Jean and daughters Sarah and Laura Jane attending the wedding of Lawrie McMenemy's daughter, Alison (on left of picture).

Below: Could this be the face of the future England manager?

another outing in the River Plate cauldron the following Sunday. But this dream changed when Revie arrived, Yorkshire chin jutting and creating totally different vibes.

Francis told David Miller of *The Times* something he had noticed during his international sessions with Revie. 'The boss liked Kevin Keegan and Mick Channon. He was very close to them and one or two of the other players, but I was not amongst them.' Francis said of Revie, 'I respected him because of what he had won with Leeds. You have to respect records. He was very hardworking, though I never got close to him during the few months before he left. He took part in everything we did, the training, the massage sessions, he was always there, always concerned for his players. At the end of the season, a year or two before the South American tour, I had gone up to him and said I wanted to work at my game, and what aspect did he think I should concentrate on. He said "heading" in a friendly way.'

Trevor Francis had not obviously worked hard enough on this aspect of his game, because Revie promptly dropped him from the England team, over-ruling Cocker's selection in favour of Mick Channon, Keegan's friend. Channon's record as an England striker (he finished eighth on the overall best scoring list) could not be queried. Yet Francis had played well against the Brazilians and deserved another chance. Don didn't see it that way, and Keegan led an England team into action on a pitch littered with strips of newspaper and confetti with Francis sitting tight-faced on the sidelines.

'I felt disillusioned and less than happy about Revie's regimental routines,' Francis commented.

In fact, Francis had been hopping mad, threatening an early exit, although he would have had far longer to go than Keegan who had simply hopped off England's team coach near St Albans. He rang his wife Helen, and moped about as Revie refused to bring him on as a substitute in the third of the tour's three draws against Uruguay. It was not until Francis successfully linked up with Keegan up front, under the new Ron Greenwood regime, that he found his international footing. Unlike the strong-willed Keegan, who had literally bounced

129

back into Revie's side after being dropped, Francis failed with his own show of frustration. Soon Keegan and his team would hear the sensational news. The boss was packing it in.

It was Jeff Powell, the *Daily Mail's* soccer correspondent, who was to get one of the scoops of the decade when he revealed that Revie had sneaked off to Dubai on an important mission before going to Helsinki. When Powell's story broke after the England party had returned from South America, there were cries of derision about Revie abandoning a sinking England ship. 'Bloody deserter' was the popular maxim for a former player and leading club manager who had accepted a four-year contract to coach the United Arab Emirates team at a starting salary of £60,000 a year. Powell's account of Revie's journey to the Middle East with a false beard and cap was almost bizarre enough to have been scripted into a film by Graham Greene with Albert Finney playing Revie, Dustin Hoffman as Powell, Herbert Lom, the football-nutty sheik, Trevor Howard as Professor Harold Thompson, Nigel Havers as Ted Croker. He would have played the part superbly, as would Finney in capturing Revie's deviousness and near-brilliance in avoiding recognition for so long. The Football Association tut-tutted until they were red, white and blue in the face, but Revie was gone. 'We had to act fast and get a successor,' Croker said. And Ron Greenwood was the FA's man. Keegan was in a bit of a quandary, moving as he was to Germany with Jean and his family. He could have done without the continual disruptions which rumbled over the affairs of his England team. The FA had slapped a ten-year ban on Revie for breach of contract. The man had been disloyal, no matter that he claimed in print that 'the job was causing too much heartache to those nearest to us (Don and Elsie). It was not worth all the aggravation. Nearly everyone wanted me out...'

Not everyone, as a matter of fact. Players like Keegan and Channon had certainly not had enough of him with England, but the lure of the Middle East and the riches involved was a proposal Revie just couldn't refuse. Many less avaricious people than Don would have done just the same. Revie had the ban set aside in the High Court – but his character and credibility had suffered too much to restore his previously almost hallowed image within the game. When he died of motor neuron disease one of the mourners was Kevin Keegan. Keegan told Jeff Powell, who was also at the service, 'I [Keegan] wanted to rectify the impression I had given as a player that Revie's dossiers were only of use as card-scorers. I was out of order and was very unfair about the dossiers. We certainly should have taken them more seriously.'

5
HAMBURG

For the Keegans, the first six months of their stay in Hamburg were inevitably disrupting. To begin with Jean, normally a reserved person, suffered from cloying loneliness when her husband was away playing in other German cities. The couple had rooms on the twenty-fifth floor of the Plaza hotel with all the comforts and mod cons available for such important guests. After all, Keegan was being mentioned in the West German and international press almost daily because of his achievements and many problems on and off the football field.

Jean plainly wanted to move into a proper home. She missed her two shaggy sheepdogs, Heidi and Oliver, to such an extent that Keegan organized their transportation across the North Sea. The couple, with dogs and many suitcases, moved to a smaller hotel in the suburbs more capable of looking after guests with canine companions.

The month of July 1977 was a time of major transition for Keegan, but it was worse for Jean because she had less to do than her restless husband, who was always preoccupied with seeing people. There were club commitments of course, including a pre-season match against Barcelona at the Volkspark stadium, at which the new arrival was able to have a long chat with the Dutch master, Johan Cruyff, before the kick-off. Cruyff only played for 16 minutes, but Keegan had already noted a good deal about what it was like playing in another country. Cruyff, of course, had been extravagantly pampered by the Nou Camp owners, but he could not resist the odd dig about Spanish referees.

Keegan appears to have been smitten by Cruyff's charm and knowledge of the game.

'Cruyff struck me immediately as a man who knew his own mind, knew his worth, and was determined to make the most of the rewards his talents brought him.'

This was very much Keegan's philosophy towards playing the game of football. It aroused a determination on the part of the Doncaster man to show Cruyff, the former king of Dutch 'total football', what a live wire he was going to become over the Rhine.

Jean was happy to break away from hotel routines and join the 40,000 crowd making their way through the surrounding woods at the Volkspark to watch the match. There was a prevailing atmosphere typical of teutonic football meetings – the sound of muffled, slightly constipated horns being blown, a smell of juicy hamburgers and hotdogs sizzling on mobile barbecue stands, and the extravagant regalia of club scarves, caps and badges so close to Germans' hearts, being offered for sale by huge T-shirt-ed men with beer bellies. Only three years before at the 1974 World Cup finals, East Germany had played the West in a unique match at the Volkspark, Jurgen Sparwasser scoring the only goal for the East against the eventual World Cup winners. Their supporters had been brought to the match under heavy surveillance, no doubt by communist KGB men, in a special train and escorted straight back again to the Iron Curtain afterwards, with barely a chance to celebrate. The Keegans, in contrast, were never far from life's Western comforts. They had brought their two cars with them, Kevin's Jaguar XJS presented by British Leyland, and Jean's Allegro. Both became familiar sights on the motorways surrounding the city and near the Volkspark stadium.

Keegan was touched by the warm reception he received from his new supporters, now that many of the Liverpool fans had turned away from him because, in their estimation, he had become an Anfield 'turncoat'. He needed all the support he could get from the Hamburg terraces. Any doubts were put right from the moment he walked on to the pitch wearing his new red shirt emblazoned on the front by the name of the Japanese sponsors, Hitachi. Hamburg varied their strip quite frequently, confusing the Englishman, and it was hard getting used to the pink jerseys they wore at home games.

Surprisingly, Barcelona were run into the ground that night by the European Cup Winners' Cup holders. Keegan scored the fourth goal amid much fuss and acclaim. It was too early, however, to assess how he would make out as a Bundesliga recruit. The club manager, Dr Peter Krohn, and his new coach, Rudi Gutendorf, had begun arguing about the best ways of utilizing Keegan's qualities, but the 6–0 rout of Barcelona diverted the issue for a short time as the Englishman was hailed as a Volkspark king.

'My heart and soul were back in the game 100 per cent for the first time in two years. I knew I still had a lot to learn about the game, but I also knew I had found the fresh challenge I needed.'

His old club found this mood burning inside Keegan's expatriate outlook when they went over to play Hamburg not long after the Barcelona match. Hamburg only managed a 3–2 win on this occasion, but what interested Keegan most of all was the news that Kenny Dalglish would be joining Liverpool from Glasgow Celtic. Dalglish commented at the time about Keegan, 'We are different players with different qualities and different strengths, but what we do have in common is a desire to see the ball in the back of the net.'

Keegan's move to Hamburg was not as catastrophic a blow to Liverpool's future fortunes as some scribes had forecasted. The departure of Keegan was certainly the end of an era, a magestic one in many ways, first under Shankly, then under Paisley. Then Paisley went off to Glasgow to pay a record £440,000 for a centre-forward from Celtic who over the years had become an irritant to large England centre-backs. He also had a tendency to speak out of the corner of his mouth, and possessed a body swerve as confusing as the nuances of a Clydebank gale. If Keegan had been Shankly's greatest signing, King Kenny was certainly Paisley's. Dalglish quickly added his name to the list of

Kop immortals by scoring Liverpool's winning European Cup goal against Club Bruges at Wembley a year after Liverpool had won the same trophy in Rome. Keegan forecasted that Dalglish would do even better at Anfield than he did, but Keegan's own achievements at Anfield were nonetheless spectacular and, acknowledged as such by Dalglish in his memoirs. It was natural that King Kenny hated the term 'the second Kevin', and he took steps to erase the very idea with a certain Glaswegian causticity. Paisley, after all, had been after his signature for a long time before he actually put pen to paper. Kenny did have to suffer comparisons because he was wearing Keegan's number seven shirt, which had become as famous on Merseyside as Pele's number ten, or Bobby Moore's number six.

'From the moment I signed for Liverpool in 1977,' says Dalglish, 'the inevitable comparisons were made between myself and Kevin Keegan. I say inevitable because it always seemed obvious to me that the newspapers and TV would seek to link my arrival with Kevin's departure, yet as far as I was concerned , I wasn't being signed to take over Keegan's role in the Liverpool team. Paisley underlined to me that what he wanted was the form I had shown with Celtic and Scotland. He didn't want me to alter my style to try and be another Kevin. The only similarity was that I took over the number seven shirt, which had been his during his time with the club. I didn't think even the fans expected a carbon-copy replacement. I honestly believe that no one could have copied Kevin when he went to Hamburg. They didn't want someone who would try to emulate Kevin Keegan and fail! It was just as well, because I wouldn't have known how to do it, even if I had wanted to. I had only played against him once; when England beat Scotland 5–1 at Wembley. There was more opportunity to play against him since I joined Liverpool. I have faced him a few times and he's a player I admire.'

Later in his book, Dalglish said of Keegan, 'He's better in the air than I am for a start, so there's one reason why I would never have been able to do the things he did at Anfield. But, and he has said this himself, probably his greatest attribute is his work-rate.

135

He just never stops. He has fantastic energy, but please don't think everything is due to that. He is quick, he plays good balls and he finishes well. Maybe that spell with Hamburg made him an even better finisher than he was before. I think going to West Germany added even more confidence. When you are asked to score goals, then a lot is down to confidence and Kevin has that. I don't know if there are areas where I'm better, than he is. People say I shield the ball better or do this or that better. It doesn't really matter to me. I was bought for what I had done, for what I was as a player. I wasn't bought to take over from anyone. Really, Liverpool made no practical changes to my style. That was something I was always grateful for.'

Dalglish's autobiographical thoughts about Keegan to his co-writer, the Scottish sports writer Ken Gallacher, made interesting reading at the time (1982) because both 'individuals' were still 'playing' at the peak of their form. Dalglish was soon savouring a vibrant new goal-scoring partnership with Ian Rush.

One of Keegan's least fond memories was a visit to Anfield, not long after joining Hamburg, when he was subjected to the taunts of some of his old fans from the Kop. His team were shattered by a 6–0 scoreline in the European Super Cup, which produced this scathing recollection by a witness, Stephen Kelly, in Ian St John's book, *Liverpool – the Glory Decade*.

'Keegan was once the hero of the Kop, but when he deserted Anfield at the height of his career for new challenges on the Continent, the Kop responded like a family whose brother had walked out. Rightly or wrongly. It was regarded as an act akin to treachery and the esteem with which he had been regarded disappeared almost overnight. Only weeks before, he had helped Liverpool to the European Cup, but his love affair with the club was over and the recriminations soon began when Keegan returned to Anfield...the Kop vocally mocking Keegan's decision to move abroad.'

Keegan had made the decision and he proved he was well able to cope with such disappointing nights when many old scouse pals turned against him. At least he retained the respect of many fans at Anfield, unlike other future old soldiers who showed they were far more susceptible to folly in creating major headlines through misconceived, wounding remarks to the media. Keegan turned his back on Anfield because, like any business-man, he wanted a new challenge.

'So many people had advised me and I had listened to what they had to say, but the decision had to be mine and I was pleased I had the confidence to make the move. If I failed, I couldn't blame anyone except myself. If I had acted on some of the advice I was given, I would not be where I am today. I managed to retain the same streak of independence as when I kicked a ball against Mrs Wild's wall in Spring Gardens as a small boy. I am grateful that I had the talent to do what I wanted to do with my life. I was late for my trial at Doncaster Rovers, and Coventry turned me down. But perhaps it was good to have had a few disappoint-ments on the way.'

At Hamburg in late 1977, Keegan got on reasonably well with his new coach, Rudi Gutendorf, who believed in the human touch, rather than a regimental sub-human bullying attitude towards players. But there could be tension when Keegan's own sponsorship concerns went against the club's. He was pulled up early in his Hamburg career for wearing a pair of French, 'Patrick' boots in pre-season training by one of the assistant coaches. He demanded in no uncertain terms that the Englander put on a pair of Adidas boots, because Hamburg was an Adidas club. 'Sorry,' Keegan replied, but he had signed a con-tract with Patrick, and he would wear their boots or bust. It was Doncaster will-power against Hamburg steel. The assistant coach wasn't impressed, but after discussing the matter with Dr Krohn, the matter was put on ice. What mattered more, Dr Krohn hinted, was getting Keegan out there on the pitch, and it didn't matter if Keegan wore brothel creepers as long as he stuck the ball regularly into Bayern and Borussia nets.

Jean was doing her Yorkshire best to settle into the North German way of life. The crowded market-day atmosphere of Welsh sheep farmers and their wives out for a bustling day's shopping had been replaced by a more ordered discipline, which German families employed, leading to spotlessly clean front drives, and a heavy fine if anyone dared to drop a chocolate wrapper on the ground. Jean had to endure Friday nights alone in front of the German multi-channel television set when Kevin went off to a local hotel to join the Hamburg squad who stayed under Krohn and Gutendorf's paternal wing before their home matches.

The Keegans generally made no secret of their sporty outdoor tastes of dog-walking, tennis, and golf. Not that they had much to hide. Kevin Keegan's name had begun to appear on German television endorsing a number of goods, under the spirited wing of his agent. Harry Swales, chairman of Kevin Keegan Ltd, and a fellow Yorkshireman, was keenly aware of the magic of 'brass'. So Kevin always seemed to have something special to wear, on duty or off, from a pair of French boots, to a colourful Kevin Keegan T-shirt which he could put on in his own back garden at weekends, or one of those grey sports jackets and ankle-flared trousers he favoured wearing during his ITV appearances on Brian Moore's panel in 1978 as a World Cup analyser. Jean could look the blonde open-air girl with a vengeance, and her neighbours, once the couple had moved into their sumptuous new three-bedroomed house, 15 minutes' drive from the stadium, observed that she liked dressing up when the English couple went out to dinner by the lake.

The Keegan life style was viewed less favourably by tetchy, envious members of the Hamburg team and although Keegan tried to make it clear he and Jean were there as friends, not snooty neighbours, the coldness some of these club members extended towards the English player, obviously worried him. Manfred Kaltz, the fast, heavyweight international right-back with wasp stings in his tackling, liked to moan about the 'Englander' and some of his remarks made the German newspapers. He wanted to know who Keegan was anyway. 'What's so special about him?. When did he last score for England?' Kaltz obviously felt the side which had won the European Cup-Winners' Cup the season before, should have retained it without Dr Krohn spending so much money on an English player who the right-back thought was greatly over-rated. But like his early experiences with Tommy Smith, Keegan rode out this storm, sensing the coldness shown to him by Kaltz and his friends was only natural. They had read in the newspapers what Keegan was being paid – an estimated £200,000 as his share of the deal.

Rumours back home that Keegan was about to walk out on Hamburg instigated a prompt statement from Keegan, 'I have a three-year contract with the club here, and I intend to honour it. I'm happy here.' What he did miss in Germany were his lager and limes. 'I'm sticking to milk and Liebfraumilch which Jean and I enjoy at meals. But I'm afraid German beer isn't for me.' Language problems, however, proved a greater chore. Keegan was bemused by the managerial verbal backbiting behind the scenes at Hamburg. Dr Krohn and Gudendorf's failure to slot Keegan into a productive position on the pitch, England's captain was tried out in five different positions in 15 games, was the complete opposite of Shanks's theory about keeping the same system running. 'It was as if I was a new toy for Hamburg to play with, but eventually I began to settle into a mid-field role, operating behind the two main strikers'.

The 'personality clash' between the general manager Krohn and Gutendorf, anticipated by the German sporting press, was about to boil over, and the Keegan question became paramount in the issue after bad results. Rudi Gutendorf was far more respectful of Keegan's shooting abilities, telling him off in training for avoiding the netting for a fear of injuring a colleague from a yard or two out. Keegan was supposed to be a goalscorer, so it was vital the Englander put the fear of death up every opposing Bundesliga goalkeeper week-in, week-out. But Krohn and Gutendorf were not to see the full fruits of Keegan's known world-class ability. Both of them got the push, Gutendorf, the sack, and the general manager forced to resign four months after Keegan's arrival. Keegan didn't raise a glass of Liebfraumilch at this news. 'I was surprised, I must say, I was on good terms with them both'.

The arrival of Gunter Netzer at Hamburg as manager, and the prickly Yugoslav fitness fanatic, Branco Zebec as his coach,

reunited the brilliant Borussia Moenchengladbach midfield vir-
tuoso with his old Liverpool opponent. In the memorable
UEFA Cup Final, Netzer couldn't help being an admirer of
Keegan. He had showed what a tiger he could be in those two
legs when Liverpool hung on to break their duck in European
competition. He decided he and Zebec were going to make
Keegan a successful operator among some German players with
international ambitions like Manny Kaltz, Holger Hieronymus,
Felix Magath and the giant Horst Hrubesch. West Germany's
abysmal failure in the 1978 World Cup finals under a departing
Helmut Schoen had given these players an incentive to win
places in the next World Cup squad under Jupp Derwell.
Keegan was also aware of his own international ratings. Playing
in the Bundesliga had been viewed with apprehension by some
huffy English scribes, but Ron Greenwood saw it differently.
Keegan, after faulty beginnings, had added a new dimension to
his play. He was far more commanding and mature, much of it
down to the fearsome Zebec.

It was no good the Hamburg players disputing Zebec's qualifications as coach, which were born out of a playing career equally as distinguished as the manager, Netzer. Zebec had been considered a world-class winger during his most illustrious playing
days in Yugoslavia, appearing in two World Cup finals. It was not
surprising he demanded such high standards at the Volkspark
stadium. Keegan's willingness to accept Zebec's torturing routines impressed the Yugoslav coach. Ron Greenwood was also
appreciative of Keegan's extraordinary fitness on his England
visits, and he felt such energy would inspire his colleagues.

Keegan had come out of another 'black' period early in 1978
when he had been suspended for eight matches by the German
Football Association for striking Lubek's left-back, Erhard
Preuss, under severe provocation. It had happened on New
Year's Eve in a dubiously titled, friendly match against
Hamburg's neighbours forty miles to the north – a port wedged
against the salty, ferry-traversed background of the Baltic Sea.
Keegan had been assaulted, both with a fist and a shoulder by the
mocking German early in the match, so after an assault which

left him badly winded, Keegan's self-control snapped and he knocked Preuss into Baltic Sea cuckooland with a right cross. The Englander had not bothered to wait for the red card.

Keegan's long suspension had the effect of diluting the other Hamburg players' animosity towards the Yorkshireman. They soon realized they badly needed Keegan's unselfish running and shooting instincts, if they were to get anywhere in the Bundesliga, which would not be that season. Hamburg had slipped down the table from fifth place into the lower reaches, losing seven matches, three of them at the Volkspark stadium. But Keegan's return would change all that. Later that summer, as yacht masts bobbed breezily around the Lake, Netzer and Zebec assembled their squad for the 1978/9 season. For Keegan a Bundesliga winners' medal to add to his three Liverpool championship medals was a challenge he couldn't resist. Again, he got down to work with a personal pre-season ruthlessness which even surprised the strict Zebec. Helping the Bundesliga in his second season at Hamburg showed just how Keegan's stock had risen, he had become even more of a celebrity which is why he and Jean spent hours learning German off instructional cassettes. Invitations to attend dinners and social functions attended by hearty city and port dignitaries were frequent, and Hamburg's wunderkid was often asked to speak. Winning the coveted European Player of the Year award twice while he was in Germany also showed what a tremendous impact the Liverpool import had made, making Manny Kaltz eat his scornful words!

One of Keegan's watching admirers at Hamburg was the 1966 and 1970 German World Cup captain, Uwe Seeler, a German hero if ever there was one. He singled out Keegan's new found attributes to John Roberts in an interview in the *Guardian*.

'For me, Keegan is like a little Volkswagen, running forever. He fights the 90 minutes with full speed and full heart. I never saw a player so professional. In his first season at Hamburg, Kevin ran too much with the ball. He looked speedy, but the game was slowed down. A player can't be as quick with the ball. In Germany, the players made the ball do the work. Keegan learnt this. Even though Keegan had a bad time in his first year. I still think when Hamburg bought him, it was one of the luckiest days for the club. Only one player was in the same condition and had a will to win from match to match, and that was Keegan. He plays with instinct and feeling, but most of all he's a hard fighter.'

Another admirer of Keegan was Chancellor Schmidt, who had been a fan of Hamburg's since he grew up in the middle-class surburb of Barmbek before the war. He came to the Volkspark whenever political and social commitments would allow. Chancellor Schmidt, with his known mania for football and Hamburg, was far more on the ball. Stories that Keegan was leaving the club saddened the Chancellor of West Germany. Could they be true? They were, because as the city of Hamburg got down to celebrate their stunning Bundesliga victory, the Keegans became more and more aware that their time on German soil as national celebrities was sprinting to an end. Only one more season lay ahead with Hamburg and after that where?

The departure of Krohn and Rudi Gutendorf put an end to Keegan's early, often unhappy indoctrination into the working of the Bundesliga. He had sat nervously as a translator delivered Gutendorf's team tactics in English. The Yugoslav, Ivan Buljan's, were delivered in French. He had got to know that drab view of the industrial area of Stellingen which lay beyond the pool area outside the dressing-rooms like a squadee facing the endless training area of pine woods at Aldershot. The new coach, Branco Zebec, was the kind of tyrant in training to make the players feel they had come under the wing of Captain Bligh of 'the Bounty'. Not that Zebec found it necessary to have his players, or even the Englander, flogged after training, but he did go out to prove that there was nothing like crash routines geared through endless running to get winning results. While the HSV players did feel like mutinying at times in Bligh fashion, their performances the following season certainly endorsed Zebec's training schedules.

Under Zebec's gruffly Slovonik spoken guidance, during which endless hours were spent simply running and sprinting, in contrast to the three- or five-a-side matches favoured by Shankly and Paisley at Melwood, Keegan grew from a Mighty Atom into a super Mighty Atom. Jean, in particular, would notice her husband's return from team training under Zebec. Even the protagonist of self-devoted physical fitness was inclined to fall back on the sofa with every muscle creaking, every sinew screaming. Training under Zebec, as Keegan admitted, was the toughest of his playing career, but there was no moaning to be done when Hamburg won the Bundesliga in 1979.

One by one, leading English sports journalists were drawn to Hamburg to interview the Keegans or watch the European Footballer of the Year playing in front of his adoring fans at the Volkspark. Kevin often gave the impression of being involved with 100 things at once. Even when he was playing he ran and ran. When Ian Wooldridge, the award winning *Daily Mail* sports writer popped over the North Sea to write a feature on the England captain for the European Championships special edition for the *Radio Times* he found the Keegans 'living in *Homes and Gardens* cut-crystal style in their £160,000 terraced house with 600 trees in the surrounds and two Mercedes parked outside.'

Keegan's rise to affluence, which British television viewers could see regularly on television commercials (as he happily splashed Brut-Fabergé over his shower-steaming frame in front of an admiring 'Enry Cooper') had turned Keegan into the sort of superstar the English loved thinking of as part of the 'furniture'. They loved the sight of the small, muscular, chatty Yorkshireman based in Germany, bossing everybody about in adverts, chat shows or on sporting panels. Keegan told Wooldridge, while they sipped vintage German white wine out of crystal glasses, that he was prepared to live his life 'at 100 miles an hour.'

'A man who does not know his worth is not worth anything.'

Here was an athlete who was pushing himself to the limit for a German football club and reaping the rewards he considered amply justified. 'If I hadn't succeeded at football, I would have succeeded at something else.' to justify his own recent achievement at winning the European Footballer of the Year award for

143

the second time, he modestly disclaimed his own qualifications to have won it twice. 'Technically I'm probably the worst player to win the award. But kids don't need to be born footballers. If they work and work, they can get to the top.' Keegan's direct honesty did much to show how much he valued his own status as a footballer. Wooldridge was impressed.

But all the beckoning and advice from Harry Swales lay in the future when Jean produced the couple's first child on 15 November 1978, a daughter, Laura Jane Keegan. The baby caused Jean and Kevin some harrowing anxiety after the birth when she was briefly, seriously ill with pneumonia. At times like these, a professional footballer must bear the agonies of waiting on hospital bulletins, like any other new parent, and Keegan had to suffer the tensions which go into keeping vigil with your wife by your daughter's cot. The crisis passed, and the Keegans were able to take the baby home, as proud as peacocks. Laura Jane's birth came a month before the first of Keegan's European Footballer of the Year awards, leaving the Doncaster scamperer in 'seventh heaven', the name incidentally of the Keegan's future home in Marbella. 'I feel so high I need oxygen,' the England captain quipped, savouring a wonderful end to the year which had seen his form helping earn Hamburg the results which would win the Bundesliga championship amid cacophonous scenes of celebration the following spring. Ron Greenwood was also on the phone fairly regularly, which Keegan liked because he desperately wanted to keep in touch with the international team now going for a place in the European Championship finals in Italy. Greenwood had plenty of opportunity to hear the proud father giving bulletins about Laura Jane, and Hamburg doing so well in the League was an added reason for the Keegans to feel content in a strange country.

Brian Glanville, the *Sunday Times* football correspondent for many years, went to the city of Brunswick to assess Keegan's progress over a year or two with Hamburg. Again the European Championships were drawing near and Hamburg were aiming, not only for a second Bundesliga championship, but also a place in the final of the European Cup in Madrid, their most likely opponents being Nottingham Forest. There is no better 'reader' of a game than Glanville, and he was not going to write about a smooth-running motor car if he noticed the odd fault behind the gloss. Glanville observed Keegan's 'endless flurry of movement'. The London correspondent decided that Keegan was overkilling his brief, as Ron Greenwood would discover when England played Italy in Turin the following summer. He made mistakes in defence, so keen was the Doncaster superstar to help out his German colleagues. 'Keegan almost gave away a goal when he mis-kicked the ball to Trimmhold in his own area'. Glanville wrote, 'If Keegan was scarcely the hero we have come to know and applaud, you can scarcely separate his performance from his team's.'

Heroes and superstars all have their off-days and Glanville happened to run into one of Keegan's, though his team did pick up a useful point with a one-all draw. During the months since Hamburg had won the Bundesliga, however, Keegan had sampled the strain of being a young father awoken by Laura's cries, with another busy season with Netzer and Zebec, to playing when he could for England in the qualifying European matches (Netzer was not always sympathetic about Greenwood's calls) and also being wooed by other clubs moving into the market for his post-Hamburg signature. This produced some hefty phone charges between agent Swales's office base on a Wakefield racecourse, and Keegan's by now much larger nook in rural Hamburg. The London tabloids had a field day about which wealthy club Keegan would choose when his £125,000 contract with Hamburg came to an end. (The Keegans had looked likely to leave Hamburg a year earlier until the player signed a new sponsorship deal with British Petroleum on 21 January 1979 which kept him at the Volkspark until the end of the 1979/80 season.) The Keegans had looked increasingly likely to move to America. Both the New York Cosmos and the Washington Diplomats were queuing up at some stage for the Englishman's services.

But it was Juventus who really came on strong with their move to bring Keegan to Turin amid fan-fares and trumpets as a second John Charles. Keegan had showed through his awards and helping Hamburg win the Bundesliga that he could survive in European football, he'd attuned well after a difficult start. And the Hamburg chairman, Paul Bentine appeared charmed by the Turin emissaries, not to mention Keegan himself who gave the impression he quite fancied making the journey south across the Alps to a lire fortune. The deal was on until Mrs.Keegan was asked her opinion. 'If you go to Italy, I'll go to Yorkshire with Laura'. That was that, and a '99 percent certain transfer went up in black and white striped smoke.' A pity in a way because Keegan's record suggested he would have made the grade in Serie A because of his will-power and determination, as Ray Wilkins, Graeme Souness and Liam Brady were able to do in the most public of football arenas. The chance went and you couldn't quibble about Jean Keegan's ultimatum. So which club would provide the vital attractions necessary to win the Keegan approval? Rumours flew around Hamburg and made their way across the North Sea as the player got on with the task of helping Hamburg win a coveted place in the European final in Madrid. Chelsea, managed for a short period by Geoff Hurst, did look a good bet to sign Keegan for a short time, while Liverpool and Arsenal also showed interest. Keegan's name was bracketed with one or two of the more affluent French First Division clubs. But who would have visualized or forecast the real headquarters where the Keegans would pack up and move to? Lawrie McMenemy's sensational signing of Kevin Keegan from Hamburg for £400,000 on 11 February, 1980 was a secret well-kept, right up to that celebrated television press conference when Keegan came bouncing back into English League football, after an absence of three years. Southampton's manager had certainly provided few clues to his astonishing coup. With Keegan being abroad he was safely out of the way from making any stray indiscretions to spoil the secrecy element. Being something of a showman, McMenemy longer to pull off the Keegan deal with the maximum amount of panache and publicity, to make Southampton an intriguing club. Getting Southampton on the map was a difficult task, even for a dedicated man like

Lawrie. He needed a big name, an entertainer, someone who everybody knew and could warm to. Keegan was the obvious one, he had spent over two years in Germany by now, and the rumours were that the player was looking elsewhere for an exciting new challenge.

With Hamburg heavily engaged in reaching the European Cup Final, and also to win the Bundesliga again, Keegan had little time to muse on which his future club might be, but he didn't see it being a German one. If Mick Channon had been rather more alert, he might have twigged why his manager asked him one morning for Keegan's home number in Hamburg. There didn't seem to be any major reason why Lawrie should want to speak to his mate (Lawrie didn't know Keegan very well) but Channon dismissed the suddenness of the request from his mind.

A fellow north country man who said he had advised Keegan on the move was his agent, Harry Swales, the bewhiskered, Jimmy Edwards-like, Wing-Commander, with RAF demob bowler hat, pin strip suit and briefcase. Swales was frequently on his travels, not only in the service of Kevin Keegan Ltd, as company chairman, but for other international England footballers including Keegan's old Liverpool mate, Ray Clemence. Swales was very much involved with the negotiations between Hamburg and Southampton, with a devotion which had much to do with his stated brief, 'I handle the money behind the boots and Kevin trusts me. It is not just a business arrangement, he's like a son to me. I always see he's all right,' Swales had been drawn in to the negotiations as a matter of course and told the *Daily Express* man, Con Coolican that apart from making sure his Kevin was looked after financially, his family's welfare should not be treated as a matter of minor importance by his new bosses. 'Of course I want to make sure Kevin is well looked after financially, but there is more to life with Kevin than just money. There is the happiness of his family. They will now live back in England, and there is also his pride in Britain. Hamburg was a great opportunity for him but he has now reached the stage when he wants to be playing for an English club again.'

Swales's business partnership with Keegan covered a far larger range of products than signed footballs. The Hamburg player had been endorsing a wide range of products from cheese to toys to chewing gum. The England player had done a good deal of German dairy product promoting during his stay, not to mention making himself look bouncy and supercharged as a superstar for shredded wheat advertisements on German television. Harry Swales might have looked like a character out of 'Carry on Up the Rhine', but he was brilliant at this particular brand of business, and the Keegans could not complain at the devoted way he made Kevin Keegan Ltd prosper. The pair had been in business for three years and a delighted Keegan told Coolican, 'Harry had done marvellous things for me. He looks after things really well and I trust him.' Swales had been employed as assistant sales manager of Warner Brothers films and had got to know the intricacies of show business on the way in. He had learnt a great deal about the blood-letting of the film business before setting up on his own in a small office near Wetherby race-course, where he made intricate plans as company chairman for the five-year future of Kevin Keegan Ltd. Swales was a perfectionist.

'It's no use to Kevin if people buy a product and little Johnny finds it keeps collapsing. That's not only bad for Kevin's image but bad for the manufacturer's. There's a lot of money involved here, and many people might think it's too much, but you've got to remember that a footballer's career is very short. Most reach their peak around 26 or 28, and by the time they are 32, their career is over. Most of them have no other trade or profession. They've been footballers since leaving school and nothing else. I'm making sure that when Kevin finishes playing he'll have plenty of money put by to start a new career. Perhaps open a few businesses...try something new but he'll always be secure as far as money in concerned.'

Swales guessed right on one matter. Keegan's career as a footballer had only four more years to go, so it was imperative his business affairs should now be peak, which is why Swales, aged 52, small and dapper, in a dark suit, stood near Keegan as he signed his contract for Southampton that memorable day in southern England.

Lawrie McMenemy tells how the deal came about.

'Kevin was top of the tree as an international player then, and to bring him in to our set-up would send Southampton onto a different planet, I hoped. His experience, for one thing, and ability to work hard and score goals. I didn't know Kevin very well at the time, so I rang him to ask if he knew where I could get hold of some lamp fittings in Germany. I had heard you could get very good ones there. It was a way of breaking the ice, so to speak. Kevin was very helpful. I was Mick Channon's boss, and he Mickey's friend, so we had that in common. Then I chatted about how his baby daughter Laura was, and then it was back to the crystal again. Kevin was very good about them, seemed to know where he could get them, and would bring them over when he was next playing for England. It took about two or three calls to get my proposal in the tank – I mentioned I had heard he might be moving to Italy and was he still interested in moving back to England. We had gained promotion from the Second Division, won the FA Cup four years earlier, and reached the League Cup final. Our prospects were sound, and Kevin seemed genuinely interested. It went on from there, comparatively easy really compared with some deals, and all the time we were keeping it that great big secret. Amazing really. Alan Ball and some of the lads thought it was some sort of "This is Your Life" set-up when I asked them to go along to the hotel. They knew nothing about it, except that Kevin would be there and there was some sort of do there involving him. They were amazed when they heard he was coming to the club. When Kevin appeared in front of the press it was a cracking story. And by the way, Kevin forgot to bring the fittings over, but he did next time. They're still up on the wall.'

The last week of Kevin Keegan's three-year spell with Hamburg well-suited his unquestioned energy. While Jean prepared the Keegan family to move back to the United Kingdom, her husband went off to Madrid with the West German club for that Wednesday's European Cup Final against Nottingham

Forest at the Estadio Santiago Bernabeau.

Forest had won the European Cup the year before beating Malmo 1–0 through a Trevor Francis goal in Munich, but their chances of emulating, Real Madrid and Benfica in winning the trophy twice on the trot looked flimsy against a strongly-knit Hamburg side in which Keegan wasn't the only known star. Quality German footballers like Kaltz, Magath and Hrubesch, a second-half substitute, were all capable of helping destroy an injury-plagued Forest. With Trevor Francis on the injured list, Brian Clough gave the impression the only way they would stop Keegan and the Germans was by boarding up the Forest goal with timber behind Peter Shilton.

To this day, Hamburg supporters who were at the game still cannot understand how their team lost. Their team spent so much of the game attacking – '84 percent' Clough said – with Kevin Keegan scurrying all over the Bernabeau pitch trying his best to inspire his sardonic German colleagues into kicking the ball at least three or four times into the Nottingham Forest net. That they failed had much to do with Peter Shilton in the Forest goal. The teams lined up as follows:

Nottingham Forest: Shilton, Anderson, Gray (sub: Gunn, 83 mins), McGovern, Lloyd, Burns, O'Neill, Bowyer, Birtles, Mill (sub O'Hare, 67 mins) Robertson.

SV Hamburg: Kagus, Kaltz, Nogly, Jakobs, Buljan, Hieronymus (sub Hrubesch, 46 mins) Magath, Keegan, Reimann, Milewski, Memering. Referee: Antonio Garrido (Portugal). Attendance: 60,000.

Brian Clough rightly assessed Forest's chances of winning would be best gained by keeping in their own half. Forest had claimed the early goal they wanted from a rare moment of adventure in the 20th minute when the Scottish winger, John Robertson, bullied a longish shot past Keegan and the keeper into the Hamburg net. From then on, Forest showed why, in Keegan's sporting terms, they were the best club side in Europe (he refrained from adding 'in defending') at getting important winning results. Keegan might have scampered around a great deal around the fringes and inner sanctuaries of the Forest box, first as an all-out striker, then moved back, but rarely did he find room to embarrass Shilton with a lethal shot. Larry Lloyd and Kenny Burns were simply magnificent at the heart of the Forest defence as the pressure grew hotter in the sheer heat of a Madrid evening. But if Keegan hoped for a penalty when he tumbled once or twice, the Portuguese referee was not convinced. Keegan had earned a penalty for Liverpool when Bertie Vogts brought him down in Rome, but there were no opportunities this time. In fact, Derek Pavis, the present chairman of Notts County, and a Forest director then, thought Keegan occupied himself that night by playing a diving porpoise in the Forest box.

'I had always admired Keegan as a player until then, especially his sportsmanship and determination, but that performance changed my view. He kept tumbling over in the Forest area. I thought it was out of order.'

In theory, Keegan did no more than other players in the Bundesliga who exaggerated their tumbles after tackles. Although the Forest defenders did manage to keep the England captain out of harm's way without being penalized by the Portuguese referee, they had no say in three Hamburg attacks which could have brought the Germans precious goals but for the flying magnificence of Peter Shilton. His first save from Bernard Nogly was the most memorable because the Hamburg defender's shot winged to Shilton's right, then decided to alter course with an alarming swerve so that the Forest goalkeeper was forced to change direction with the crowd screaming 'Ole'. He still managed to make contact at the last second. Keegan could scarcely avoid giving 'Shilts' a murmured congratulatory sigh. Shilton had two more saves registered on his evening's work, the second pleasing him most of all because of the way he reacted so quickly for such a big man. He had to punch the ball away before Milewski could get his head to a flick-on from the massive Horst Hrubesch who had made contact from a corner. Keegan was involved in the third save which ultimately broke the Hamburg team. He found room, for once, in the crowded Forest box to chest the ball down for Milewski to deliver a half-volley which was directed towards the left-hand corner of

Shilton's goal. 'That's OK,' Keegan thought momentarily, 'now we'll do Brian's lot in extra-time.' But somehow, Shilton once again proved the master, leaping to palm the ball away in panther-like style.

Game, set and match to Clough and Taylor and no bitterness from Keegan who warmly shook hands with his British teammates. It was a blow to Gunter Netzer's team to be beaten by a closed door, and a blow especially acute for Keegan who had wanted to leave Bundesliga football with a European Cup winners' medal.

Despite his disappointments, Keegan could not complain about the klaxon-blaring, flag waving farewells he received from his German fan club when Hamburg beat Schalke 4–0. 'I wanted to play in the second half,' he said, 'but the trainer thought it best that I should rest the knee. I could run straight but when I turned I felt a shot of pain. The club doctor suspects ligament trouble, but I think it might be a cartilage. I'll be having a second opinion on Monday, when I join the England team, preparing for the European Championships.'

Keegan was sorry to miss the second half. 'There is no such thing as a nice farewell,' he said. 'The fans were great to me, but then they always were. As for this knock, I'll be in Italy if I have to go there on crutches.'

Keegan's knee injury would be worrying news for Ron Greenwood. With Trevor Francis already lost to the England squad through injury, the hint of Keegan knee troubles had to be taken seriously with the European Championships just over a week away. Hopefully, the injury would not prevent him playing in the opening match against Belgium in Italy. But Keegan had played a formidable amount of football recently and knees tended to be very sensitive. He flew to London early on the Sunday morning for England duty on a Lufthansa flight from Hamburg to avoid a tear-jerking farewell at the airport. He was met at Heathrow by the national press, eager for his views on the knee injury which could have put him out of the European Championships. It was a major scare, but Keegan, following a knee scan, made a remarkable recovery in time for England's first match against Belgium in Turin.

Kevin Keegan's Merseyside flit to Hamburg coincided with Ron Greenwood's arrival as England manager to succeed Don Revie, whose disloyalty the new appointment thoroughly disapproved of, though Greenwood still admired his predecessor's great gifts as manager of Leeds United. Keegan had been fairly untried as a senior international when Revie took over, with only two caps won under Ramsey's regime. But the Doncaster kid had won a full quota of caps under Revie, as a leader and captain, able to face the new boss on fairly equal terms without being overawed or unnerved by him. Greenwood wasn't that type anyway. He liked to get on with players. He was open and friendly, but being slightly shy, he could withdraw, especially from the media when he felt obliged.

Greenwood admired Kevin Keegan. He had seen enough of his performances for Liverpool to know how valuable such leadership would be. Greenwood noted that Keegan quickly added a wider dimension to his all-round game after joining Hamburg. However, like the German club, Greenwood was not always certain whether to give him a striking role or play him in midfield. It was a cross which Keegan had to bear for most of his career. It was while up-front for England under Greenwood that he looked most effective. As Trevor Francis noted, 'It was difficult to fathom things out. For example, I really enjoyed playing with Keegan up-front against Hungary in May 1978, when we got four goals. Yet the manager didn't seem happy about this. There was a time when he seemed to think Keegan was better in midfield, yet his best position is up-front. I wish I had been given the chance to play with him more often. There was a four-year gap before we played together against Northern Ireland and again England got four.'

If Keegan and Francis were rarely seen playing in striking partnership, the uncanny understanding between Keegan and Trevor Brooking would become a feature of England's mixed performances in the European Championships and the World Cup qualifying matches. Both obviously enjoyed playing together, and took part in two wonderful defence-splitting moves which defeated Italy in a World Cup qualifying match at Wembley, unfortunately, to no avail because it was Italy who qualified for Argentina.

Keegan thought the goal he scored in that World Cup qualifying match against Italy was one of his very best.

'Trevor Brooking fired a beautifully flighted cross deep into the Italian penalty area. I raced towards the near post to meet it with my head and sent the ball wide of the goalkeeper, Dino Zoff, inside the far post. I was able to return the compliment later in the game when my through-ball let Trevor through for his first international goal.'

But while goals like these provided happy foretastes of the momentum Greenwood and the nation hoped the team might achieve in the European Championships and the World Cup, two years later too many obstacles combined to destroy any chance of the manager going out in style. Obstacles like injuries to Keegan and Brooking in Spain in 1982 were the final straw. While Greenwood had to shoulder some of the blame for failure, he and his assistant, Bill Taylor, who died tragically young, and his replacement, Don Howe, did not always get the expected commitment from their squad players. As Don Howe once said, 'Perhaps we should worry less about what they are used to when they are with their individual clubs and concentrate more on what we require of them in an England shirt.' Keegan, of course, was never less than willing to work himself 100 percent for the Greenwood cause. But the many fickle performances around him tended to drain his energy and the ultimate killer instinct which mattered.

In one that didn't, against West Germany in Munich on a snowbound pitch, Keegan impressed the German crowd by matching the explosive Rainer Bonhof in the many tussles they had in midfield. It was not until Keegan came off that Bonhof shot a goal past Ray Clemence which caught a deflection off Mick Mills. Keegan's form was enough to show the German audience he really did have the world-class qualities that had eluded him at Hamburg early on in his first season.

The Wembley crowd had plenty of opportunities to see the

Keegan–Brooking combination working in the European Championship qualifying games. The only match Keegan missed – in a group containing Denmark, Northern Ireland, the Republic of Ireland and Bulgaria – was against the Bulgarians when the match was postponed because of fog until the next night, when Keegan had to fly back for first team duty to Hamburg. That disappointed him, because he had been scoring goals at Wembley including the winner against Denmark and two against the Republic, while Greenwood could never swear on getting a settled side out because of injuries and club commitments. Keegan, for instance, had missed the British Championships before England left for Italy in May 1980, because Hamburg were involved with League matches.

Somehow there was always a feeling that Keegan and Brooking in tandem would be the players with the say. It's a chemistry hard to define. Keegan and Brooking, when they were playing especially well together, nursed each other's special gifts. It didn't always come off, and the soufflé often went flat, but they worked at their partnership during hours of practice with Ron Greenwood. As Brooking said, 'As a midfield player, when I got possession I would hope to have two or three alternatives to give the ball to. I would look up, and more often than not the best option was Kevin because of his tremendous work-rate and his eagerness to shake off his markers. From his point of view, he said that having watched me at different times, he would have an idea of what I was going to do. And he started reading me as I started reading him, and in the end there was such an appreciation of each other's style that we were able to read and anticipate each other's game very well.'

Keegan was equally appreciative of Brooking's awareness of how to get his partner into goal scoring positions.

'Trevor thinks quickly, plays balls into space and I understand him. He has put goals on a plate for me during international games. Some people think Trevor's a luxury, because he doesn't fall back too often or pick-up opponents. I think he is a luxury every team ought to afford, because he creates goals, entertains and delivers the sort of pass that makes good players better.'

With his stocky build and muscular strength, Keegan reminded Brooking of Diego Maradona and enjoyed the moments when Kevin would scurry past some bemused defender on receipt of Brooking's perfectly weighted pass and deliver one of his deadly salvoes at goal. In Brooking's opinion, the Bundesliga made him much sharper.

'The three years that Keegan spent at Hamburg enhanced his game further, teaching him in particular not to be overcome by man-to-man marking, and his status in the game was acknowledged when he won the European Footballer of Year title in consecutive seasons. His years abroad inevitably broadened his character. He as a comedian and motivator in the dressing room and a good captain who always conducted himself as befits a top sporting personality. Kevin was a great example to youngsters, just as Bobby Charlton had been, years before.'

The real proof of such an understanding between two fine athletes should certainly have taken place in Italy during the 1980 European Championships. But Keegan's ligament troubles, which had needed a medical scan of his right knee on his return to Britain following that farewell match in Hamburg, slowed him up a vital yard or two, as England went out in the first round. They drew with Belgium, lost to Italy and beat Spain. The continuing failure of England to score goals was shown by the constant changes Greenwood made up-front. David Johnson played against Belgium, Garry Birtles was substituted by Paul Mariner against Italy and Keegan found himself thrust into the strike force for the last match against Spain as a partner to Tony Woodcock in Naples. Keegan looked far more at home in this position; he had irritated his manager by playing far too defensively in midfield against Italy.

Trevor Brooking had been left out of the Italian match in favour of Ray Kennedy because Greenwood said, 'Trevor tended to float a bit, following his nose and instinct, while Ray's presence was more solid. I could see him filling our left area as he did for Liverpool.' But it was Keegan who tended to drift back into his own defence in a tense match at the Communale Stadium, Turin. Such indulgences by Keegan left his manager open-mouthed. Keegan would go scurrying back to help his defenders in a way he would never have done under his beloved Shanks or Paisley. This allowed his tenacious marker, Marco Tardelli, to work on a few options of his own, like forgetting Keegan from time to time, and going off on raiding mission of his own. Greenwood declared Keegan's defensive mission 'a responsible desire, but he overdid it. He was always dropping back, and the deeper Kevin dropped back, the more Tardelli pushed up. He was constantly in a position to threaten us.'

Without Brooking's inspirational probing in midfield, which Greenwood re-instated for the next match against Spain, England lacked passion in the area where it mattered. Birtles struggled on his debut, and although Kennedy hit the Italian crossbar with a volley which utterly defeated Dino Zoff playing in his own Juventus arena, there was more likelihood of a goal for the home team as the match entered its final stages. Phil Neal sold himself through a woebegone tackle on Francesco Graziani, leaving the Italian forward time to streak through and lay on a splendid, low cross for Marco Tardelli to smash his shot past Clemence. Greenwood faulted Keegan for allowing the Italian to break away from him in the first place.

'I felt very sorry for Keegan because he had the burning desire to do well, but a long, hard and eventually disappointing season was telling against him. His time and comments were much in demand. There were always people around who could see profit in him.'

Keegan had attended a press conferences at England's training camps up near the Swiss border at Asti, and at Salerno, on the coast near Naples and there was bound to be the odd unscrupulous operator around to make a fast buck out of the mildest verbal slip-up by the English captain. There was also a cunning move by some photographers to have Keegan photographed with an attractive model, but the plot was put down before any embarrassing photographs could be sent to Milan and Rome for lurid reproduction.

With the World Cup qualifying games coming up and a new berth at Southampton at the start of the 1980/1 season, Keegan's final match in these championships against Spain proved much more enjoyable after the first two disappointments against Belgium and Italy. The Belgium match was drawn 1–1, with England's goal coming from perhaps the most polished performer in the England squad that summer, Ray Wilkins. The game was marred by the familiar sight of England fans rioting in the Communale Stadium. Ray Clemence was overcome by tear gas fumes burning his eyes, and Keegan and the rest of the players had to stand-by while the goalkeeper was treated by the medics. Keegan, like his manager, was enraged. The afternoon had not gone well, with a Tony Woodcock goal dubiously ruled out, and defensive slopiness allowing Belgium to equalize. Keegan made a statement saying: 'I have aways been very proud of our fans. But today I'm ashamed to be English. Ninty-five per cent of our fans here in Turin are great. Five per cent are just drunks.' Later, after England had failed to reach the next round, Keegan was prepared to accept the inadequacies of his team. 'We failed abysmally in our group, but now we have a gauge for the 1982 World Cup.'

Keegan's reference to a 'gauge' applied ironically to his own form, as he left Italy cheering his fellow Hamburg forward, the giant Horst Hrubesch, as he scored the winning goal for West Germany against Belgium in the Rome final. The eyes of England's captain hardly sparkled with that customary Keegan optimism and self-confidence. There were hints, though fleeting ones, that England's captain was concerned about his own future as an international player. His manager's habit of shuffling his options, with Keegan moved to midfield and back again into a striking role, had achieved most success in the last game against Spain after Keegan had moved up-front as part of a Brooking–Woodcock–Keegan triangle. With players like Terry McDermott, Ray Wilkins, the maturing Glenn Hoddle and Bryan Robson in the team, there were plenty of skilful colleagues around to give Keegan the ball. Keegan did not score, but Brooking and Woodcock did, as the other members of the triangle. So Keegan could feel pleased that some success had come out of an overall England performance he had called abysmal. How long, however, could Greenwood afford to include Keegan in his team with a fully-fit Trevor Francis back on the availability list again, and Glenn Hoddle working hard to prove he must become a regular with his large lobby of admirers? The harshest critics were already saying Keegan was over the hill a year before his 30th birthday. No longer capable of that inexhaustible energy and industry he had shown for Liverpool in the mid-1970s under Paisley. Keegan knew the knives were out in some quarters, but first he had to see through a major move from Hamburg to Hampshire where he had acquired a new house.

Keegan said goodbye to Greenwood knowing they would meet more regularly now Keegan would be performing in the First Division at the Dell for Lawrie McMenemy. Greenwood appreciated this because with the World Cup qualifying games due to start in five weeks time with a match against Norway at Wembley, he needed players to be in close contact with Lancaster Gate. Greenwood knew the qualifying matches ahead against Norway, Switzerland and Hungary would provide many problems and many difficulties. He would be putting his neck on the judgment mantlepiece and Keegan, with his general optimism and cheery good humour, would be invaluable to Greenwood when difficulties cropped up.

6
SOUTHAMPTON

Kevin Keegan's first season at Southampton was predictably given a rapturous reception with American-style razzmatazz, and, along the south coast, a rush to buy season tickets. Lawrie McMenemy saw to it that, as Kevin Keegan's manager, his most spectacular of soccer signings should wear his red and white Saints shirt for the maximum possible media exposure.

Keegan was happy to settle among the old faces he had known since his earliest days with England – Dave Watson, Alan Ball, Charlie George and his best friend of all, Mick Channon, back after playing for Vancouver in Canada. All looked rosy at the Dell for McMenemy, Keegan, and the team. They were raring to go, but as often happens in big-time football, somebody stuck a small spanner in Keegan's works, the spanner being a succession of tiresome injuries.

There had been no hint of trouble when Keegan first started kicking a football in earnest for Southampton. His arrival, after three years in West Germany, was welcomed by the media, naming Keegan as just the 'knight in shining armour' to bring some sanity to a game being suffocated by crowd violence. The riot at Turin had sickened television viewers at home and the game desperately needed leaders like Keegan to show that Saturday afternoons should be enriched by entertainment, not the crunch of battered skulls. The high attendance, over 20,000, which Southampton attracted during those early months of the 1980/1 season was proof of Keegan's high regard as a crowd-puller and known superstar. For example, at an early match at Highbury with Southampton, the visitors proved an irresistible attraction to the crowd of over 40,000 crowd squeezed into every corner of the ground, turning the stadium into one of those concentrated, claustrophobic, corned beef tins that was a regular sight during the mass attendances following the Second World War. Stanley Matthews was the star attraction then – now it was Keegan who was on show. The atmosphere was enough to make youngsters like Nick Hornby feel frightened for the first time at the pressure put on them by the surrounding hoards anxious for a glimpse of Kev.

In *Fever Pitch*, his absorbing 1992 autobiographical ramble recalling the joys and hazards of being an Arsenal fan, Hornby made mention of that August evening.

'Something went wrong. They hadn't opened enough turnstiles, or the police had made a pig's ear of controlling the crowd flow, and there was a huge crush outside the North Bank entrances on the Avenell Road. I could pick both my legs up and remained pinioned, and at one stage, I had put my arms in the air to give myself just that little bit more room and to stop my fists digging into my chest and stomach. It wasn't anything that special really. Fans have all been in situations where for a few moments things look bad. But I remember struggling for breath when I approached the front of the queue (I was so constricted that I couldn't fill my lungs properly) which means it was a little bit worse than usual. When I finally got through the turnstile I sat down on a step for a while, gave myself time to recover, and I noticed that a lot of other people were doing the same.'

Mercifully, there were no serious casualties. As for Keegan, his performance on the night of Hornby's great crush was hardly world class. Brian Glanville in the *Sunday Times* hinted that Keegan was turning from a busy ant into a grasshopper.

'Keegan needs to pace himself, and play to his true strengths – he should stay up front despite a temptation at his age to pull out of the front line where it hurts.'

Keegan did start getting hurt, and often. McMenemy lost the services of his new star through a number of injuries, serious enough to keep Keegan out of the England team, who had started their World Cup '82 qualifying matches. It was no consolation to the manager that Keegan should have been awarded the coveted Best Dressed Man of the Year award for his all-round dress sense (not including the famous perm) by the esteemed Menswear Association of Great Britain. It was all very well for Kevin to look smart, but too many matches were going by with a reserve player in his place in the team.

Keegan's absences were alarming. He only missed 16 matches through injury during his entire career at Anfield, but in his first season at Southampton he was forced to pull out of eight of the first 20 matches before Christmas. It seemed the sleek, physically awesome trunk of Keegan's physique, which was about to celebrate its thirtieth birthday, was beginning to develop a few cracks in its superstructure. Keegan's injuries were not confined to one special region of pain. During those early months at Southampton, his problems ranged far and wide. First, a damaged left-ankle ligament, then a pulled hamstring, then a left-eye knock, a right-hamstring strain, and finally a cut on his right shin. The injuries came and went, with Keegan moping in the stands. Results were hardly marvellous, although there were occasions when Keegan's presence did help to bring some welcome victories. February saw Keegan free from injury again, and welcoming his part in a run which saw Lawrie McMenemy's team gain six consecutive wins and remain unbeaten for 12 matches. Their first unbeaten run had lasted up until 13 September when, without Keegan, they were beaten 1–0 at Norwich.

Charlie George revealed the sometimes tetchy, prima-donna-like side to his nature, by shoving the ball into the face of an *Eastern Daily Press* photographer, Jack Spencer, who had retrieved the ball for him to take a corner. George's manager took Spencer into the Southampton dressing room after the game where George apologized and shook hands with the offended photographer. It was not the last of the upheavals involving the Southampton stars, but Lawrie McMenemy's prompt action showed he was not going to stand any nonsense from his players, even if they were famous stars on large salaries.

The Keegans had moved into an isolated, rural Hampshire world of gymkhanas, pony academies, bridge parties, and tennis-club barbecues on the Solent. Keegan was never far away from the resident golf courses available to him, while Channon rarely allowed a day to pass without discussing the day's turf form. Their home at Chandlersford near Romsey was one of those large, red-bricked mansions overlooking the statutory green, gleaming stretch of lawn and fronted by a first-floor balcony on which the England captain and his wife could sunbathe. On the lawn below was a slide for Laura Jane, and numerous toy gadgets. Access could be gained to the lawn through two sliding glass doors on each corner of the house. Here, Lawrie and Anne McMenemy regularly came to dine as the manager and his head-boy became close in everything to do with Southampton FC. Lawrie's wife, Anne, provided valuable advice about New Forest life, and the best ways to not get on the wrong side of some of the snooty colonel's widows or colonial civil servants who ringed the area.

While Keegan sometimes had to vacate this bricked paradise to go off and play football, one date at Anfield was especially circled for Keegan's benefit on the Dell manager's calendar. Although Keegan had been back to Anfield with Hamburg when his team had received a 6-0 drubbing, the chance of playing against Bob Paisley's side in a proper League match was irresistible. Keegan could barely wait to get up North – despite the risky outcome from the visitor's point of view. Liverpool were on their way to winning the League Cup after a replay against West Ham, and the European Cup, for the third time, through Alan Kennedy's goal in Paris. Their eventual fifth place in the League, one place ahead of Southampton, was not of the standard normally expected from them, but goals had not come frequently enough. Ian Rush was about to change all that once he had earned a regular first-team berth in Kenny Dalglish's company the following season. Keegan felt bloated with nostalgia on that late February afternoon at Anfield, when at least the Kop was more respectful of his bounding arrival from the tunnel from where he used to come out almost drenched with verbal hero worship. The *Sunday Telegraph* representative recorded another sad afternoon for Keegan, and for his team which went down 2–0.

Over 40,000 were at Anfield to give a guarded but polite welcome to the 1977 Liverpool European Cup hero of Rome. Kevin Keegan was back, playing his first League game at Anfield since leaving Hamburg. But Keegan was well policed by Alan Hansen, one of the three regulars returning to Liverpool's first strength side since 5 November, and produced only limited reminders of his epic career at Anfield. Not that an improved Liverpool side achieving a fairly comfortable victory after six matches without a win were especially concerned about nostalgia yesterday, or, indeed the presence of their old star. An overriding topic was their European Cup first leg quarter final against the Bulgarian military yeomen of CSKA Sofia...'

Liverpool won the match by two clever goals scored by Keegan's former colleagues Ray Kennedy and Terry McDermott. If Keegan was subdued, there was much to admire in the play of two less famous members of the Southampton team, the Yugoslav Ivan Golac, and overlapping right-back Graham Baker. With these two fitting in so well with some of the better-known names McMenemy assembled for the new term, Southampton progressed towards the next season in which they had qualified for the UEFA Cup with optimism. Although Keegan was worried over Lawrie' s lack of reserve in depth, there was every indication that Southampton would enjoy a good run in the League.

For England, Ron Grenwood handed the captaincy to Emlyn Hughes until the time he decided Hughes was no longer part of his team selection plans and told him so by phone, when he handed the captaincy back again to Keegan. Keegan had half-agreed with Greenwood about his geographical status being wrong for England, but not when he brooded more about it later.

'I couldn't pretend not to be disappointed. Once a captain it is natural to want the job permanently and, without contradicting

Greenwood, the most important thing about a captain is not the number on his shirt, but the amount of respect the other players have for him.'

Unlike Alf Ramsey, who had the invaluable leadership of Bobby Moore on the pitch during most of his managerial spell, Greenwood was playing ducks and drakes on the Hove sea front with his own captaincy choices, the problem still being injuries to Keegan, and Ray Wilkins. Mick Mills would eventually get the captaincy during the World Cup finals in Spain with Keegan again injured. And why not? Mills was a superb leader at Ipswich Town and popular with his team-mates. Just the right credentials to make him suitable for the job. But knowing Keegan and his ambition and pride, he must have been envious of Mills.

Keegan didn't show at all in Greenwood's World Cup qualifying teams until after the friendly against Spain in March 1981, but he was fit and available to play in the important summer World Cup games which were of major importance if England were to travel to Spain. At Wembley, they had beaten Norway comfortably enough by four goals and also Switzerland, but suffered a 2–1 defeat to the mean Rumanians in Bucharest. In some national newspapers, Greenwood's job was still very much on the line. There were calls for Greenwood's head to roll as quickly as possible – much the same as there would be with his successors, Bobby Robson and Graham Taylor. Greenwood was in a stew – and clinging on. But he was hardly comforted by such tabloid entreaties as 'For God's sake, Ron, pack up'.

Thus it was a relief to know Keegan was stripping off again in the Basle dressing rooms for England's next match against Switzerland. Greenwood gave Keegan, the born leader, a midfield role with Trevor Francis and Paul Mariner up front. When the Swiss got down to business, all the old creaking imperfections in England's game began to show up and the old jinx, which had played havoc with visiting England teams in the past, told again as Greenwood's team were given an embarrassing beating. Despite Terry McDermott scoring, Keegan and his team-mates had to face the bludgeoning roar of disapproval of the English press after the 2–1 defeat. Keegan hated losing, and what a game at which to earn a recall. As Trevor Francis said after being substituted by McDermott at half-time:

'It was a terrible result. We conceded two bad goals. The feeling was we would have liked to have gone home and prepared for our match against Hungary on English soil.'

Greenwood decided to keep the England squad in Zurich, making his players work harder than they had ever done under him. Unknown to Keegan and his colleagues, Greenwood had already decided to quit the England manager's job and planned to make the announcement when the team returned home after the Hungary game in Budapest.

'The Swiss result threatened to torpedo our chances of reaching the World Cup finals. My 'first' retirement (the second came officially after the finals) came during a period of failure and bitter criticism that made me feel I had somehow let my country down.'

Don Howe, Arsenal's assistant manager, was particularly fastidious, shouting orders which demanded respect, no matter how valuable an international thought himself worth. Howe, unlike Greenwood, was not an ardent Keegan fan, and it was always thought to be his vote which swayed the manager into not picking Keegan to start the World Cup match against Spain in Madrid a year later.

When the England party flew to Budapest, players and media alike were unaware that the manager had already told Dick Wragg, the chairman of the FA International Committee and Ted Croker that he would be retiring from his post directly after the match against Hungary. Enough was enough. The embarrassing defeat in Basle had been the last straw. Although Wragg and Croker had both asked him to change his mind Greenwood was adamant.

What must have surprised Wragg and Croker was Greenwood's optimism about the outcome of the World Cup match in Budapest. There was something Keeganesque in the way he confidently forecasted an England win without spluttering, coughing, or mumbling. Greenwood was clear in his mind, England would win the match, and he would make sure they did.

In Hungary, there was much bowing and scraping for Keegan, with interviews galore, and Don Howe trying his best to round up players wandering towards enticing gift shops, full of the gypsy magic of the Hungarian plain.

When Keegan retired to the hotel room he shared with Trevor Brooking, the last thing on his mind was the odd rumour that Ron Greenwood might be packing in the England job. Greenwood had looked confident and relaxed at dinner. He was not a quitter, and the very idea that he might have become so disillusioned and demeaned sailed way over Keegan's head. The most important topic was the team that Greenwood, with Howe's advice, would select. Players who had not done well in Basle had every reason to expect the axe. Keegan retained his place, although Greenwood switched him into a striking role up-front with Paul Mariner. Trevor Francis took his own omission more calmly than he had in Buenos Aires under Don Revie, but Kenny Sansom was deeply aggrieved at being dropped – Don Howe, his coach at Arsenal, having come to the rescue as Sansom behaved like an affronted warrior. Sansom had never been dropped from the England side before, so the experience was a shattering blow. But unlike Keegan, who felt similarly about being dropped by Don Revie, Sansom did not have home comforts to run off to. He moped in his room with Keegan and the players who had actually been selected, trying their best to keep the South London boy's spirits up.

Greenwood, who was still sitting on his own personal retirement bomb, had happy memories of recalling Trevor Brooking, who in the past had linked up so well with Keegan. He could afford to take a chance since they had played so devastatingly well together. They were friends and they knew each other's games like kid brothers. Francis, another Swiss discard, watched England's 'make or break' match from the bench.

'There was a time when Hungary equalized just before half-time when it didn't look too great for us. Brooking had put us in front. Yet I wasn't looking forward to the second-half. Ray Clemence was to blame for the equalizer, and he spent most of half-time in the shower area, he was feeling so low. But it all

167

came right, Brooking silencing the crowd with a fantastic left-foot shot, the best he has ever hit, to put us in front again, and it was all over when Kevin Keegan scored from a penalty, 18 minutes from the end. I have no doubt it brought immense satisfaction and relief to Greenwood, especially against Hungary, the country which for so long had been his inspiration.'

Brooking's goal was a peach. Greenwood still relishes the memory of it.

'Trevor's second goal was certainly a pearl. Phil Neal found Keegan in space on the right and he picked out Brooking who was coming up in the box at speed. Trevor's left foot made perfect contact and the ball went into the net with such power that it forced its way behind a stanchion and lodged there. Keegan deserved a goal for that pass alone and he eventually got one that was all his own. He was brought down by Garaba and, as the penalty was given, he kept hold of the ball, placed it quickly, picked his spot and put the game beyond Hungary's reach. Brooking was now signalling that his groin was giving him trouble and we sent on Ray Wilkins in his place.'

The manager had every right to be pleased. As Francis had noted, the preparation for the Hungary match had been as right as the Swiss one had been wrong. Now Ron trudged off the pitch looking almost happy. As soon as he reached the dressing-room area Ron started looking around for the two heroes, his warriors of old, Trevor and Kevin. Where were they? He couldn't find them. Somebody waved a thumb towards the cacophony of the crowded corridor area. 'Television interviews'.

Greenwood was pained, he wanted his two stars to be there. Only a minute or two would have been enough, but neither had shunned their manager on purpose – they'd simply been swept away in the euphoria for television interviews. Keegan was delighted to tell the England supporters back home, how happy and relieved the team was when it saw Trevor score that classic, second goal. It finished Hungary 1, England 3 – now the pressure was off Greenwood at least until the autumn.

When the players heard the manager's decision to go, there were rumblings of disbelief. Kevin Keegan's response was short, but thorough in its surprised reaction to a man walking out of a job – something, ironically, he almost did himself eleven years later. 'You're out of order'. While other voices were more abstract in their answers, hoping the boss would change his mind. Keegan was more positive, 'We want you to reconsider your decision.' Greenwood smiled wryly. He was already reconsidering.

Once again, an airport collection area would become a place of drama for Kevin Keegan. It was Keegan, in his capacity as a senior England player and captain, who joined Mick Mills and Trevor Francis in trying to persuade a reluctant, though persuadable, Ron Greenwood to change his mind on the management issue as they wheeled their empty trolleys towards the luggage arrival ramp. There was no Frank Worthington around on this occasion to walk through a plate-glass door with his trolley as in Budapest in 1974, which had alerted every security guard in the area before Keegan was beaten up by menacing Yugoslav police. At Luton there was a celebratory atmosphere in the arrival lounge – wives and families parading for the big welcome. Keegan and the two other players had time for a quick chat with Greenwood as they waited for the luggage to appear. Kevin issued an authoritative message: 'We started this thing together – let's finish it together.' Mills said in mock seriousness, 'If you do retire, I'll never speak to you again.'

By the time the luggage appeared and customs were waiting to be cleared, Ron Greenwood had changed his mind. 'All right', Greenwood told the trio and a number of other England players who had joined them. 'I'll tell Mr Wragg. I'll give it until after the World Cup.' Half a dozen English voices, including Keegan's, murmured a unified 'Great'. But although the victory against Hungary had been a superb one, warding off some overreactive media criticism, the manager would not escape more savagery, particularly when England lost 2–1 to Norway in Oslo, the following September. It was a lamentable result, which caused Kevin Keegan to suffer more than a few bouts of 'black dog' depression afterwards, so elementary had England's performance been against the Scandinavians.

As Greenwood said afterwards, 'Our victory in Hungary brought me some of the finest moments in my life. Our defeat at Oslo provided some of the worst.' Trevor Francis remembered meeting Keegan in a Manchester hotel following the Norwegian fiasco – and they could barely speak to each other out of embarrassment. Playing for England was still a great honour, but if this was going to be the end-product, was it worth it? England finally did get to Spain, clinging to a tightrope all the way, helped intrinsically by the sweet-and-sour Swiss, who proceeded to take three points off Rumania and England were able to keep their second position in Group Four behind Hungary. Keegan savoured the victory over Hungary, achieved through a Mariner goal at Wembley, which stamped their passport for Spain in the last qualifying match of the programme.

For Keegan, there was still a full league programme ahead with Southampton, one of the main contenders to take the title. But warning clouds were beginning to hover over the Dell, making any thought of the approaching Espagna '82 almost minuscule in the England player's mind.

There had been no sign of the stresses lying ahead as Keegan assembled with Lawrie McMenemy's team for the 1981/2 season. Keegan had settled into a way of outdoor life in Hampshire, almost Utopian compared with the back streets of his Doncaster youth some 25 years earlier. Keegan could lean on the sympathetic, paternal shoulders of Lawrie when he wanted advice – the pair's friendliness could not be questioned. They travelled together a great deal on charity missions to the Northern stations near their birthplaces, McMenemy gaining much support from Keegan in promoting his friend Brendan Foster's new athletics stadium venture at Gateshead. Southampton were often on tour, including one memorable trip to the United States, when Keegan, Ball and Channon, Southampton's 'Three Musketeers', found themselves flat broke after losing all their cash at the tote during a race meeting. It was Channon's fault, mixing up number of the horse and getting a losing ticket.

'I remember going back to Kevin and Bally, and they couldn't believe it.' Ball's squeaky reaction could be heard from LA to

New England.

Channon and Keegan were not always lucky with their gee-gee ventures, although their joint love of horses provided the pair with an ideal hobby away from the pressures of the First Division. Southampton were occupied by UEFA Cup commitments as well. It was great having their gee-gees so close at hand after leaving the intensely patriotic Hampshire atmosphere of the Dell, where crowds of 22,000 regularly turned up to watch them take part in some exciting, high-scoring matches. McMenemy had put together a potential trophy-winning team. Apart from the Revie-discarded Ball, and Greenwood-discarded Channon, there were a number of match-winners including the balding David Armstrong, who had arrived from Middlesbrough, Chris Nicholl, the former Aston Villa centre-back, Nick Holmes, Graham Baker, Steve Moran and Steve Williams, a precocious midfielder who eventually moved to Arsenal.

Williams was arrogant and difficult to get on with, but he found Keegan a hard nut to crack. Channon recalled him once turning on Keegan and asking, 'Who the hell do you think you are?' and Keegan replying, 'I'm something you'll never be, son.' Keegan was right about that – Williams' list of England caps between 1983 and 1985 amounted to six, a modest total for a player with so much potential, and lip.

Horse-training gossip at the New Forest barbecues was all-right for summer nights, but not at training sessions which, as usual, Keegan took very seriously indeed, driving himself beyond the call of duty. McMenemy, his assistant, John Mortimer and coach Lew Chatterley hardly had to gee-up Keegan, whose devotion to duty went beyond reasonable limits. But did Keegan, last back on the coach after training, really have to drive himself so ferociously? Players like Ball and Channon, who knew him well, were not unduly surprised, unless Kevin missed the first race at Goodwood or Plumpton.

Southampton had been going well in the league, impressing visitors to the Dell like Greenwood, and earning such glowing comments as this report in the *Sunday Telegraph* after their 1–0 victory over Everton on 6 September.

'Kevin Keegan, with his third goal in three games, a 53rd-minute penalty, gave the watching Ron Greenwood a warm indication of his present verve at the Dell. Greenwood's sprightly captain not only set up the chance which led to Lyons fouling Channon to give away the spot-kick against this promising Everton side, but he improved after a quiet first half so that he was quite the outstanding performer at the end.

'Everton under their new manager, Howard Kendall, had made a fair start to the season and often looked as if they might out-flank the Southern opposition, but once Keegan got going, Kendall had to abandon his seat in the director's box to organize operations from the trainer's bench.'

Keegan was happy. During a ridiculously tense match against Ipswich Town in early October, he scored his eighth goal of the season, again from the penalty spot at the Dell, when a Keegan-inspired Southampton came back to win 4–3 after being 3–1 down at half-time to beat the UEFA Cup holders. That was almost the style of Liverpool, and Keegan left the Dell that late afternoon with memories of Anfield again, the Kop roaring the Reds on. Now it was the Dell crowds' turn to chant 'Kee-gan, Kee-gan'.

While the Dell roar might lack the Merseyside crescendos, there was a Southern fervour attached to its bark, and Keegan found himself carried along by a large section of the crowd who had found the wee, darting dragonfly an almost irresistible attraction. Everyone hoped Kevin would stay for a good while longer under Lawrie. The Southampton outfit were beginning to look like a team on the brink of a prize they had never won before since they entered the Third Division as founder members in 1920 – the League Championship.

When Malcolm Allison brought his Sporting Lisbon side to play Southampton in a UEFA Cup first leg match at the Dell that autumn, he ran into a home player he admired since his days with Joe Mercer at Manchester City. Before an England match against Wales in 1972, Allison showed he had joined Keegan's admiration society by telling *Express* man James Lawton what 'bubbling promise' Keegan was enriched with. He thought Ramsey would 'introduce Keegan slowly' into the England team, although Ramsey, reacting rather quickly to the lure of Keegan's talents, picked him the next day for his debut against Wales.

Now Keegan was making his way jauntily down the long dressing-room corridor area leading to the director's tea-room. There was Big Mal giving the bubbler a warm smile and handshake. Keegan was very much a pest against Sporting Lisbon, running rings round some tall defenders, but he became frustrated at times by the brilliant goalkeeping of the Hungarian national goalkeeper, Ferenc Meszaros. Sporting lost the first-leg by two goals, Keegan scoring with a penalty driven against one of the Dell stanchions he had been peppering of late, and a diverted shot by Mick Channon, making it 2–0.

The real fireworks lay ahead at the end of September however, when, in the space of eight days, Southampton beat Liverpool at Anfield by a single goal, and after a few days recuperation in the Spanish sunshine, beat Ron Atkinson's expensive, all-star Manchester United 3–2 at the Dell, winning in the final minutes when a move set up by Kevin Keegan led to Steve Moran's cheeky final pass to David Armstrong, who showed what a dangerous striker he had become by hitting the ball beautifully past Roche. It was Keegan's goal which did not count that Southampton supporters talked about on the way home. A goal which, had it counted, would have been among his career best. Few could remember a better one, not indeed the thwarted striker who was naturally upset that the referee annulled such a perfect moment with one stark blow of the whistle after a linesman raised his flag for offside.

There was a touch of Pele in the way Keegan had soared up to meet a centre from Mick Channon, hooking the ball back over his head into the top corner of the net. The United team were dumbfounded, world-class players like Ray Wilkins and Brian Robson letting their mouths hang open with astonishment at the strike. Yet, it did not count and both Channon and Armstrong owned up later to being the guilty offside players.

With England at last having qualified for the World Cup finals, Keegan had every right to feel cock-a-hoop that Christmas. New Year trouble was brewing though and would endanger the great harmony between Big Lawrie, whom Channon had nicknamed 'The Ayatollah', and the superstar from Doncaster. It didn't come straight away, because the Southampton side performed so well they were seven points clear at the top of the First Division at one stage. But Liverpool, slow starters that season, began to make up ground after winning only six of their first 16 games. Ian Rush, making a regular scoring impact for Liverpool, had been on the payroll at the Dell. Southampton would almost certainly prove catchable, but Rush wasn't, and Southampton fell back.

To see Southampton slipping in the championship race worried the superstar to such an extent that he began seeking out his manager to warn him that the side needed strengthening on the way. No offence was meant towards the current Southampton squad, but a critical injury to Steve Moran had put the striker out of action and his replacements failed to deliver.

Keegan has always been a firm believer in going into the transfer market if a side is in need of fresh faces to see them through a tricky situation in late season. (As manager of Newcastle, he soon began asking for new first-team blood on the payroll – and almost walked out when his board failed to react.) At Southampton, Keegan believed Lawrie should have taken his advice and by not doing so, blew a great chance of winning the title. However, McMenemy didn't react, and Southampton started losing games they would have won earlier on in the season. They were getting nervous, nothing was going right. Meanwhile, Keegan was fuming. McMenemy tried to look calm, putting on the charm to alleviate fears that his team had blown the championship – but draws at Notts County and Coventry were not good enough results to win championships.

After one particular match, which Southampton lost at home to Aston Villa, McMenemy really did react with fury. He accused the team of not pulling their weight, and went for Keegan too, who was astonished by the allegation. Keegan, always tried, and was ready to run himself into the ground for the team. What McMenemy had said was grossly unfair. From then on, things went downhill and as Keegan told Bob Case of the *Sun* after he had joined Newcastle the following season, their former close relationship was finished. McMenemy had accused Keegan of 'cheating' and although Keegan kept on pushing the manager, to buy new players, the close season was approaching and Keegan was already on his way to another club.

Keegan certainly over-reacted to McMenemy's show of temper in the dressing rooms. While McMenemy was wrong to suggest, in the heat of the moment, that Keegan wasn't pulling his weight, Kevin was silly to create the storm he did. Like many such rows, however, the pair made things up eventually. Sadly, the whole business looks, in retrospect, to have been an unnecessary squabble between two usually level-headed friends. In McMenemy's case, he had taken on a tough assignment as Southampton's manager and had signed some well-known stars, in the Indian summer of their careers, who had a tendency to give quotes to Fleet Street at the slightest murmur of discontent in their own headquarters. Peter Osgood proved he could chat away when he wanted to, and Alan Ball, who had spent a successful period playing for Vancouver in the North American League, wasn't exactly a retiring personality when asked to give his cantankerous views about the game. McMenemy was highly skilful at treating his older players as 'distinguished professionals', but like so many edgy 'artists', they needed their egos constantly massaged, not realizing that but for McMenemy they might have been in the dole queue.

Ball would soon become manager at nearby Portsmouth, but as the senior citizen of the Three Musketeers, he was inclined to take Keegan's view that an opportunity was being wasted just at the time that Southampton were on the brink of their finest hour. The trouble was that Southampton were not in a position at that time to spend freely and McMenemy had to make the most of the players he had already. The irony was that Keegan was picking up awards galore at the time Southampton were going downhill fast. He won the Professional Footballers'

Association Player of the Year Award, and won the Golden Boot Award as leading scorer in the First Division with 26 goals. He couldn't have complained about his own performances that season, probably some of the finest of his career, but his relationship with McMenemy and the club became unworkable. Not that his loyal Southampton fan club noticed the split coming. Season ticket sales for the following season were up again owing to the expectancy of seeing Keegan and the team capturing the big prize at last. When they heard Keegan would not be around, there were cries of outrage.

McMenemy doesn't like to discuss this particular part of Keegan's short but eventful stay at Southampton, preferring to heap praises on Newcastle's new manager whom he respects both as a friend and former player.

'He [Keegan] does things that haven't been done before. He had those hallmarks as a player. He is always determined to make things happen.'

As Southampton were not peaking quite as Keegan's ambitious nature had wanted, the likelihood of Keegan leaving the Dell became more plausible, even though his life with Jean in Hampshire seemed so cosy. Meanwhile, Liverpool were celebrating their 13th League Championship victory and the England party were preparing to leave the following month for the World Cup finals. McMenemy remembers Keegan's departure vividly.

'Manchester United came in first – they must have remembered that incredible goal he scored against them. But then my old pal at Newcastle, Arthur Cox, and chairman Stan Seymour came in. It was incredible really. Newcastle had always been my team – I stood on the terraces and watched them as a kid. So there we were, playing a pre-season friendly at Utrecht with our new goalkeeper Peter Shilton, whom I had bought from Nottingham Forest with the money we had got for Gerry Baker, who went to Manchester City. It was Keegan's last match for Southampton, and while we flew back to Southampton, he flew to Newcastle. It was the start of a great two years for him. He could have retired straight away – but he decided to give it a go as another challenge in another place, which was just like Kevin.'

McMenemy was criticized by the Southampton following for not holding Keegan to his contract – the Mighty Atom having signed a new one only in the previous November. They felt let down, and when their discontent was made known, it could have scarcely failed to reach the notice of the departed player, who moved to St James's Park for the modest sum of £100,000. Keegan did show remorse at moving on so suddenly because he had always been conscious of the need to consider the season-ticket holder or the man on the terraces. But he could be tough when he needed to be. Sentiment would not allow him to linger. Before then, another campaign with England was in store for Keegan.

7
WORLD CUP '82

*T*he most important football prize in Kevin Keegan's career, was offered tantalizingly to him as the World Cup '82 finals were about to start in Spain. For the big event, the England party was gathered in Bilbao in early June for their Group Four matches under Ron Greenwood.

The Northern port of Bilbao was not one the most salubrious venues for Keegan and his colleagues to be based. In Estepona, millionaire playboy country, the Scotland squad managed by Jock Stein had settled in comfortably. There were jokes about the polluted beaches up north, Basque tummy-wobbles, and inclement weather. The odd scribe who came down to visit the Scottish camp confirmed they were staying in paradise compared with the English boys. Constipation and diarrhoea appeared to be rife in Bilbao compared with the shark-fishing, golf-playing paradise of the Costa del Sol. It wasn't a touch of tummy-wobbles which was to cast doubts on Keegan's own dream of getting to the Madrid final with this much-improved England team. A back injury, aggravated in training, blew up to such a degree that there were doubts as to whether Keegan would appear in the first Group Four match against cultured France. Keegan was in despair and becoming increasingly agitated with press enquiries and mass world-media attention. Where Bobby Moore might in his benign, unflappable way have got the interviews out of the way with the minimum of fuss, Keegan overdid the Greta Garbo reaction. His room-mate and friend Trevor Booking, who was also out with a recurring groin strain, did his best to keep the situation in order with his usual East End charm and diplomacy, but Keegan was in a bother, the pain was increasing, he was off his food, and the chances of him playing in the next match against Czechoslovakia were remote. Both Keegan and Brooking played for the second team in a practice match behind closed doors, but Greenwood was already clear in his mind what his selection would be. Trevor Francis, a Revie reject, was one player to benefit by the absence of the two heroes of Budapest, and he publicly said so to David Miller.

'Five days before the opening game, Kevin Keegan hurt his back at the training ground. He carried on but by the end it was troubling him. I didn't think much about it, but 24 hours later he was obviously in real difficulty, with it affecting his walking and movement. I suddenly realized I had a chance of playing, that there was doubt and Kevin himself told one or two of the others that he was pessimistic. It was difficult to put my feelings into words. Having had injuries in the past which cost me caps, I could imagine what he must be feeling. It could not have come at a worse time, yet on the other hand I was delighted now to have a chance of playing. I'm sure any professional would tell you the same.'

Keegan had already got himself into a spot of bother with the Football Association by making comments, during the height of the concurrent Falklands War, concerning his views on the possibility of playing against the enemy, Argentina's football team in Spain. On 7 May he said, 'We are living in this country and must accept its laws. I would be disappointed if we didn't go, but I would support the decision.'

There had been much debate as to whether England should actually take part in the tournament. A strong, patriotic lobby stirred by Mrs Thatcher's frenzied-flag waving had come out against England making the trip, but the Football Association sensibly decided to go through with the tournament whatever the politicians might say. By making his opinions known, Donny socialist Keegan irritated the travelling secretary, Ted Croker.

'Kevin's remarks fuelled the campaign against England taking part. It was an example of Keegan saying the wrong thing at the wrong time. When a person has as much publicity as Kevin, he has to be careful about every word he utters. The year before, his comments about being willing to play for England in Belfast had put us in an embarrassing position as we had received sound advice that it would be inappropriate for us to go.'

Fortunately, such diverting matters, caused by marked hostility towards the English camp in some Spanish newspapers, calmed down once the Argentine forces had surrendered in the Falklands, the day before England played France. Of more concern was the sight of a T-shirted Keegan trundling dispiritedly around the England hotel area, whenever he had abandoned the rooms he shared with Trevor Booking. Croker consulted Greenwood about the two vital injuries and it was decided to fly out Brian Roper, West Ham's honorary consultant surgeon, to give Brooking an injection. Roper's arrival at the England camp was cloaked in a veil of secrecy. The surgeon had already treated Brooking for a similar injury two years before with an injection which worked. So the pair kept their fingers crossed this time. Such an extravagant way of doing things irked Croker, if not Greenwood and Brooking, and he insisted that the FA party, in future, should travel with an orthopaedic specialist as well as a doctor.

Keegan, meanwhile, was desperately spending a night in a Bilbao clinic under the supervision of a football-mad specialist, John Gonzalez, but X-ray analysis failed to show any reasons for the the player's condition. Keegan wanted a game as much as his old Liverpool team-mate, Ray Clemence who had lost his place to Peter Shilton. While Keegan was obviously in too much pain to even contemplate turning out against Czechoslovakia, Ray Clemence was fretting round the England complex almost willing Ron Greenwood to give him the nod, possibly in the game against the weakest team in the group, Kuwait. But Shilton had other ideas and told Greenwood he wanted to keep in maximum shape for the games which were going to matter if England were to reach the final. Poor Clemence's dream subsided and he spent the rest of the competition as a spectator.

The England camp was by now surrounded by pettiness and intrigue, and the accompanying press was in a sour mood about Keegan and their failure to get news of his condition from the manager and coaching staff. What was going on? What happened was that late one night, Keegan cornered Greenwood when he had been out for a stroll. Kevin was fed up, he had been trying in vain to sleep. 'I'm letting everyone down. Do you think it would be better if I went home? Would I be best out of the place?' Keegan was insistent. And he had one major idea he hoped his boss would agree to. It was probably the only way he would get fit enough to play again. Greenwood was curious. The lateness of the hour made Las Tamarises hotel seem like a Hollywood film set with Humphrey Bogart and Peter Lorre locked in a sinister whispered conversation by a moonlit parking lot. 'I want to go to Hamburg,' Keegan said, as if Hamburg was just down the road beyond the first cafe. He had a regular specialist there who had looked after him in the past. If he could get to Madrid there would be a plane waiting there to take him to Hamburg. Keegan remembered making the journey two years before when he played for Hamburg against Nottingham Forest in the European Cup Final. It was fairly quick. He would zip into his old football home and back again in a day or two. Some managers may have laughed this idea off as totally mad; a long trip in an aeroplane could have made the injury worse and besides, how the hell was Kevin going to get to Madrid in the early hours of the morning? It turned out to be easier than either Keegan or Greenwood must have expected. An attractive receptionist offered him her two-seater car, which was at that particular time in the hotel garage. Keegan roared off out of Bilbao, his pockets loaded with pesetas from his manager to be used as expenses.

Greenwood was anxious and disliked lying to the press about Keegan's whereabouts. A World Cup base was hardly the venue to be playing James Bond-style games. His task was to get England through to the Final, and they had started well enough, compared with the Scots, who had been honourably thrashed in Seville by the rampant Brazilians. A chance to play Brazil might come later, in the Final even. A wonderful prospect, and one to aim for, as Keegan turned up four days later, back to his old form. He told Greenwood his Hamburg specialist had done a good job, and he felt better already. Keegan's cover was blown fairly quickly with the world's media groaning for copy about his strange disappearance. Glen Kirton, the FA press officer and normally the most unflappable of human beings, told the press Keegan had simply gone off for treatment somewhere out there, waving his hands in the general direction of the Spanish frontier. Scribes put their heads together. Hamburg could be an obvious place for Keegan to go. Or, on the other hand, he might have gone to Madrid where the medical facilities were first-class. But why the secrecy? Again, Graham Greene should have been flown out from Antibes to write the script as he should have done when Don Revie put on dark glassses and a workman's cap and flew to Dubai.

In the end, Keegan was confirmed to be where he was in the usual bizarre circumstances. Brian Scovell, an experienced *Daily Mail* soccer reporter, remembered how he found out about Keegan's whereabouts. 'I saw Ron coming down the steps of a church in Bilbao. He must have been sightseeing.' Scovell asked Greenwood outright where Keegan was, and expected a shifty answer. 'After all, the whole business had been shifty from start to finish.' The pair stood on the church steps for a moment as Spanish traffic roared by, and dark shadows clung to alleyways. 'Kevin's in Hamburg,' Greenwood said, almost biblically. If the England manager had been wearing a cap, he would surely have touched it with a forefinger and moved discreetly on to buy a postcard or two. 'In Hamburg, back soon'.

Scovell returned to the press centre where Jack Charlton, England's 1966 World Cup centre-half, and future manager of Newcastle United and the Republic of Ireland, was enjoying a stint as a television match analyst. He knew what to do. He had Keegan's home number and dialled. Jean answered and Jack came straight to the point, hanging his accent with a mixture of sympathy, while proceeding with his enquiry. Charlton had his answer straight away, and the news focus switched to the North German port, where the state of Keegan's progress was now of public concern. Greenwood had quietly retired back to running the team in preparation for the next match against West Germany in Madrid, in a second-round Group B match. England's old World Cup foes had been paired with them along with a disillusioned Spanish side, who had been beaten in their own little snake pit at Valencia by Northern Ireland, the surprise team of the competition. There had been unqualified rumours of 'rifts' between Greenwood and Keegan, but this again was almost bound to happen. The single-minded miner's son from Doncaster liked to put his own views forward, something which he had done as a recruit in Alf Ramsey's days, prompting the older boys to wince at such cheek.

Ted Croker was still smarting over Keegan's remarks about playing Argentina, and then to cap it all, Keegan went shooting off on a solo expedition to Hamburg. England should have brought Westminster hospital along with them. It might have been cheaper. 'The Keegan business baffled me,' he wrote huffily later.

The players began feeling the pressures as they strove not only to win matches (they drew in the last of their Group A matches against Kuwait, although England were still confirmed as Group A winners), but sought to keep their walking wounded to a minimum. Bryan Robson, after his splendid performance and early goal against France, had been forced to miss the next two matches. Greenwood had pleased a number of Hoddle admirers by including Glenn against the Czechs and the weaker Kuwaitis, who had brought a camel with them to present to Madrid Zoo.

Keegan had returned from Hamburg, his back no longer being so stiff and painful. The England party moved their headquarters to Navacerrada, a more private oasis in the mountains North-West of Madrid. Brooking's groin strain was also on the mend so Greenwood could bank on having the two 'Royals' back. (Brooking had just received his MBE, Keegan his OBE.) The other players, including Trevor Francis, who had been very much part of the action, had been watching these developments, wondering if Keegan and Brooking's recovery might cost them their own places against the Germans.

Greenwood kept an unchanged team for the German match, which did surprise some of the players with Brooking and Keegan now available. Says Trevor Francis, 'Ever since Keegan had first played for England, almost 10 years before, there had been no more industrious a player, and almost 18 months before he had seemed irreplacable. On the morning the team was announced, he was as enthusiastic as ever in training, giving all in a ten-a-side practice match; but at the finish he was off to the sanctuary of the hotel in a flash to avoid the cameras (some photographers had been literally camping out by the England quarters). To be yesterday's hero is sometimes tougher than attempting to be tomorrow's.'

Keegan's back problem wasn't remotely new among sportsmen of his increasing years. Now, just when it mattered most, he was being held back as he was about to apply full throttle. Off he rushed to his room ahead of Trevor, who would also miss the German match. It was hell for both of them, but they knew full well Greenwood would not have been doing his job had he messed around with a winning team. Keegan did make a statement the day before which helped clear up his own hazy situation.

'Realistically I have no chance of playing against Germany and if the lads go out and win, and I hope they do, then there is no chance of the team being changed except through injury. Hopefully they will carry on winning and that could mean I don't play in the tournament. I have always believed in the old maxim that you don't change a winning team. I've profited from it in the past and now sadly I'm a victim. I'm surprised how I have been able to accept the disappointment. I try to look as if I'm happy. I almost feel like an actor, the way I have to hide my feelings.'

This was true up to a point. Keegan had tried to play down his morose feelings, but not always as successfully as he imagined. Some of his playing colleagues were heartily fed up with his moaning on the training pitch, and moaning off it, but they could see how a player who had always appeared incapable of sitting still must feel, being chained to a Spanish wall by a back condition. However, there was still a World Cup to play for. Or was there? So lifeless and dreadful was England's goalless draw against Germany that Greenwood's team might simply have packed their bags and gone home. The Danish newspaper *Extrabladet* called the match 'a funeral'. It cost England dearly in the end, because the Germans went on to beat Spain while England could only draw 0-0 with the host nation. England didn't have such a positive plan, in fact they seemed almost pleased and honoured to get a draw, and it made Keegan fume.

There was plenty of press speculation about the English team Greenwood would ultimately choose for the match against Spain at the Bernabeau Stadium on the evening of 5 July. Trevor Francis had expected their manager to pick Kevin Keegan to play up-front with Paul Mariner after Steve Coppell's knee had swollen up after the German match. Francis had taken Coppell's place in that match on the right, and that was how Keegan's possible inclusion appeared likely to be accommodated. But Greenwood decided to delay his selection until the last possible moment, because he wanted to play an unchanged team, hoping the frustration caused by the Germans would boil over into an England goal glut against the dejected Spaniards. But Coppell's knee showed no signs of improvement and on the Sunday night, Greenwood made the surprise choice of Tony Woodcock to play up-front alongside Mariner, with Francis on the right, and Graham Rix keeping his place despite Trevor Brooking's availability on the left. Greenwood briefed Brooking and Keegan alone about their role as 'Royal' substitutes. 'If things are not going well I'll send you on,' he told them. 'I'll try and get the moment just right and then you'll set them fresh problems when it matters.' Keegan was disappointed at not starting the game of course, but while Francis had expected him to get the nod, Greenwood's mind must have altered over 24 hours. Francis believed it was his assistant Don Howe who talked him out of selecting Keegan over dinner on Saturday night. All that was mentioned in his own autobiography, was simply that Woodcock had been the one change, and Keegan and Brooking selected as 'two trumps' on the substitutes bench he wanted to keep up his sleeve.

Howe was at pains to deny this old rumour, however, when the author spoke to the former England coach. 'Ron picked that team – and Ron alone. He was the manager. It wasn't an easy decision. He had Brooking to think about as well as Keegan.'

Greenwood's team was the same as the one which had achieved the excellent start against France, apart from Woodcock's inclusion rather than Keegan's. Greenwood and Howe might have been influenced by the fact that Francis and Woodcock had scored a goal each against Spain in Barcelona two years before. The argument still rages on as to whether Keegan's sheer relief at getting back into the action would have turned the match England's way in the first half when they laboured to score a goal. David Lacey of the *Guardian* believes that Greenwood was right to show caution.

'Keegan had looked a bit "over the hill" in a warm-up match against Finland before the World Cup. His best international days had been earlier under Revie and the earlier days of Greenwood when he looked much sharper.'

But some of Keegan's colleagues and close friends, like Mick Channon, thought Keegan was far from being over the hill at the time. Channon thought that Keegan was an even greater player with Southampton than he had been with Liverpool and Hamburg – 'Because he had to carry Southampton more as a team'. Keegan had gone down with a nasty back injury, but having recovered, he would have been in the position of being a positive leader in what looked like a tight situation.

FIFA's much criticized second round arrangements were based on an ambiguous 'classification' system in which England and Germany would have to draw lots if England won by 2–1 to gain a semi-final place. This had brought an official protest from the Football Association, which an appeals board threw out after an hour's meeting. It was utterly logical to think, like Greenwood, that England would deserve to go through because they had a better overall classification than the Germans, who had lost to Algeria. But FIFA didn't see it that way and England's task now in the oppressive heat of Madrid was to beat Spain by two clear goals, or by 3–2 or 4–3 to get through.

Keegan hadn't brought his calculator along to the English dug-out but he had certainly brought his southern Yorkshire voice. His instructions were certainly noticed by the team, but not always welcomed by international players with long-established international careers behind them like Mick Mills, Terry Butcher, Ray Wilkins and Bryan Robson. Keegan was desperate to be sent on and Greenwood's ears began to zing as the match went into the second half with both sides having missed chances, and England still looking as goal-bankrupt as they had been against Germany. The home crowd, angered and frustrated after all the pre-season tournament hype about the host nation cakewalking to the final, abused their own players with whistling. The match grew scrappy with David Miller observing in the *Daily Express*: 'Many of our set pieces were speculative, unplanned or simply inaccurate.'

The bad habits, which had given England problems in their qualifying matches against Switzerland and Norway, had returned for this repeat of their disastrous night against Poland in October 1973 when they failed to reach the finals. Chances, if not glaring ones, were tossed away, while Spain although less inclined to go forward, might have sneaked the odd poached goal but for the forbidding Shilton between the posts. For the players, the conditions were taxing to say the least and Francis for one lost ten pounds in weight during the game. But Greenwood's gamble of using Woodcock had not paid off. His experience as a lone striker with Nottingham Forest and Cologne hadn't produced the razor's edge on this occasion, while Graham Rix, whose performances for England had certainly earned him great respect, found the occasion too much for even his indefatigable resources.

The sight of Keegan and Brooking making an appearance in the 63rd minute, after all those nagging injury bulletins, had varying effects on the armchair television viewers at home surrounded by mountains of lager cans. Keegan's scurrying run into the centre of the pitch, and Brooking's imperial stance, were by no means unfamiliar to the nation's viewers, but their doubts as to whether the pair would produce the vital breakthrough increased as the minutes ticked away. Now Keegan and Brooking had to prove they were not 'over the hill' and mere walking crocks; they had to show what a dangerous pair they had become in unison.

Indeed, the Spanish players were soon to feel the effects of the two players' arrival. Brooking almost staged a breakthrough within seconds. The West Ham man found himself galloping behind the Spanish defenders with a freedom England had rarely found, before he tried a shot which Luis Maria Arconada blocked. Then Trevor Francis reaped similar havoc with the Spanish defence, but there was nobody in a white shirt to apply the finishing touch. Greenwood, like Ramsey in 1973, tried his stiff-upper-lipped best to keep his emotions at bay.

Robson set up Keegan's chance brilliantly, a cross from the left that put the ball on to Keegan's forehead in front of an empty net. But he placed it wide, and to this day he can't explain how or why. Brooking, who immediately injected a new level of skill into the game, made his opening in a way I had seen dozens of times since I first knew him as a boy at West Ham. It was a great chance but somehow Arconada, the Spanish captain and goal-keeper managed to get in the way. 'Normally you just screw that sort of chance in', I said to Trevor afterwards. 'I was going to ,' he replied, 'but the ball ran away from me at the last moment and I had to poke it instead of wrapping my foot around it.' Spain nil, England nil. It was all over.

All over indeed for the England team – for that tournament, and for Greenwood and Keegan as international celebrities. Greenwood knew it, Keegan didn't. Greenwood didn't grumble, he praised his team for their efforts which in a way had been much better than expected. Like the winning side, Italy, who beat West Germany in the final with another inspirational performance from Paulo Rossi, England had remained unbeaten. This warranted praise from the manager. 'It's the end of my career as a football manager, but I don't think I would have been any prouder of my lads had we won.' It was a nice gesture and a loyal one. No bitterness, no sulks, only the players who had shelved their tears, were in a position now to contemplate how close they had come to glory. Meanwhile, Keegan moved from room to room knowing that he had missed his chance.

The 'Malvinas oppressors' had to endure the taunts of nationalistic anti-British, pro-Argentinian factions on the way back to base camp in the mountains, but even the tossing of a brick through the window of England's coach failed to divert that bitter taste of the goalless draw against Spain.

Keegan was dejected, of course, like everyone else, but analytical as well. The angling of his header had been precise enough, only the aim was out. It was too late now though. 'I couldn't believe it when the header went wide. No excuses. I should have buried the chance.' Of course he should have, but although Keegan was brutally honest about his failure, many saw it as a chance to write him off from the international scene. Keegan did not look his true self at the Bernabeau that night, compared with his room-mate who was far quicker and aware of Spanish weaknesses. Ron Greenwood, as dispirited as he was, was asked repeatedly why he had not brought on Keegan and Brooking from the beginning.

'The fact is that neither Kevin or Trevor were perfectly fit at the time. They wouldn't have lasted the full game so how would I have handled my substitutes if someone else had been injured? It was a risk sending them on at all, but at that point risks were worth taking. And this one nearly paid off.'

There are goals missed which stick in the memory, and goals missed which stick forever in the memory. Jeff Astle's extraordinary miss in 1970, when playing for England against Brazil in Guadalajara after coming on as substitute, is one that will stick forever in the memory. With Brazil winning 1–0, and facing the width of two farm-gates, with goalkeeper Felix out shopping, Astle shot wide. That game, which England lost, didn't spell disaster for Alf Ramsey's team because they went on to reach the quarter-finals regardless. Keegan's miss was one of those which will live forever in the memory because it was Keegan who missed, the player you relied on to get you out of a hole when it

189

mattered. The self-confident, trusty player Shanks always knew on Saturday afternoons would do the business for him, even if it meant working until he dropped. Shanks had died only the year before and what he might have said, had he watched the television that night, could well have been unprintable.

What the miss did was to set off Keegan's warning bells. A loyal player whom Greenwood described at their parting as 'a rare and brilliant little chap', Keegan had failed – and he hated failure. He was fidgety, although he put on a brave face as the lads flew home, being friendly and signing autographs. As he and the team said their goodbyes to Greenwood, there was already a strong feeling inside Keegan's ambitious head. He needed a new challenge, a drastic change if he was to recapture all those tremendous highs he had reached in the game, seemingly without undue mental toil. This drastic change would not take long in coming. But when it did, the football world was again caught totally by surprise.

8
NEWCASTLE PLAYING DAYS

*T*he idea of a flourishing manager–player partnership between Arthur Cox and Kevin Keegan at St James's Park in the late summer following the 1982 World Cup would have been dismissed as a mad joke a mere two years before when a crop-headed Cox arrived to take over as manager of Newcastle United. The once proud Second Division 'Magpies' were by now thoroughly broke, their cupboard was bare of real talent, and there seemed little prospect of an immediate change, let alone enticing a national superstar like England's former captain to sign for them.

The Tyneside fans would have scoffed at the very idea. Kevin Keegan was a wealthy star with too much money, in their opinion. He had just signed for Southampton, which was a long way south and managed by that Lawrie McMenemy from Gateshead – a bit stuck-up, they argued, for a Geordie. So was that Keegan, 'Mr Hamburger Moneybags'. Cox wasn't exactly a novice in the management field, or without professional playing experience. His major club as a player had been Coventry City, but it was as coach and assistant manager at Sunderland that Cox experienced one of his finest afternoons under Bob Stokoe when the Wearsiders beat the mighty Leeds United 1–0 at Wembley to win the FA Cup in 1973. Cox had arrived at Newcastle from Chesterfield to take over from Bill McGarry. McGarry had been sacked after the club had taken a flimsy 13 points from 19 games in a disappointing finale to the 1979/80 season after they had

191

looked promotion prospects. Cox's fortunes the following season were hardly sensational, but he stuck to the job, some said dourly, as Newcastle finished eleventh in the Second Division and ninth in the next.

Cox's major acquisition on a budget was to buy Imre Varadi from Everton for £125,000. This represented a bargain for a striker with known pace, and an accuracy and flair for goalscoring not always appreciated at Goodison Park. In striking parnerships with Alan Brown from Sunderland and then David Mills from West Bromwich Albion, Varadi began to get a reaction from the St James's Park crowd. They took to his showmanship and they cheered themselves Tyneside-hoarse when he scored. There was also a young kid on the wing who worked in a sausage factory and played as a part-timer for Tow Law. Chris Waddle played 42 games for Newcastle that season in the number 11 shirt. He was promising and he ran with a deceptive swerve, although he looked ungainly at times, and kept his head bent down when he didn't have to. In his regimental way, Cox told him to get a move on, but that was the cry of the club at the time. The whole place was waiting for something to happen. Cox, believe it or not, had Keegan's arrival planned all the time in one of the coups of the century on Tyneside.

Even though the prospect of paying Keegan's wages would surely be a hindrance when Cox and his board sat down and trashed out the idea, Stan Seymour, the chairman of Newcastle, thought his manager's idea worth pursuing. Could the goalscoring master of the New Forest be lured so far north, given he had endured a personally disasterous World Cup in Spain? Could Keegan really be expected to sign for a middle-of-the-road Second Division club with money problems, and limited prospects? Cox thought the answer was yes.

A secret Newcastle boardroom meeting was arranged to thrash out whether Cox's proposal had been caused by too much summer sun on his receding hairline. After initial murmurings, Cox's idea to sign Keegan began to take root. Keegan's salary would be geared to his match appearances and attendance figures. England's former captain would, thus, all but pay for himself as the central cog of the deal. There would also be considerable financial gain from commercial interests. The Newcastle board decided to call in the club sponsors, Newcastle Breweries, to get them quickly involved.

Keegan hadn't expected to move so soon from the south where the horse-race-punting world under the tenacious guidance of his friends Ball and Channon, mingled with a settled family life and all its rural comforts. Although McMenemy had accepted he would not be able to hang on to Keegan for much longer, it did surprise him when Newcastle expressed an interest.

McMenemy gave Keegan permission to hold secret talks with the Newcastle board and brewery officials at the Swallow International hotel in West London. After hearing what the Second Division club had in mind for him and his family's future, he was inwardly raring to go at St James's Park. He held back on the question of what number shirt he would wear for the first match, but the Northern visitors sensed they had all but got their man. 'It took Kevin seven and a half minutes to make up his mind to join Newcastle,' Cox recalls. 'I would have locked him in the hotel until he did sign.'

'From the moment I met Newcastle's officials and shook hands, I knew that was it,' Keegan recalled. 'I only talked to two clubs, Manchester United and Newcastle United, but I could have talked to 30. I knew Newcastle wanted me, and I have never felt so excited in a long time, since I first met Bill Shankly.' Being bracketed with Keegan's mentor gave Arthur Cox a special feeling of pride. He was to form the same kind of uncanny understanding between himself and Keegan that had existed between Shanks and Kevin at Anfield a decade before.

Newcastle's signing of Keegan at the Gosforth Park hotel on 19 August 1982 attracted all the front and back-page hype expected when a national sporting celebrity decides to go down a peg and join a club enjoying only moderate success in the Second Division. Splashed pictures showed Keegan seated wearing a smart grey suit, white shirt, Newcastle club tie, and signing the papers. Keegan looked half-happy, half-bemused by all the media fuss going on ahead of him – it was only 11 years since he had arrived for duty at Anfield against Nottingham Forest when his name was virtually unknown. If Keegan hadn't seemed the right name for a footballer then, it did now.

Mick Channon, who knew Keegan's moods and philosophies almost better than anyone in the game, was in no doubt about his friend's commitment to the challenge.

'Challenges had always given Kevin his kicks. Without them he would never have been the player he was. He took Newcastle by storm. When I went up to Tyneside for a brief stay as a player (on loan), his name was on everyone's lips. I know the Geordie supporters have always had a great reputation for getting behind their teams, but it was Keegan who galavanized them into becoming such fantastic followers of the team in recent times. He brought out their passion and fervour better than anyone else could have done.'

The opening match against Queen's Park Rangers at St James's Park showed the full new power of this passion rarely seen at this famous ground since the eras of Hughie Gallacher and 'Wor' Jackie Milburn. There were other people present that afternoon like a full Fleet Street press corps, and the new England manager, Bobby Robson, himself a Geordie. The audience was ethnically linked to that rousing Tyneside legions many of whom had queued round the club car-park and out into Gallowgate to buy season tickets after the Keegan story had broken.

'Keegan fever' had built up before the Rangers match as these season-ticket holders thronged to where the folk heroes of Tyneside were still talked about. Keegan, as this *Sunday Telegraph* reporter found, had yet to find a niche. There was caution among some senior fans, although the arrival of a real star was obviously welcomed.

'There are a number of mundane, everyday things Kevin Keegan will not be required to do on Tyneside now that the former star of Liverpool, Hamburg and Southampton has moved into residence at St James's Park as prospective saviour and Geordie folk-hero. Like queuing on cold winter evenings for a

32 bus to the Montagu Estate via Barrack Road, or asking the way in Newgate Street to the nearest employment exchange. What our Kev will have to do is to work like blazes to show his new following that he's got the something extra, that fizz that made Hughie Gallacher, and later 'Wor' Jackie Milburn, Tyneside gods of their eras.'

All over town, Keegan mania persisted. As Milburn himself volunteered: 'The sleeping giant of North-East football will be resurrected. Every kid kicking a football wants to be Kevin Keegan in Newcastle now.'

Malcolm Dix, an often disgruntled club shareholder in the past and founder of the Newcastle Supporters' Association in the mid-1970s, could barely restrain his relief.

'We've been the laughing stock of football for too long. Once again, we have a special player worthy of the fans. The last was Supermac.'

For Kevin Keegan, the grandson of a mine inspector at Hetton-le-Hole, County Durham, the responsibilities of a new job in soccer were about to begin – a job he might find the most demanding.

The Tyneside doubters were soon made to think again when Keegan scored on his debut in what turned out to be the winning goal. Like Jimmy Greaves in his heyday, Keegan liked scoring on his debut, to show his new fan club how goals should really be scored in the quickest possible time. It wasn't as quick as the 12th minute goal he put away for Liverpool, but it came in the second-half and it satisfied the crowd, chanting the name of their new captain.

John Gibson, executive sports editor of the *Newcastle Evening Chronicle*, and a supporter of Newcastle United since boyhood, reported the impact of the crowd's adoration on their new signing and what it felt like to be at St James's Park on that memorable afternoon.

'Queen's Park Rangers, who were to go up at the end of the season, provided the opposition, but on this day they were merely to be the chorus line…Keegan was the star. United lost their record signing John Trewick with a bad injury inside a quarter of an hour. The tension could be cut with a knife as gladiators fought for supremacy. The shouts of 'Kee-gan Kee-gan' rolled down the terraces to spill over on to the pitch and the little man with the 100 mile-an-hour engine was not to be denied. The match wasn't a classic, more a memorable occasion, but Keegan's winning goal elevated it to a higher plane. Turning quickly and assuredly at inside-right in the second half, Keegan stole forward to drive a low shot past the helpless Hucker and, in his delight, kept running to be swallowed up by the delirious fans at the Gallowgate end. It seemed as though they were never going to give up their hero as he was submerged under welcoming arms and black and white scarves, but eventually he emerged, grinning widely, to take the applause from the rest of the crowd.'

Arthur Cox knew that such stardust would not feature on St James's Park every week. He had to build a team around Keegan, without splashing too much money out. Keegan had always enjoyed playing with talented players around him at Liverpool, Hamburg and Southampton, not to mention England.

Cox responded by building a new defence around Jeff Clarke, a talented, intelligent defender acquired the previous season on a free transfer from Sunderland. So dedicated to Newcastle's cause was Clarke that Keegan proclaimed the centre-back should have been awarded the North-East Player of the Year award instead of himself; a touching gesture and typical of the warmth Keegan had for players who were not endowed with fame and fortune during their short professional careers. Newcastle didn't exactly conquer the world that first season, despite Keegan's 21 league goals in 37 appearances. An unpleasant eye injury, sustained in a testimonial match, kept Keegan out of the team for five matches during November and Newcastle's promotion aspirations were checked. By now, Keegan had been joined by some familiar faces from the top division; two of them, Terry McDermott and Mick Channon (on loan), were his old colleagues at Liverpool and Southampton respectively. David McCreery, who had been playing soccer in America after making a name for himself with Manchester United and Northern

Ireland, was certainly an asset. Surprisingly, the talents of Chris Waddle, noted by Keegan, had been discarded for the time being by Cox. Varadi, however, formed a useful striking partnership with Keegan, scoring 22 league and Cup goals, one more than the star attraction himself. But Varadi was then transferred to Sheffield Wednesday, with Keegan assuring worried Tyneside fans he would be signing a new one-year contract. Newcastle had finished fifth in the Second Division behind Queen's Park Rangers, Wolves, and Leicester City (all of whom were promoted), with Fulham in fourth place. The Newcastle fans certainly felt secure now with the prospect of having Keegan knocking them in at the Gallowgate end next season. However, it had been touch and go. Keegan was worried, and said so in an exclusive interview with Gibson. His words were directed at the management who had brought him to Newcastle.

'I'm not holding a gun to their heads, but I want to see some movement from the club. I want to play with a better all-round squad next season so we gain more success. It's as much for the benefit of the fans as for myself. They deserve so much after all this time. The boss and the chairman know exactly how I feel, so I'm not talking behind their backs.'

Gibson's interview with Keegan was eagerly gobbled up by his huge fan club, because like Hughie Gallacher 50 years before, Keegan had become the 'people's hero' on Tyneside – the showman and entertainer which a recession-plagued area craved for. If he had a grudge, the people would side with Keegan's grudge.

'I joined Newcastle because I have always put my faith in people – not bricks and mortar – and neither Arthur Cox nor Stan Seymour have let me down. But at this stage of my career I don't want failure.' Keegan remained supremely loyal to his manager, declaring he would leave if Cox was ever dismissed.

These fiery words alerted, rather than inflamed, the Newcastle board to their own maximum priority; the retention of Keegan for one season at least, when promotion could well have been gained. Only the gods would tell what would happen after that, but Keegan had to stay for another season. He was mindful that if things went wrong during the season, and Newcastle found themselves languishing at the foot of the Second Division table, he wanted away.

Keegan's contract reeked with emergency clauses, linked to transfer fees. If he departed at Christmas, for instance, his outward-going fee up to end of the season would be £75,000. United would get £50,000 and Keegan's reward would be a free transfer at the season's end. The Newcastle board found themselves up against a tigerish negotiator in a business transfer market which was once nicknamed 'the white slave trade'. Newcastle had developed a reputation as a club notorious for buying and selling their bewildered footballers.

Keegan was determined to make something special of his time at Newcastle. This had much to do with the low morale he had suffered by being left out of the England squad by Bobby Robson, a rejection which prompted his immediate retirement from international football in September 1982. He had craved the international action, but he brooded over the rejection, and his restlessness was either transferred to his energies on the pitch, or to tossing away newspapers carrying news about Robson's selections. Jean noticed how deeply Kevin felt about Robson's snub, and so did close friends like Channon.

Channon used to accompany Keegan to training and became aware during his short loan spell at St James's Park how depressed Keegan could get, despite all the idolatry he was getting as superman of the North East. Keegan had expected a letter or a phone call from Robson, but had heard nothing and there was the strong likelihood that Denmark would qualify for the European Championship finals in 1984 instead of England. Keegan knew in his heart that the strong-willed Georgie in Robson (another miner's son) would not allow another Keegan return. But Keegan's attitude to Robson altered from then on. You could sense how quiet he became when accompanying England football tours after his retirement but he remained rational and professional as the good commentator he was, refusing to wash dirty linen in public. Throughout that final season of promotional triumph at St James's Park, his career worried him. Meanwile, there was a job to do for the Tyneside fans, and the treat was not so far away.

A number of red herrings confronted Cox in his efforts to build a team worthy of Keegan's high standards. The selling of Varadi to Sheffield Wednesday had not gone down well with many Newcastle fans, because although he did not have Kevin's charisma and class, he could knock the ball into the net – 42 times in two seasons, which wasn't bad going at all. There was, however, the problem of clashing styles, with Keegan preferring a marker alongside him to play some classic one – twos.

Varadi's style was in the old centre-foward tradition of belting down the pitch to catch long balls played over the top of an opposing defence, and at times the fans loved this type of poaching. The old ones said it reminded them of Vic Keeble, who won an FA Cup winners' medal with the Magpies in 1955 against Manchester City. Vic was a former Colchester United player with greased streaky hair, who liked galloping away into the Tyneside mists. When you have a player like Keegan around, whose feathery first touches required a closer response than Varadi's greyhound sprints, Cox was justified in making a change. His idea of replacing Varadi with the tall George Reilly was aborted when the player went off to Graham Taylor's Watford. So the manager decided to give a chance to a Geordie football nut who literally slept with a football by his bedside table, and took his kit bag everywhere with him just in case there was a game on somewhere. To say Peter Beardsley was mad about the game, was to underestimate his truly insane schoolboy love of soccer which the majority of people could never really appreciate or understand. Keegan could, and was keen to indulge Beardsley's youthful ambitions. Beardsley had arrived at St James's Park following a spell with Vancouver Whitecaps in Canada and one with Carlisle United.

Beardsley was a Geordie through and through, with an expression which always seemed to be asking for the football scores on 'Sports Report'. That was back in the days when he turned out for Wallsend Boys' Club near St James's Park and managed to get a third-team trial for the Magpies which came to nothing. Now, at the start of the 1983/4 season, the boy was – ready to don the first-team colours of his beloved Newcastle United, and to play beside Kevin Keegan to boot. When he ran out on the pitch accompanied by the frenzied roar of the Tyneside crowd, he almost heard the squeaks and shouts of unbroken voices as they played on a waste dump. He had been one of them not long before. Now here he was alongside Keegan, who was doing those flexing exercises in the penalty area as a loosener, as the crowd roared 'Kee-gun, Kee-gun' – a chant which one day soon would become 'Beards-ley, Beards-ley.'

Cox introduced the elusive Chris Waddle into the side, and almost at once Newcastle began to click; not by magic, but by the sparks which seemed to generate between a vastly experienced, former England captain and his two younger cohorts. By October, and the first falls of elm leaves by the river Tyne, Newcastle had won six consecutive games, and Cox and Keegan were starting to be written about as 'the Magpies' Wings of the Tyne'. Both were philosophical about the prospects of winning promotion so soon in the season, but the team was responding far more around Keegan than it had the season before when certain players simply did not have the class to respond to Keegan's quick thinking. It had at times exasperated the eternal schoolboy, but he rarely showed any inclination to whine on the pitch.

One match at St James's Park against Fulham lured Bob Paisley to watch his old employee, inspiring his new formation on the promotion trail. Paisley had retired as manager of Liverpool at the end of the previous season, joining the Liverpool board, and keeping close contacts with his successor Joe Fagan about emerging talent, though not half as obtrusively as Shankly had with him at Melwood. Paisley saw Liverpool to another Football League Championship and Milk Cup victory the previous season and there was a certain awe about his presence in the director's box at St James's Park. Kevin Keegan was pleased and touched that Paisley had dropped in to watch his old pal playing, although he wasn't foolish enough to think Paisley was on Tyneside solely for a sentimental journey. Peter

Beardsley was beginning to interest other clubs up in the First Division and Paisley had every right to have a look at some of the thrilling things young Peter was achieving. After the match, which was attended by a massive crowd of 31,568 and won narrowly by Newcastle 3–2, to complete an 18-point run, Paisley took steps to praise Keegan in a press interview in the car park. It was in this same car park that he could remember playing against another Geordie hero, Gilbert Stubbins, before the flaming red-head joined Liverpool for the first post-war League Championship season, both Paisley and Stubbins gaining winners' medals.

'If Newcastle win promotion forget about making Kevin Keegan Player of the Year. He'll deserve to be named Team of the Year. They should rename Newcastle, Keegan United. He took throw-ins, free-kicks, doubled up as a striker, and midfield player, scored one goal, and created another. He had more touches of the ball than the rest put together. Keegan's playing as well as I've ever seen him at an age when most players are looking for a less demanding stint.' Here was Paisley's snub to Bobby Robson.

Such an accolade didn't fool Keegan, even though it came from a manager he once said he felt closer to than Shankly himself. He knew he wasn't Mr Newcastle. It takes a football team to do the job, so after reading Paisley's article Keegan cut down his thrown-ins. It was never recorded, but what was recorded fully in the national press was that great players can be made to look foolish just at the time their hopes and egos are taking on an extra polish. It was worth bearing in mind, a warning perhaps, and it happened at Stamford Bridge one murky November afternoon following the Magpies' illustrious run of six consecutive victories. Chelsea had missed out on promotion, under the chain-smoking former Wrexham and Middlesbrough chief John Neal. Yet, with some considerable emerging talent in the side since their doldrum years, when their new stand had almost sent them into liquidation, the arrival of their saviour, the vigorous tongued new chairman, Ken Bates, in 1982 had changed the team's course. They now had a side to climb into the top division, but Kevin Keegan could not have expected the humiliation which lay in store for his team that afternoon. So much had been expected of him and the team.

Chelsea, with the quicksilver Pat Nevin, ripped the Magpie defence into shreds before the end as they emerged comfortable 4–0 victors. Another Chelsea executioner was Peter Rhodes-Brown from Hampton, and David Speedie from Barnsley, who both helped destroy Cox's team in front of a 30,628 crowd. 'A dazed Kevin Keegan left the ground saying he didn't believe there was a side in the second division capable of inflicting such a defeat on his team,' Bates recalls.

Keegan had hoped this visit to London, his last as a player, would be, if not all conquering, at least positive proof that his team was budding First Division material – especially as King Olav of Norway was a spectator at the match. Instead, the crowd was treated to some insolent dribbling skills by the Scot who was bought by Neal for a song from Clyde during the closed season. Newcastle were handicapped as early as the ninth minute, when McCreery had to go off with a knock sustained when he challenged Rhodes-Brown. From then on, they were deprived of a player capable, like Keegan, of bringing order to disarray. They had gone behind to a beautifully dipped shot from Nigel Spackman, and the seeds of destruction had been planted, though Keegan almost scored with a nicely flighted free-kick which went close. There were rare signs from either Beardsley or Waddle of the damage they would impinge on rival defences later on in the season. They remained mute as Chelsea scored more goals from Rhodes-Brown and Speedie. On the way home to the North East, Keegan gave a pat on the back to his goalkeeper, Thomas, who had helped keep the score down, but now Cox and Keegan had some thinking to do. The team, almost gloating after six straight wins, had been rudely found out by the Second Division leaders. A loss like the Stamford Bridge massacre wasn't part of his mission. Keegan and Cox knew after Stamford Bridge that the defence had to be strengthened if Newcastle were to keep in contact with the top three clubs. Cox went out and bought Queen's Park Rangers' captain and centre-back, Glenn Roeder to boost the defence, while the strongly built Wharton moved back to play well in the number three shirt. With the Chelsea calamity well behind them, Newcastle picked up points galore in the New Year and were on the promotion course by February, losing only one game at home to Grimsby. This one-off loss was compensated for by efficient wins away at Portsmouth and Manchester City. The possibility of Keegan leading Newcastle back into the First Division now looked on, fanned by the adulation of supporters praying for the story-book ending to celebrate the eternal schoolboy's last League season. On St Valentine's Day, his 33rd birthday, Kevin Keegan OBE announced he was hanging up his boots for good. Many thought it a hasty decision. Keegan was still very much the class player and showing it for Newcastle. Being strong-minded, Keegan wouldn't be swayed. The time had come to pack it in and it wasn't the Chelsea rout which had brought it about, rather it was a player called Mark Lawrenson.

The Chelsea result might have sounded the odd alarm bell in Keegan's mind about being left behind once or twice by some nippy Stamford Bridge performers, but a major decision lay not too far ahead in January when Newcastle played Liverpool at Anfield in the third round of the FA Cup. Keegan went back to Anfield, ten years older, and very much the elder statesman. He was warmly applauded, and treated with almost venerable respect by his once-devoted Kopites. It was a very different Liverpool line-up from the one Keegan had bid farewell to in Rome in 1977 although Phil Neal was still a regular at right-back in the team. Playing against Liverpool was a daunting prospect with such formidable first team regulars as Graeme Souness (in his last season before joining Sampdoria in Italy), the best centre-backs in Europe, Mark Lawrenson and Alan Hansen, Kenny Dalglish, Ian Rush, the Australian Craig Johnston, Ronnie Whelan and Steve Nicol. There was also the great eccentric Bruce Grobbelaar in goal, and Paisley's successor, loyal Joe Fagan on the sidelines. Keegan didn't have to be told what a challenge his team had to face that Cup afternoon at Anfield. Liverpool were rolling over everyone.

It was an incident during the match which went a long way to deciding Kevin Keegan's future. He went for a 50–50 ball, but found Lawrenson – also quick, so alert, so powerful in the tackle – coming in to perform a snatch job from the Newcastle player. It was the type of opportunity Keegan might have gobbled up with similar brashness ten years before, but not now. Keegan said later that being left for cold by Lawrenson really erased any doubt he had about hanging up his boots at the end of the season. He was a yard too slow. He knew it better than most.

Lawrenson's recollection of that particular incident is naturally indistinct – he remembers the game, he remembers Keegan, he remembers Liverpool winning easily.

The Republic of Ireland international was then half-way through his most triumphant and satisfying season culminating in the European Cup triumph in Rome against the local team on penalties. His centre-back partnership with Alan Hansen was as secure as two bridled shire-horses.

Keegan had admired Lawrenson and Hansen playing as a pair during one of their rare confrontations on the pitch, and it was Lawrenson who had brought about this decision of Keegan's to hang up his boots. He had lost his place in the England team, he was a Second Division player, whatever the kind things people were saying about him being the Magpies' saviour. He wanted out, and hang the consequences. There was nothing to stop him, Jean and their family enjoying a slice of premature retirement in the Spanish sunshine. After all he was mad about golf, with a good handicap of eight. It was time to go and time for hand over his shirt to another younger recruit. When he made his famous announcement on St Valentine's Day, he made one vow – to help Newcastle win promotion with every drip of sweat his body could summon up during the remaining weeks of the season.

Channon believed his friend could have played for another two or three seasons as a First Division player despite the harsh realities discovered at Anfield.

'Kevin would have gone back into the First Division with Newcastle. The whole area idolized him and the club had a few better players to help him. His know-how was greater than it had ever been. He became a wily old fox. His speed, or lack of it, didn't matter because he was still so sharp over five or ten yards, and that's where it counts in the highest class. Of course, he was going to get isolated in certain situations, having to go on the occasional run where he was going to be shown up. You are a lot more astute at 30 than you can ever be in your early twenties and Kevin could have steamed on.'

There was, however, that dreaded 'black dog' feeling Paddy Crerand used to talk about at Old Trafford; the fear of losing your grip on the game, the depression brought on by seeing old age creeping up. 'The trouble with Kevin is that he dreaded going downhill as a player,' Channon sensed. 'He hated the thought of ending up a shadow of his former self. He wanted to get out at the top and he certainly did. There is no going back for Kevin Keegan once he has made his mind up. Once he has decided to do something, he's very single-minded and goes ahead and does it.'

If there was one matter Keegan was single-minded about in the spring of 1984, it was clinching promotion, and the crowds rolled up at St James's Park as the prospect began to ripen into summer fruit. There were 33,386 inside the ground when Newcastle beat Carlisle United 5–1, through goals from Keegan(2), Beardsley (2), and Waddle. At the next home game on 3 May, a near rejoicing Tyneside crowd of 35,850 saw Derby packed off to the tune of 4–0 with goals from the same three players. Even Keegan was injured from time to time, and this meant his absence from the 2–2 draw at Huddersfield although he would return for the final match against Brighton and Hove Albion, when only a point was needed to secure promotion. A great party was planned for that extraordinary last Saturday afternoon of the season. Brighton, who had reached the FA Cup Final the season before, would surely not dare to get in Newcastle's way. Keegan had led his team out for a lap of honour before the start, the little man looking crisp and Peter Beardsley, beside him, giving off one of those broken-front-tooth smiles directed towards the fans chanting on the terraces. Brighton lost 1–3 to goals by Keegan, Waddle and Beardsley. It was all over. Now the pandemonium set in even louder.

John Gibson, up there in the St. James's Park press box, tried to repress his feelings as a Newcastle fan as he wrote his report, but it was difficult with Arthur Cox and Keegan leading the celebrations on the pitch.

'So Keegan had scored in his last match there as well as his first, and his personal lap of honour at the end gave the season an unforgettable glow. An official farewell against his old club Liverpool was staged later, adorned with unfettered sentimentality and topped off "by the great man" being hoisted from the centre circle into the skies above St James's Park by a helicopter. He had more farewell appearances than Frank Sinatra, but no one was complaining, especially at the club where more than a million people watched Newcastle's 42 Second Division games that season. To seal his illustrious career, Keegan scored 27 league goals in 41 appearances and finished top scorer ahead of Peter Beardsley with 20 in 34 matches.'

Now it was time for King Kev to depart, for an exile from the game which spanned eight years. For the time being, Newcastle United were back in the First Division, and at his new desk Jack Charlton didn't have to worry about Keegan's welfare.

He was already playing golf. Bless the bugger!

9
FAREWELL TO SPAIN

So what did Kevin Keegan do with his life during all those years in Spain? He surely couldn't have played golf all the time.

Once Keegan had settled into his spacious residence overlooking the seventh green of the Rio Real club, a few kilometres east of Marbella, Jean and their young daughters, Laura Jane and Sarah, would have ample opportunity of seeing him armed with golf clubs, making his way to and from the nearby clubhouse. The Keegan's house wasn't called 'Seventh Heaven' for nothing. For Keegan it meant relaxation away from the screeching pressures he had experienced over the years in international, first and second division football. He had always promised Jean that one day they would move away from all that and make a settled family life for themselves. Marbella was ideal – Keegan had his family around him, and he had his daily golf. As his caddy friends are still happy to point out, Keegan was a 'fanatico' on the course. He became so good that some days he dazzled them with his form. A five handicap could be lowered to two or one. The still boyish England football hero simply wouldn't let up. He was a winner; every morning, that lush green course with tropical plants and trees and the odd black and white wagtail for company, act as a challenge Keegan could not resist.

Derek Pavis, the Notts County chairman, recalled playing with Keegan while on holiday in Marbella.

'Kevin put as much into his golf as he put into his football. He wanted to win and to perfect his game in doing so. I enjoyed our games together, but there was only one winner, and that was Kevin.'

The Keegan family life style was certainly one adopted by many wealthy households with blue swimming pools dotting the hillside around the golf course. Privacy was imperially kept, with Spanish maids and gardeners, two or three large cars in the front drive, tennis courts and equestrian clubs at the ready, and the elegant Los Monteros hotel five kilometres or so away on the other side of the pounding Costa motorway. Kevin Keegan may have had the odd day by the seaside at Cleethorpes in his youth, but as he admitted, 'When I lived in Marbella, I never went to the beach.'

This was hardly surprising from Keegan's point of view. He was an international celebrity, like his golfing neighbour, Sean Connery. To have taken his family on to one of the scruffier Marbella beaches would have meant an afternoon signing autographs in a wide expanse of public sand. Once he started signing autographs, Keegan had the reputation for going on and on signing them. It was in his nature, but being famous now and living in Spain meant moving in private circles with waiters who knew you well in 'Silks' and other Marbella eating places, and in corners away from nodding celebrity seekers. The Americans were allright, but with the Costa del Sol become a growing settling point for English residents, that small discreet corner table did have its value away from the madding crowd.

Ian Woosnam, the Welsh 1991 US Masters champion, who had displayed the same kind of tenacious Keegan-esque qualities when battling to take that coveted title at the 72nd hole, noted the footballer's golfing skills when dropping into Marbella between international competition.

'Kevin is a first-class golfer – that's for sure. He works very hard to improve his game. If he hadn't been a brilliant footballer, then he might have done well in golf. He works so hard.'

'Wee Woosie', as he was nicknamed by the American magazine *Sports Illustrated*, has spent time coaching Keegan's mentor, Johan Cruyff, but despite the Dutchman's flair for winning major trophies, his golfing abilities fall far short of Keegan's. 'Cruyff still has a lot of work to do in the game. Keegan has been playing for a long time'.

Keegan was not the first professional footballer to fall passionately in love with the game of golf. Many British players and managers have reached a very high standard on local greens after training, including Alex Ferguson, the Manchester United manager, who heard his team had won the 1993 Premier League Championship while playing golf with his son at his local club. But it was Keegan's obsession, witnessed often by his Spanish caddies, that drove him to greater heights. The perfection he sought, however, was not always there. In one pro-celebrity tournament in the Home Counties, Norman Fox, the *Independent on Sunday* soccer correspondent, was out walking the dog, when he found Keegan alone in a vast landscape trying to unearth a golf ball from a scraggle thicket. Keegan was obviously in trouble, and told Fox so. 'I could do without this pressure,' a sweaty Keegan said.

Such Keegan lapses on the international greens of the world were rarely offered for public viewing. As Fox recalled, 'Seeing Keegan alone in that large patch of open landscape trying to unearth a golf ball from what looked like a warren covered by gorse was quite a surprise.'

Keegan did not have to worry about being caught in such uncompromising positions on his own patch of green in Spain. From the moment he left the motorway on the Mediterranean, the hill-road leading to his own villa and the clubhouse led a casual driver up and down into a silent zone of privacy awash with cash. Rules of etiquette on the club scorecards could also have been written by the Mighty Atom himself in one of his motivated moods which could leave everyone else breathless.

'Players must avoid unnecessary delays. If a player does not keep his place on the course and misses a hole in relation to those preceding him, he must give way to the player following him. When a ball is being looked for, the group following must be given way to.'

The Walter Mitty element in Keegan did get a response from

time to time when Keegan began to grow restless from the sheer tedium of staring over at tropical landscapes with the nearby Sierra backdrop purple at sunset leading away towards Ronda, the old bull-ring, and the deep gorge Hemingway often referred to with wonder in his toro letters. The urge to be at Aintree, not only backing the runners and riders after playing in the morning for Liverpool, but also (as he disclosed) actually riding in the Grand National became an obsession not always doused with a cold sponge from the pool by Jean. Brough Scott, the racing commentator, sports columnist and former amateur jockey, did reveal on a number of occasions that Keegan was active in getting a ride in the National.

'I think much to all our relief, he abandoned the idea, but for some time he was prepared to gallop at Beechers Brook. Knowing him, he would have got over somehow, even with only one foot in the saddle.'

Living in hot countries can have a marked effect on restless expatriates like Keegan, and the desire to pack in the good life on the Costa del Sol would show itself from time to time through the odd outburst in the national press. He had many excuses to air his concern in print about managers and players and the English game, in general. The Heysel and Hillsborough disasters involving his old club took place while Keegan was still in hibernation in Spain. Two events covered by local press, and both tragic enough to arouse restrained feeling of disillusionment from someone who cared so much about the game. When Keegan felt particularly unhappy about the running of the England team, of which he had been such a proud member, he was ready to say so, once sounding off at Bobby Robson. He told Bob Cass in the *Sun*, 'I dream of Bryan Robson holding up the World Cup trophy, but it remains a dream. I've seen nothing to suggest it will soon become a reality.' And on another occasion, Keegan actually suggested, in 1989, he wanted Robson's job, accusing the former Ipswich manager of 'ruling England over the years'. Keegan staked his case for the job.

'I can motivate players, I have the respect of players.'

But Keegan had been far more cautious earlier about entering

210

management. 'It takes a certain type to be a manager,' he said at cocktail time in an Andalusian glade. 'It's foolish to think that because you're a better-than-average player, you are going to make a good manager. I'm not scared of failure, but I would sooner not do it than fail.'

So what promoted that major change of mind when Newcastle came in with their offer? Derek Pavis was in no doubt in his mind that Keegan saw the route could lead to his becoming England manager. He had, after all, stated in print he wanted Robson's job. Now Robson had moved on, and Graham Taylor was two years into his four-year England contract, the time had come to put himself in the running for a post he had certainly craved for from time to time. The team that mattered now to Keegan was Newcastle United Football Club, but knowing his ambitious and restless nature, the England job could rest in some future cubbyhole, to be gazed at as a personal challenge. Pavis knew why Keegan came back when he did not have to involve himself in a decidedly dodgy profession. 'Pure and simple. Kevin wanted to be manager of England. And the only way he could get it was to become a club manager, to allow himself four or five years in the front line. He didn't waste time at St James's Park, and having done so well in gaining promotion to the Premier League, I believe it won't be long before he becomes a powerful contender for the England post. It's all linking up nicely.'

Football management, even at the very highest level, remained very much a pipe-dream in Keegan's worldly ambitions as he and Jean prepared to leave Spain in 1990 and resettle at their other home in Hampshire. 'I hadn't thought about managing a club when we packed up and came home. It was the last thing on my mind. My future seemed to lie with doing commentaries on radio and television. We would make our farm in Hampshire our base, breeding horses, enjoying life without being involved in the real game.'

Keegan had always seemed a 'natural' in the commentary business from his early days at Liverpool which, as BBC Radio commentator Bryon Butler remarked, he responded to with 'an eager, volatile mind'. Perhaps, he had been just a little too shy in one of the first television interviews he gave at Scunthorpe, but once Keegan got under Shankly's wing his media responses were timed almost to the rhythm of the Kop's roar. He was articulate and certainly no longer nervous. His first agent when he was at Liverpool, Vic Huglin, did much to bring the young Scunthorpe man out of his withdrawn shell. Huglin and members of his family were benefactors of Merseyside wit and wisdom, while helping the young footballer to sort out his early public engagements and the odd appearance on radio or television. As Keegan matured, Huglin's role became progressively redundant, and as Keegan's outside interests spiralled, Huglin found Keegan a new agent in Paul Ziff at 'Public Eye' in Leeds. So it went on, with Keegan becoming more and more the superstar until, by the time he was transferred to Hamburg, the vigorous Harry Swales was running the Keegan radio show. When Keegan made his major breakthrough as a television personality, on Brian Moore's ITV World Cup panel in June 1978, Moore's panel included four managers – Brian Clough, Peter Taylor, Lawrie McMenemy (Keegan's future Southampton chief) and the Norwich City boss, John Bond. Player representation came from Keegan, his England colleague Trevor Brooking, and the future commentating sage of Sky Sports, Andy Gray, with Manchester United's old stalwart Paddy Crerand backing up. It was during the introductions off-screen that Clough made his famous backhander at Keegan who had just finished his first season at Hamburg. 'And who are you putting your Deutsche Marks on, Kevin?' Keegan's response was quick. 'And where did you get your suntan Brian? Not on an English beach.'

The England captain was quick and assertive with his observations about the state of play being funnelled in from Buenos Aires and other World Cup venues. He could be a bit of a kingfisher with the television boys, nevertheless, disappearing at crucial moments. As he pointed out, his schedules in those days hardly offered a minute's respite. He would dash into the studios, and dash out again.

'Kevin was always so busy we started worrying about him

cracking up under the pressure. He never rested but never seemed to want to rest. I mentioned the fact once to his manager, Gunter Netzer, who waved my anxiety away. "It would be wrong to try and stop him. Ever tried to stop a champion racehorse?" Kevin told me once his programme in Hamburg was so busy he and Jean would get back home late at night, and realize they hadn't eaten all day, and there was nothing in the fridge.'

But Keegan's appearance on the panel did not suggest he was under any timekeeping deadlines. He was relaxed and with his fellow-players prepared to add a certain authority of his own when the managers grew too long-winded from their own self-importance, especially when the Scottish team were having a bad time of it in Cordoba and Mendoza. 'Kevin's contribution was very professional and brought him to the notice of viewers who hadn't really heard about him before, being non-football fans drawn in because this was the World Cup.'

Peter Batt, the *Sun* columnist had a wry dig at the management side of the panel, for being over-patronising during 'a staggering 120 hours of airtime on the box'. Batt suggested that the two world leaders of the period, President Carter and Mr Brezhnev, might also have been 'subject to delusions of grandeur' during that World Cup in June.

It was Keegan who came to the rescue, according to Batt, with an impish imitation of Clough which toned down all the self-important ballyhoo rampant on the panel bench. Keegan was noted for his ability to knock down any displays of gross self-importance, and so it proved on the last day of the Brian Moore World Cup show.

'Sure enough, on World Cup final day, after Argentina had beaten Holland 3–1, the perceptive and intelligent Kevin Keegan finally gave the game away when, with almost the last kick, he gave a bitingly satirical impersonation of Cloughie. Leaning forward with the confident air of a man who had won his fight against self-doubt, he prodded a pencil towards the chest of Brian Moore and intoned, 'Correct, correct'. It was vintage Clough, and before the cameras could make a discreet retreat, Keegan and his mate Pat Crerand dissolved into a bout of mischievous nudging, winking and grinning.

'By way of retribution they received a stern, disapproving look from Clough, but for this viewer, anyway, it was a warm, light-hearted moment, a release from the patronising that had gone on and on before...'

Keegan's wit greatly amused the nations' viewers, and brought the Hamburg dynamo further invitations to appear on various panels and big match specials from then on. His long, extravagantly-permed hair falling down on the open collar of his white shirt provided a fashion trademark for what young footballers out on the town should look like, while his Doncaster in-built warmth charmed more than a few fireside grannies. But even though Keegan did look relaxed, he admitted his schedule was 'a killer sometimes'. The 'Mighty Atom' was near bowled over by one of them.

'The classic case was the Saturday when I arrived at Heathrow at 8.40 pm after playing for Hamburg in the afternoon. A BBC limousine whistled me off to "Match of the Day", then I went to the Sportsman club for dinner with a sheik who wanted to name a life style after me. I left there at 1.00 o'clock for the Heathrow Post House, rose at six and met my agent (Harry Swales) to discuss contracts. My next call was the offices of the *Sun* where I teamed up with a photographer who took me round central London for a two-hour picture session. It was only 10 am when I set off to the National Exhibition Centre at Birmingham to do a personal appearance at the Toy Fair, then it was straight back to London for talks with a film producer before dashing to the airport for my return flight to Germany. That was all crammed into 24 hours.'

Such trips helped pay the family bills, of course, while the hectic tempo which was to remain with Keegan long after his Hamburg spell, tended to make Mr Ubiquitous impatient when he found his own schedules, in his view, disrupted by fellow players having a natter into the microphone in Keegan time. Barry Davies remembers being put out by Keegan's regal attitude one afternoon following a Southampton–Stoke match.

'It was one of the first times I had come into contact with

Keegan as a commentator. I was interviewing Southampton's Chris Nicholl, after the game which went overtime. Keegan was next on, but didn't show. Someone asked me to go down and collect Keegan from the dressing room. I said I wouldn't, he was being paid by the BBC to speak. Kevin did show eventually, saying he had come up but saw Chris Nicholl was being interviewed so he went away again. It was OK, we got on very well afterwards. I always found him a very nice guy to work with after that, and very professional.'

Keegan hadn't exactly been in a rush to get back to England or the world of commentating when he parked his Range Rover in a lay-by on the M5 at Reigate Hill overlooking the Weald in Surrey, after driving from Spain via the Channel ferry one night in April 1991. Uncharacteristically for Keegan, he decided to have a snooze. The tight schedules seemed to have passed him by, the millionaire former captain of England's soccer team now contemplating a comfortable life addressing the nation on various aspects of football on the box while helping his wife Jean and daughters Laura and Sarah run their Hampshire stud farm. He could relax in the darkness as cars whizzed past on the motorway only yards away.

It was, therefore, a severe shock when his many fans read and heard next day that the superstar had been attacked by intruders while he slept, so severely that Keegan admitted he was 'lucky to be alive'. It turned out to be a frightening experience for the sleeper, far more frightening than being kicked by Welsh fans at Ninian Park, or being rouged-up by Belgrade airport police, because the incident happened so suddenly and was proof of the senseless violence rampant in the homeland he had returned to. Three youths with baseball bats and a lump of concrete smashed their way into the Range Rover, robbing Keegan of £1,200 and a credit card. The victim was taken to hospital with cuts, after being hit on the head, shoulders and legs.

The youths responsible got three years apiece when they appeared in front of Recorder, Edward Southwell, 'A disgraceful use of criminal violence against a defenceless individual,' he observed, with Anglo–Saxon indignation. The sentences were

215

considered far too lenient by those who saw the beating-up as another case of the cynical rise in crime erupting in the country. At least Kevin Keegan's name gave prominence to the problem and made people realize how close criminal activity was to their own front gates.

Keegan suffered the indignity of such a nightmare in the relative privacy of his Hampshire home, choosing not to vent anger through revengeful, over-hysterical pronouncements which would make headlines. He suffered, certainly, but it was with the civilized air of a country squire.

Besides, Keegan was busy settling back into the more normal and settled ways of English domestic life down in rural Hampshire. He and Jean were pleased to be back with their daughters for a sheltered outdoor life. Dad took off from time to time for the commentary box. It all seemed ideal. Then one day, very early in 1992, when leafless New Forest trees were looking distinctly jaded after the autumn fall, and surrounding golf courses were soggy and damp with the odd pony loping across a sombre third green, Keegan received that important message from the North-East. If his heart didn't pound, then it should have done. If his sense of reason didn't become a little disconnected, then it should have done. If his feelings of not wanting to be disturbed were suddenly dashed, then they should have been.

It was to Jean that the still-boyish professional footballer had to convey a small piece of news which would totally alter both their lives and lure Keegan back into the world of soccer headlines again. Newcastle United wanted Keegan to become their manager. Would he kindly discuss it? As in the past, when he had always asked his father, Joe, about such important matters, Keegan now spoke to Jean.

Mrs Keegan hardly paused with her reply. She knew Keegan could hardly restrain himself from jumping up and down with excitement. It was like his clerking days at Pegler Brass Works in Doncaster when he heard he might get a place in the first team. 'Then you'll go,' said Jean. It was that look in his eyes. She knew he had to go to Newcastle.

Kevin Keegan did just that.

CAREER RECORD

1951 14 February: Born Joseph Kevin Keegan – second child of three to Joseph and Doris Keegan of Elm Place in the mining village of Armthorpe near Doncaster, South Yorkshire.
Educated: St. Francis Xavier Primary School, Doncaster, St. Peter's RC Secondary School, Doncaster.
1966: Joined Pegler Brass Works, working as a clerk in central stores.
1968 2 January: Signed apprentice pro forms for Scunthorpe United.
1968 16 September: Made first team debut at Peterborough United. Peterborough won 3–2.
1968 20 December: Signed professional forms for Scunthorpe. Made 124 appearances, scoring 18 times.
1971 10 May: Signed for Liverpool FC for £35,000. Bill Shankly later called the deal 'robbery with violence'.
1971 14 August: Makes first team debut at Anfield against Nottingham Forest. Liverpool won 3–1, Keegan scoring the first at the Kop end after twelve minutes.
1972 16 February: First representative honour. Keegan, 21, won an under-23 cap against Scotland at Derby.
1972 1 June: Sent off playing for the England Under-23 team against East Germany for retaliating.
1972 12 August: Awarded the Football League Managers' 'Best Young Player of the Season'.
1972 7 November: Keegan won first full cap in a World Cup

qualifying game against Wales in Cardiff. England won 1–0.

1973 April: Keegan won his first major trophy as Liverpool take the League championship for the 8th time. Keegan scored 13 goals.

1973 May: Liverpool rounded off a memorable season by winning the UEFA Cup, beating Borussia Moenchengladbach 3–2 on aggregate. Keegan scored twice in the 3–0 lst leg victory at Anfield.

1974 4 May: Liverpool beat Newcastle United 3–0 at Wembley to win the FA Cup. Keegan scored two goals in one of the most one-sided finals in years.

1974 10 August: Both Keegan and Billy Bremner of Leeds were sent off at Wembley in the annual Charity Shield after coming to blows. Liverpool eventually won 6–5 on penalties after extra time.

1974 September: Keegan and Bremner were both fined £500 and suspended for eleven matches.

1974 23 September: Married Jean Woodhouse at the St Peter-in-Chains Roman Catholic Church, Doncaster.

1975 20 May: Dropped by Don Revie for international against Wales at Wembley. Keegan immediately walked out on Revie claiming 'its the end of my international career'.

1975 24 May: Recalled for next game against Scotland. Keegan admitted later that what he had done was a mistake. England won 5–1.

1976 24 March: Captains England for the first time against Wales in Wrexham for a Welsh centenary match.

1976 April/May: Voted Football Writers' Association Player of the Year.

1976 4 May: Liverpool clinched the League championship on the last game of the season with a 3–1 win at Wolves. Keegan equalized with only 16 minutes remaining, setting up his second championship medal and Bob Paisley's first as manager.

1976 April/May: Liverpool won the UEFA Cup for the second time, beating Bruges 4–3 on aggregate, Keegan scoring the winning goal in Belgium.

1976 August: Keegan revealed his first wish to leave Anfield at the end of the following season.

1977 10 May: Liverpool retained the League championship with a goalless draw with West Ham at Anfield.

1977 21 May: Hopes of an historic treble were dashed as Liverpool lost 2–1 to Manchester United in the FA Cup Final.

1977 25 May: Keegan played his last game in a Liverpool shirt when Paisley's team beat Borussia Moenchengladbach 3–1 in Rome to win the European Cup for the first time. Keegan made 321 appearances for Liverpool, scoring 100 goals.

1977 3 June: After much transfer speculation, Keegan signed for SV Hamburg for a then British record of £500,000.

1977 27 July: Keegan scored on his debut for Hamburg in a friendly against Barcelona.

1978 15 November: Laura Jane Keegan born.

1978 December: Voted European Footballer of the Year. 'I feel so high I need oxygen'. Voted West German Man of the Year.

1979 May: SV Hamburg won the Bundesliga Championship.

1980 January: Became the first man to be voted European Player of the Year in two successive seasons.

1980 11 February: Southampton announced they had signed Kevin Keegan for £450,000 for the next First Division season.

1980 28 May: Nottingham Forest beat Hamburg 1–0 in the European Cup Final in Madrid.

1981 18 November: England qualify for the World Cup in Spain, beating Hungary 1–0 at Wembley.

1982 April: Voted PFA Player of the Year.

1982 April: Confined to bed suffering muscle spasms in his back. Doubts about his World Cup availability.

1982 6 June: Sarah Marie Keegan born.

1982 12 June: Awarded OBE for his services to football.

1982 June/July: World Cup in Spain. Due to back injury, Keegan played a very small part, only appearing as a 63rd minute substitute against Spain, which England drew 0–0 and went out of the tournament.

1982 August: Keegan signed for Second Division Newcastle United for £100,000. Keegan made 68 appearances in two seasons for Southampton, scoring 37 times.

1982 28 August: Scored the winner for Newcastle in his debut at home against QPR. An instant rapport with the fans. 'I've seen it all…but playing before thousands of passionate Geordies will equal everything in my life'.

1982 September: Left out of England squad by new manager Bobby Robson and immediately retires from international football after 63 caps and 21 goals.

1984 May: Leads Newcastle back to Division One in his last season before retiring.

1992 5 February: Sensationally returns to football as the new manager of a Second Division Newcastle United. He replaces the sacked Ossie Ardiles.

1992 May: Newcastle narrowly survived relegation.

1993 May: Newcastle champions of the Barclays League First Division. A marvellous season capped with a 7–1 home victory against Leicester. 'We are not far away from being good enough to win the Premier League'.

BIBLIOGRAPHY

The following books have proved invaluable in researching
Kevin Keegan: Black and White

Brooking, Trevor *100 Great British Footballers* (Macdonald
  Queen Anne Press, 1988)
Channon, Mick *Man on the Run* (Arthur Barker, 1986)
Croker, Ted *The First Voice You Will Hear Is* (CollinsWillow,
  1987)
Dalglish, Kenny with Ken Gallagher *King Kenny* (Stanley
  Paul, 1982)
Francis, Tony *Clough – A Biography* (Stanley Paul, 1987)
Francis, Trevor with David Miller *The World to Play For*
  (Sidgwick and Jackson, 1982)
Gibson, John *The Newcastle United Story* (Arthur Barker, 1985)
Greaves, Jimmy *Goals! A to Z* (Harrap, 1981)
Greenwood, Ron *Yours Sincerely* (CollinsWillow, 1984)
Hackett, Keith *Hackett's Law* (CollinsWillow, 1986)
Hodgson, Derek *The Liverpool Story* (Arthur Barker, 1979)
Hornby, Nick *Fever Pitch* (Gollancz, 1992)
Keegan, Kevin with John Roberts *Kevin Keegan* (Arthur
  Barker, 1977)
Keegan, Kevin with Mike Langley *Against the World* (Sidgwick
  and Jackson, 1979).
Keating, Frank *Sportswriter's Eye* (MacDonald Queen Anne
  Press, 1989)

Law, Denis with Ron Gubba *Denis Law* (MacDonald and Jane's, 1979)

Miller, David *Stanley Matthews* (Pavilion, 1989)

Pawson, Tony *The Goalscorers* (Cassell, 1978)

Pead, Brian *Liverpool – A Complete Record* (Breedon Books, 1988)

Ponting, Ivan *Liverpool – Player by Player* (The Crowood Press, 1990)

Powell, Jeff *Bobby Moore – The Authorised Biography* (Everest, 1976) Reprinted and Revised, Robson Books, 1993)

Rollin, Jack, Ed *Rothmans Football Yearbook 1992-93* (Headline, 1993)

Soar, Phil and Widdows Richard *Spain, 82* (Hamlyn 1982)

St John, Ian *Liverpool – the Glory Decade* (Sidgwick and Jackson, 1990)

VIDEO *Keegan on Keegan* – Watershed Pictures – 1992)

INDEX